# Prosaics and Other Provocations
*Empathy, Open Time, and the Novel*

Ars Rossica

Series Editor: David BETHEA
(University of Wisconsin — Madison)

ACADEMIC
STUDIES
PRESS

# Prosaics and Other Provocations

*Empathy, Open Time, And The Novel*

GARY SAUL MORSON

BOSTON / 2013

Library of Congress Cataloging-in-Publication Data:
A catalog record for this book as available from the Library of Congress.

ISBN 978-1-61811-809-7
ISBN 978-1-61811-183-8 (electronic)

Cover design by Ivan Grave
On the cover: "Harvest at Black Walnut Inn,"
photograph by Steven Blumenkranz, 2008.

Published by Academic Studies Press in 2013
28 Montfern Avenue
Brighton, MA 02135, USA

press@academicstudiespress.com
www.academicstudiespress.com

*For Jonathan and Fran*

# Table of Contents

# Acknowledgments

When Academic Studies Press asked me to put together a collection of my theoretical essays, I thought the task would be easy: just pick out the ones that have (or in my view should have) attracted the most interest. But when I sat down to do so, I found that my method of thinking through a problem—keep approaching it from different angles and see what ideas emerge—created a lot of overlap from essay to essay. I eventually decided to combine different essays into a single coherent statement, drawing on already published ideas while making connections between them and tracing new implications.

And so the only essay that can could arguably called a reprint of one that appeared earlier is "Contingency, Games, and Wit," which originally appeared in *New Literary History*'s special issue on play, vol. 40, no. 1 (Winter 2009). Alicia Chudo published a version of "An *Onegin* of Our Times" in *Formations* vol. 6, no. 1 (Spring 1991).

\* \* \*

Developing ideas that have been with me since the early 1980s, this book reflects debts of many kinds to several people. It owes most to my wife Katharine Porter, who read every line and was there for me every moment. Emily Morson and Alexander Morson were always in my thoughts. Jane Morson helped me develop many primitive insights.

David Bethea suggested I do this volume and was tireless in guiding it through; Caryl Emerson encouraged me; and Sharona Vedol made it all happen.

I often discussed time, contingency, and the unpredictable with the late Aron Katsenelinboigen, who remains one of the great intellectual influences of my life. The same is true of the late Stephen Toulmin, with whom I co-taught three courses at Northwestern University.

Elizabeth Allen, Nava Cohen, the late Helen Brenner, and Gayle Washlow-Kaufman helped many times in ways far beyond what I had any right to expect.

As a graduate student at Yale and long after, I learned from the late Victor Erlich and Martin Price, and from Robert Louis Jackson and Michael Holquist. I did not meet the late Thomas Greene until I was an assistant professor, when his ideas about anachronism helped direct my thinking. At the University of Pennsylvania, Alfred Rieber contributed to my awareness of the ways in which disciplinary presuppositions can blind one. The late Elliot Mossman's encouragement kept me going at dark moments. At Northwestern I profited much from dialogues with Leonard Barkan, Sanford Goldberg, Robert Gundlach, Gerald Graff, Lawrence Lipking, Barbara Newman, Mark Ratner, Kenneth Seeskin, and my colleagues in the Slavic department.

Time and again, I looked to Robert Alter and Frederick Crews of Berkeley for their corrections of my work. They suggested changes that made my books better than they would have been, and did so with grace as well as wisdom.

I owe a special debt to Joseph Epstein, who not only commissioned my first extended meditations on prosaics but also inspired me through years of conversation. Ralph Cohen and Herbert Tucker provoked me to write several articles for *New Literary History* which initiated extended creative projects. With Caryl Emerson I thrashed out theme after theme.

Over the past three years I have had the singularly illuminating experience of co-teaching an interdisciplinary course with Morton Schapiro. His relentless sharpness and unfailing broadmindedness made learning about economics, education, and many other topics an adventure.

The late Michael André Bernstein not only inspired me with his amazing erudition and intellect but was also an incomparable friend since we met as students at Oxford in 1969. Not a day goes by when I do not miss him.

I dedicate this book to Frances Padorr Brent and Jonathan Brent, not only for their guidance, editorship, and wise readings, but also for a deep personal understanding that has made all the difference.

# PREFACE

*David M. Bethea*

In her inspiring TED Talk (http://blog.ted.com/2008/03/12/jill_bolte_
tayl/), Harvard neuroanatomist Jill Bolte Taylor reprises how it feels
to experience a stroke "from the inside out." As someone who had
deep personal reasons for dedicating her life to brain science—her
brother had suffered from schizophrenia and had not been able, in her
words, "to attach his dreams to a common, shared reality"—Taylor
knew exactly what was happening when she awoke on the morning
of December 10, 1996, with the symptoms of a serious stroke. She had
a blinding pain above her left eye and her body was having difficulty
obeying simple commands. The right and left hemispheres of her brain,
which normally communicate with each other through the 300 million
axonal fibers of the corpus collosum, were experiencing a kind of
power outage in their back-and-forth circuitry. "Reality" was entering
Taylor's consciousness more and more through her right hemisphere,
which can be likened to a "parallel processor" that operates exclusively
in the present moment. Her body belonged, suddenly and weirdly,
yet pleasantly, kinesthetically, to the energy flow of the universe; she
sensed that her extremities were permeable edges where her molecules
were intermingling with the molecules of the larger world in a massive
oneness, and the pictures, the sounds and smells, that attended on this
euphoric merging were beautiful.

At the same time, the left hemisphere, the "serial processor" that
provides the sense of "I am" and that "thinks in language," was in
deep trouble. Without this left-hemisphere serial functioning Taylor
literally could not picture herself as a discrete body in time and space,
as a separate mind that could cast back into the past and project into
the future. The left hemisphere's "chatter," which is to say its mode

of linking the individual to the external world (our proverbial "to-do" lists), was falling silent, surfacing only rarely and spasmodically amid the otherwise overflowing feeling of "Nirvana." Fortunately, Taylor was ultimately able to dial the phone and communicate to a colleague her distress, after which she was rushed to Mass General and stabilized. Two and a half weeks later the surgeons removed a golf-ball size blood clot that was pressing on her language centers; it then took her eight years and Himalayas of pain and patience to be restored to her pre-hemorrhage state, although truth to tell, with her story, the state to which she was ultimately returned was in many ways a new world. As she says in her talk,

> So who are we? We are the life force power of the universe, with manual dexterity and two cognitive minds. And we have the power to choose, moment by moment, who and how we want to be in the world. Right here right now, I can step into the consciousness of my right hemisphere where we are—I am—the life force power of the universe, and the life force power of the 50 trillion beautiful molecular geniuses that make up my form. At one with all that is. Or I can choose to step into the consciousness of my left hemisphere, where I become a single individual, a solid, separate from the flow, separate from you. I am Dr. Jill Bolte Taylor, intellectual, neuroanatomist. These are the "we" inside of me.

I begin my comments here with Jill Bolte Taylor's story because it seems to me that to read this splendid collection of essays by Gary Saul Morson is to experience in a particularly vivid verbal form the two-cognitive-mind dialogue that lies at the center of Taylor's amazing "aha" moment. Also, because Taylor's story is actually many stories in one, and because it is all about narrating one's position in time and space at a given moment, it is Saul Morson's special province and intellectual homeland. The only individual in our rather small and often insular Slavic/Russian studies discipline who is a true public intellectual, and someone whose very substantial body of written work and pedagogical performance speaks uniquely to the larger world of ideas and contemporary culture, Morson is one of the most advanced "serial processors" of ideas of our generation. His passion is to place ideas in a series, but that series is not closed, and it merges palpably with the external world and a future that contains multiple options. "Contingency" is his best ideational friend. Fierce in his own reading of things and ever eager to go against the grain of received thought, Morson also celebrates *what works*, so to speak, which is a most refreshing turn in today's academic landscape. He is willing to stand on the shoulders of giants, but he insists that they *be* giants. Thus, he is willing to celebrate when the occasion demands; however, that celebration will normally be expressed in a rather unorthodox, "misanthropological" (as he would put it) way.

In my remarks to follow I highlight ideas that are central to Saul Morson's approach to the study of literature, culture, and, more pointedly, the seam separating the social sciences and the humanities. These ideas, I would like to suggest, are not just compelling in their own right, which they are, they are also heuristic "therapies" for dealing with the discursive "stroke" that, à la the story underlying Taylor's TED Talk, has virtually paralyzed discussion (as in productive dialogue) in our time between the worlds of "scientific thinking" and — for lack of a better word — "spirituality." Whether what happened to Taylor on that December day in 1996 took place inside her head or outside of it makes no difference to Morsonian thinking. The human brain contains something like 100 billion neurons, of a thousand varieties or more, and those nerve cells are capable of making at least 100 trillion connections. In the modern world we have established that neurons fire and are connected, but how exactly they act in concert to govern behavior remains a mystery. Reading Morson and following him through the epistemological thickets of contemporary thought is, while perhaps not the same as reading neuroscience, a very good place to go to frame correctly the mystery of consciousness as it happens. Few thinkers are better at addressing the "'we' inside of 'me'."

### Prosaics, Bakhtin, Misanthopology

More a philosopher than a literary critic/scholar, Mikhail Bakhtin made a career out of developing terminology that took on a life of its own and spoke with particular authority to the modern condition. Heteroglossia, chronotope, dialogism, polyphony, carnival, "outsideness," "unfinalizability," "word with a loophole" — these terms inevitably opened speech acts that had seemed closed, made fluid narrative hierarchies that had seemed fixed. Morson has not only analyzed Bakhtinian thought, often and to great effect, he has also built on the master's terminology, and in the process coined a powerful vocabulary of his own. Prosaics is, broadly speaking, the methodology Morson has developed over the years as an antidote to "poetics" and "structuralism," which latter tend to look at a literary artifact as constructed "from the end" in such a manner that every part fits tidily into the whole and that when the work is completed, it seems to be held in mind almost spatially (the late Joseph Frank's term), all at once, beginning to end. It is in this sense that he means "structure is the literary counterpart of providence" and "in God's world and the literary masterpiece, optimality—the best state of affairs or the best structure—reconciles free will and providence." From the structuralist perspective, all detours along the way to the final product, all rough drafts and resets, serve as a kind of hologram that the creative brain holds in limbo until the finished product presents itself. The reader who applies this approach casts himself or herself in the role of the author's implied psyche, foregrounding details and selecting out thematic and semantic parallels of which the originating creating mind may not be aware. In other words, in Morson's version of a careful structuralist reading of a poem or a play or a novel (it is clear he prefers novels, following Bakhtin, as the form most accommodating to process) there is an engulfing intentionality that is always present, even subconsciously, as the writer composes his work. No afterthoughts, only forethoughts.

The problem with this view is that it doesn't accurately reflect how the mind operates as it interacts with recalcitrant reality. Reality throws curve balls. For Morson, whether we are looking at the reality of a verbal artifact or the reality of the three-dimensional world, the puzzle is not Leibnizian (the contingent is possible, but only if it implies no logical contradiction), but Tolstoyan (the contingent is so unexpected and so inherently contradictory that to claim God can "foresee" it is to attenuate the divine mind out of existence, which may be the point to some believers). What is needed to understand Tolstoyan reality is "not a poetics of structure but a prosaics of process." Here I would only say, not necessarily disputing Morson's underlying thesis but engaging it along a slightly broader spectrum, that a very tightly constructed lyric poem, say Pushkin's "I recall a wondrous moment" (Ia pomniu chudnoe mgnovenie), does *tend more* to a spatial arraignment of part to whole, where the interplay between and among sound, grammar, meter, rhyme scheme, stanzaic form, subtextual allusion, and so on strongly suggest, if not a completely closed, then a "closing" structure.

If we take prosaics and translate it into the moral realm we get "misanthropology," Morson's witty term for the study of the "cussedness of human nature." It is clearly, as the name implies, a turning on its head of anthropology and the cultural relativism that often attends on that discipline. Here Morson examines the, in this case, social scientist's tendency to present the other that is distant in time or place with a phony neutrality, as in Margaret Mead's famous study of Samoans who in their sexual mores seem to have found a way out of western bourgeois repression. "Misanthropology," writes Morson, "focuses on human evil, and so by its very nature rejects relativism." Evil is fundamental to our nature, as is good. We develop as social animals, our identities being formed through speech with others that is internalized into thought (Vygotsky) or composed of innerly persuasive voices that become "accented" into personhood (Bakhtin). There is no state of human cognition or consciousness that is not already social. The difference between the misanthrope and the misanthropologist is that the former, say Jonathan Swift, is a "reverse sentimentalist" and a frustrated utopian—believing that humanity is simply perverse, like the Yahoos—while the latter, say Dostoevsky, sees "both the evil and good in human nature as 1) irreducible to each other, 2) ineradicable, and 3) fundamentally social." The process that brings one to view humankind misanthropologically is in effect the same process that brings one to read a novel dialogically, as a series of events involving human beings who can, in their present, evolve in different directions depending on the specific context and the choices that are made.

## Aristotle, Part to Whole

One of the reasons prosaics is a potentially productive approach to a variety of topics from the humanities to the social sciences is that it looks at culture as an evolutionary process with "intelligent feedback loops." Of course, the "misanthropological" optic means that the feedback does not always happen and is not always intelligent.

As with all genuinely original thinkers, the originality of prosaic thinker is itself firmly contextualized, growing out of something and toward something else. What is fresh about such thinking is not that it takes place in a vacuum, but that it uses what has come before in ways commensurate with, and sometimes exceeding, the power of the precursor. One senses this especially keenly in Morson's case, with his comments about Aristotle, which eventually lead to analogous comments about Darwin, which are then themselves leveraged into forays into the social and psychological. Microeconomic theories about how an individual's choices in the marketplace are part of larger patterns of consistency, or Freud's argument that the mind doesn't simply make mistakes but creates "slips" that are still meaningful, are precisely what is wrong, in Morson's opinion, with a modern scientific episteme that claims to follow Darwinian logic but in fact does not.

First, Morson's summation of Aristotelian versus Platonic thinking:

> For Aristotle, form is inseparable from matter, because it inheres in matter and gives it shape. Form does not exist on its own, any more than there can be color or shape without a thing that is colored or shaped. Believing in the independence of forms, as Plato did, is like supposing that because we can mentally abstract the properties of color, somewhere, in absolute purity, color must exist by itself.
>
> For Aristotle, soul shapes the matter of living things. Psyche is Aristotle's term for the form of the living object, and psychology is the study of the formal factor that makes a living object what it is. Psyche is therefore not separable from body. More accurately, form (or soul) is a shaping power, an entelechy, that is in the process of shaping matter. Thus, in nutrition (performed by the "digestive" soul), food becomes assimilated into flesh. Living involves not just form but forming.

This is an elegant encapsulation of the ancient philosopher's understanding of the origins of intelligent life: Aristotle's psyche is the feedback loop that joins form to function, organ system to consciousness (voluntary/involuntary response), without separating them from each other, since to do so is to end life. Disgust, on the other hand, as Morson argues elsewhere, is that moment when we see this living ensemble compromised: the guillotined head that blinks and stares, the compound fracture where the bone pierces the tissue.

### Darwin, Solov'ev, William James

Darwin enters the picture by placing Aristotle's form/function correlation into at least two important nineteenth-century intellectual frames of reference: Thomas Malthus's views of the dangers of population growth (hence the "survival of the fittest" terminology) and Charles Lyell's discoveries about geological formations (including fossils) and their relations to continuous change over time (uniformitarianism vs. catastrophism), from which Darwin would extrapolate his ideas about species formation and natural selection. The distance from Aristotle to

Darwin is that between a "soul" which "shapes the matter of living things" and a panda's thumb (made famous by Stephen Jay Gould), which is not really a thumb at all but an extension of the radial sesamoid that is *good enough* to function as an opposable digit and help the panda eat its bamboo. It is the logic of this "good enough" that is everything. It is also this same logic to which Morson keeps returning in his essays. Prosaics are, one might say, Morson's "panda's thumb."

Two other thinkers with whom Morson is in constant, though largely implicit, dialogue are the Russian philosopher Vladimir Solov'ev and the American philosopher-psychologist-humanist William James. Once again I suspect the touchstones are Aristotle and Darwin, with Bakhtin's leitmotifs of structure as open-ended (i.e. *evolving*) and consciousness as dialogic (i.e. always already *socially situated*) added in. In his amazing 1889 study of Darwin ("Beauty in Nature"), Solov'ev fully endorses the great naturalist's argument that species adapt and change through time and therefore are not created once and forever by an omniscient deity. The aesthetic, which is also one of Morson's favorite topics, arises in nature when matter is "enlightened" by spirit into something potentially new and beautiful. A lump of carbon is pure matter and light by itself is pure air, but rearrange the carbon molecules through intense heat and shine light on the result and you get a diamond. In the animal world we hear the aroused tomcat caterwauling on the rooftop and the nightingale singing its song. For Solov'ev, these are not the same thing. The sex drive, the explanation from origins, is insufficient to capture the full charm of the notes produced by the nightingale. There is something extra there, something more than a mating call.

On the other hand, a worm (say, an acanthocephalan) appears "ugly" (*bezobraznyi*, "lacking form") because it is all feeding (endosmosis, *vsasyvanie*: i.e. it sucks nutrients along its entire surface into the hollow cavity inside) and reproducing (the "complex structure" of what Claus terms its "mighty genitalia"). The other parts of an organ system that might constitute a complex configuration of form and function are not found here, and thus the aesthetic as a potentially transfiguring element has not yet done its work. (To be fair to Solov'ev, messiness does happen and all is a work in progress.) Indeed, the aesthetic for Solov'ev is most present, most seen and felt, when the sex and feeding drives are not, when the latter have moved into the background and appear veiled: e.g., the elaborate design on a tortoise's shell that hides and protects the unprepossessing and vulnerable creature underneath.

These ideas in turn find stimulating parallels in Morson's statements about disgust and voyeurism.

One also imagines inviting William James to this symposium-like roundtable led by Morson and joined in by Aristotle, Darwin, and Solov'ev. "By their fruits ye shall know them, not by their roots," writes James in *The Varieties of Religious Experience*_(1902). With the first part of this sentence James quotes Matthew 7:20, while with the second part he makes the case for a spirituality worthy of the name and endorsed by the exacting standards of American pragmatism. "The *roots* [James's emphasis] of a man's virtue are inaccessible to us," and so why try to define that virtue by those roots? Curiously (is this the intellectual world absorbing Darwin deeper and deeper into its consciousness?), Solov'ev had argued exactly the same thing a decade earlier: "The question '*What is* a known object?' never corresponds to the question '*From what* or whence *came* this object?'" James, however, trained in medicine at Harvard and fascinated with the discipline of psychophysiology, moves discussion into the area of personal spirituality. As opposed to a Richard Dawkins, he does not want to deny from the outside the validity of an individual's experience of the divine, but he also wants to argue that that experience does exist in time, regardless of the protestations of the prophet or the saint. There is a "before" and "after," the serial processing of which Morson often reminds his reader. James tells us matter-of-factly how notions of the "deity" have been historicized, and his tone, almost magically, manages to be both urbane and compassionate:

> In any case, they [i.e. the founders of different religions—DB] chose him [the deity] for the value of the fruits he seemed to yield. So soon as the fruits began to seem quite worthless; so soon as they conflicted with indispensable human ideals, or thwarted too extensively other values; so soon as they appeared childish, contemptible, or immoral when reflected on, the deity grew discredited; and was erelong neglected and forgotten.

Is this not Darwinian logic, the "good enough" of the panda's thumb, as applied to religious experience? Is this also not what Morson brings to the contemporary discussion of how the God of the Old and New Testaments (i.e. His scribal traces) *changed over time* and was therefore *not outside it*. Thus, concludes James, "it is the voice of human experience within us, judging and condemning all gods that stand athwart the pathway along which it feels itself to be advancing."

Once more it is what works in the here and now and what makes sense for our existential choices that is James's quarry, but also Morson's. Culture, including the spiritual side of human nature, moves forward the same way that Lyell's work moved forward and Darwin's work moved forward. We need to be cautious about those James called the "medical materialists," who today would be in the camp of Dawkins and the hard science atheists. If Saint Teresa's experience of revelation is too vague, too ecstatic to be taken seriously nowadays, then we should look more carefully at Tolstoy's conversion experience, which James certainly does and which Morson, one of our most eloquent students of the Russian author, might see as a process, an unfolding story, rather than a one-off turning point. In a word, our understanding of spirituality needs to be more intelligent.

## Teaching

It is probably no exaggeration to say that Saul Morson is one of the great teachers in the history of Northwestern University. He has won awards for his brilliant presence at the podium, his classes routinely attract some of the highest humanities enrollments in the country, and he has been known to team-teach a course with the university president himself. This is all doubtless laudable, but is not really the point. It (the teaching "aura") is not a cause of anything, except perhaps local accolades; instead it is the byproduct of other choices, of "walking the walk" and living Prosaics in one's professional life with students. To fully absorb the lessons of Mikhail Bakhtin is to become at some basic level the intelligent anti-theorist. College students are not trained in theory and will in all likelihood never "apply theory" in their future lives. Reaching them and turning them on is, or should be, the goal of our pedagogical travails.

In his spirited chapter entitled "What is a Literary Education?" Morson explains why great literature, especially great novels, are needed on our campuses (and in our society for that matter), and why that literature is not being done any favors by the widely held practices of today's academy. It is not for the professor to "tell" Shakespeare what he "meant" to say with the help of Freud. Better to turn the tables and imagine how the creative genius Shakespeare might read the overreaching Freud. Going line by line through George Eliot or Tolstoy creates, as it were, organs of empathy in the individual who "lives into" each character's story. Morson encourages his charges to view unfolding events as containing various possible futures. Novelistic characters are neither literary constructs (the formalist view) nor real persons (the so-called pathetic fallacy); they are rather "possible people." Thus, Mary Garth of *Middlemarch* may share personal qualities with Mary Anne Evans, which is interesting and relevant in and of itself, but the more important exercise is "practicing empathy" by living with Mary as she experiences the ups and downs of her relationship with Fred Vincy. Each event in their lives presents a series of choices. How does Mary remain Mary while making those choices? How does Fred improve on Fred by coming under Mary's influence? Here we see a glimpse of Tolstoy's famous idea that great literature "infects." Morson wants his students to "feel ideas" and to enjoy fully the process of "first-time reading" (not the "re-reading" of the literary critics). He encourages them to make use of the right hemisphere (*Anna Karenina*'s Levin mowing with the peasants) and the left hemisphere (that same Levin undergoing confession prior to marriage) and the chatter between them that tries to make meaning in our time.

## Quotations

Last but not least, Saul Morson is a student of quotations and sayings as well as a uniquely talented producer of them. There is a distinct pleasure in reading Morson, not only because his thoughts are inherently stimulating, but also because they turn out to be eminently quotable. I close with some of my own favorite quotes from these essays, as, saying more with less, they capture the texture of his thinking better than a long-drawn-out argument.

- "Men's work becomes meaningful when it partakes of the spirit of women's work."
- "Sinners love fatalism."
- "Prosaics assumes that the natural state of the world—at least, the human world—is mess, and that it is order, not disorder, that requires an explanation."
- "History is not a riddle with a hidden solution."
- "True holiness, which never fits a pattern, grows out of the particular situations of daily life."
- "One has a science when one no longer needs a story."
- "Darwin offers us an example of non-Newtonian science, one that requires narrative."
- "Social scientists practice Leibnizism without God."

- "Re-reading almost inevitably diminishes suspense. . . . Literary critics are by necessity re-readers."
- "Modern atheists are haunted by a theology they do not recognize as such."
- "Superstition is the social science of others."
- "By process I mean not just a sequence of events extending over time but a sequence in which multiple paths are open at multiple moments."
- "One becomes a genuine 'personality,' rather than a thing, when one is not just the sum of one's experiences and qualities. A personality retains the capacity to surprise."

Now, find your own favorites and enjoy!

# Abbreviations

Where no source of a biblical quotation is given, it is drawn from the King James version.

1984 George Orwell, *1984* (New York: Harcourt Brace, 1961).

AA M. M. Bakhtin, *Art and Answerability: Early Philosophical Essays*, ed. Michael Holquist and Vadim Liapunov (Austin: University of Texas Press, 1990).

AP Aristotle, "Poetics" in *Critical Theory Since Plato*, ed. Hazard Adams (New York: Harcourt Brace, 1971), 47-75.

AWD1 Fyodor Dostoevsky, *A Writer's Diary*, volume 1, 1873-1876, trans. Kenneth Lantz (Evanston: Northwestern University Press, 1993).

BK Fyodor Dostoevsky, *The Brothers Karamazov*, trans. Constance Garnett (New York: Random House, 1950).

BoG Gary Saul Morson, *The Boundaries of Genre: Dostoevsky's "Diary of a Writer" and the Traditions of Literary Utopia* (Austin: University of Texas Press, 1981).

BWA *The Basic Works of Aristotle*, ed. Richard McKeon (New York: Random House, 1941).

C&G John B. Cobb, Jr., and David Ray Griffin, *Process Theology: An Introductory Exposition* (Philadelphia: Westminster, 1976).

C&P Fyodor Dostoevsky, *Crime and Punishment* (New York: Random House, 1950).

CAID Sigmund Freud, *Civilization and Its Discontents*, ed. and trans. James Strachey (New York: Norton, 1961).

CWA2 *The Complete Works of Aristotle: The Revised Oxford Translation*, vol. 2, ed. Jonathan Barnes (Princeton: Princeton University Press, 1984).

DL Diogenes Laertius, *Lives of Eminent Philosophers*, vol. 2, trans. R. D. Hicks (Cambridge, MA: Harvard University Press, 1995).

DD Ambrose Bierce, *The Devil's Dictionary* (New York: Doubleday, n.d.).

DJ Lord Byron, *Don Juan*, ed. Leslie A. Marchand (Boston; Houghton Mifflin, 1958).

EAHB Gary S. Becker, *The Economic Approach to Human Behavior* (Chicago: University of Chicago Press, 1992).

FTOS Alexander Herzen, *"From the Other Shore" and "The Russian People and Socialism,"* trans. Moura Budberg and Richard Wollheim (Oxford: Oxford University Press, 1979).

GDR Katie Salen and Eric Zimmerman, *The Game Design Reader* (Cambridge, MA: MIT Press, 2006).

GPR Elie Halévy, *The Growth of Philosophic Radicalism*, trans. Mary Morris (Boston: Beacon, 1955).

GT *The Portable Swift*, ed. Carl Van Doren (New York: Viking, 1963), 489.

HC *The HarperCollins Study Bible*, ed. Wayne A. Meeks (New York: HarperCollins, 1993).

HIPV Gary Saul Morson, *Hidden in Plain View: Narrative and Creative Potentials in "War and Peace"* (Stanford: Stanford University Press, 1987).

HIQ M. J. Cohen and John Major, *History in Quotations* (London: Cassell, 2000).

HoD Fyodor Dostoevsky, *The House of the Dead*, trans. Constance Garnett (New York: Macmillan, 1959).

I Fyodor Dostoevsky, *The Idiot*, trans. Constance Garnett (New York: Modern Library, 1962).

L&S Gary Saul Morson, *The Long and Short of It: From Aphorism to Novel* (Stanford: Stanford University Press, 2012).

LaR *The Maxims of La Rochefoucauld*, trans. Louis Kronenberger (New York: Random House, 1959).

M George Eliot, *Middlemarch* (New York: Modern Library, 1984).

MB:CP Gary Saul Morson and Caryl Emerson, *Mikhail Bakhtin: Creation of a Prosaics* (Stanford: Stanford University Press, 1990).

MDQ *The Macmillan Dictionary of Quotations*, ed. John Dainith et al. (Edison, New Jersey: Chartwell, 2000).

N&F Gary Saul Morson, *Narrative and Freedom: The Shadows of Time* (New Haven, CT: Yale University Press, 1994).

NFP Martha C. Nussbaum, *Not for Profit: Why Democracy Needs the Humanities* (Princeton: Princeton University Press, 2010).

NFU    Fyodor Dostoevsky, *"Notes from Underground" and "The Grand Inquisitor,"* the Garnett translation revised by Ralph E. Matlaw (New York: Dutton, 1960).

ODQ    *The Oxford Dictionary of Quotations*, sixth edition, ed. Elizabeth Knowles (Oxford: Oxford University Pre, 2004).

OoS    Charles Darwin, *On the Origin of Species: A Facsimile of the First Edition* (Cambridge, MA, 1964).

QOK    *The Quatrains of Omar Khayyam: Three Translations of the Rubaiyat*, trans. Edward Fitzgerald, Justin McCarthy, and Richard Le Gallienne (California: Bardic Press, 2005).

P    Fyodor Dostoevsky, *The Possessed*, trans. Constance Garnett (New York: Random House, 1963).

PDP    Mikhail Bakhtin, *Problems of Dostoevsky's Poetics*, ed. and trans. Caryl Emerson (Minneapolis: University of Minnesota Press, 1984).

PI    Dan Ariely, *Predictably Irrational: The Hidden Forces That Shape Our Decisions*, revised edition (New York: HarperCollins, 2009).

PL    *The Riverside Milton*, ed. Roy Flannagan (Boston: Houghton Mifflin, 1998).

PSS    L. N. Tolstoi, *Polnoe sobranie sochinenii* [Complete Works], 90 vols., ed. V. G. Chertkov et al. (Moscow: Khudozhestvennaia literatura, 1929-1958).

R&E    Leo Tolstoy, *Recollections and Essays*, trans. Aylmer Maude (London: Oxford University Press, 1937; reprinted 1961).

RtR    Stephen Toulmin, *Return to Reason* (Cambridge, MA: Harvard University Press, 2001).

SEM    Gregory Bateson, *Steps to an Ecology of Mind* (New York: Ballantine, 1972).

SMW    Gary Saul Morson, *"Anna Karenina" in Our Time: Seeing More Wisely* (New Haven, CT: Yale University Press, 2007).

TS    Laurence Sterne, *The Life and Opinions of Tristram Shandy, Gentleman*, ed. James Aiken Work (New York: Odyssey, 1940).

VH    Niall Ferguson, *Virtual History: Alternatives and Counterfactuals* (New York: Basic Books, 1999).

W&P    Leo Tolstoy, *War and Peace*, trans. Ann Dunnigan (New York: Signet, 1968).

WoO    *The Words of Others; From Quotations to Culture* (New Haven, CT: Yale University Press, 2011).

YBQ    *The Yale Book of Quotations*, ed. Fred Shapiro (New Haven, CT: Yale University Press, 2006).

# Introduction

Looking back over decades, one can hardly avoid the fallacious impression that one was already there at the beginning. Retrospectively, it seems as if I tacitly knew all I ever would know even if it took me a lifetime to write it down. All those thrilling moments of creativity were so many illusions. At best, they were mere discoveries. Numerous critics have written biographies of authors from this standpoint, and when one becomes a critic of oneself, it is hard not to adopt the same narrative approach.

If so, how smart I was when young! On the other hand, how pointless the years have been!

I think the view of life as mere unfolding is mistaken. After the fact, a pattern appears, and so we think it is the only pattern that could have appeared. But if another pattern had emerged, we would have deemed it inevitable as well. You only see the road you took. Irrevocability is easily mistaken for inevitability.

The winner of a lottery feels chosen by fate, but, if someone else had won, he too would have felt chosen. The only thing really fated is that someone is bound to misconstrue his good fortune as fated.

The idea that outcomes are not inevitable even if they seem so has constituted one of my favorite themes. Time is open, the present moment makes a difference, and whatever does happen, something else could have. The dominant tradition of Western theology held that God foreknew all, and from the seventeenth century on, science has been mistakenly seen as proving determinism. Iron-clad laws of nature have played the role of a God substitute. We are still held captive by a vision at odds with our own experience. But other theologies and other views of the world are possible. Science, properly understood, does not dictate to the world what it *must* be like.

I believe deeply that at any given moment, more than one subsequent moment is possible. We live in a field of possibilities. It is not true that given all the facts about any moment, one could in principle predict every future moment and retrodict every past moment, as Leibniz, Spinoza, Laplace, and Einstein all believed. I think of myself as developing the ideas of the opposite tradition of thought, which holds that there are more possibilities than actualities. This counter-tradition includes thinkers as diverse as Aristotle and Tolstoy, who believed in genuine contingency, and Dostoevsky, who believed in human freedom. It is implicit in the temporality of the realist novel as a literary genre.

The greatest novelists, and especially Dostoevsky and Tolstoy, posed what the Russians called the "accursed questions" (*proklyatye voprosy*): are we responsible for what we do or is it all determined for us? Are our choices real or do they only seem so? Does the objective view of the world include everything, or is it essentially incomplete? Does it in fact omit what is most valuable to us, our direct sense of a subjective self? Is our selfhood given to us by outside forces, or do we in part make it ourselves? Do we change in unpredictable ways or merely reveal already given qualities?

The tradition of posing such questions in novels, drama, and poetry characterizes Russian literature. It is reflected as well in Russian literary criticism, which has tended to raise philosophical problems by analyzing fiction. Russian philosophy often takes the form of commentaries on the great writers, Russian and foreign. To Westerners, Bakhtin's *Problems of Dostoevsky's Poetics* and *Rabelais and His World* best exemplify this peculiar tradition.

Like many earlier Russian critics, Bakhtin located the value of literature in its contributions to psychology, philosophy, and, especially, ethics. But he saw ethical and philosophical implications in the very shapes of works. Each kind of plot, for instance, represented a model for how events happen. With such analyses, he reconceptualized formalism as ultimately a matter not of form but of "ideology" (complexes of ideas).

Thus Bakhtin approached genres as palpable philosophies. In his view, each genre constituted a "form-shaping ideology," a view of the world seeking expression through appropriate forms. The way novels represent heroes and heroines, their exploration of the way society and individual psychology interact, and their inclusion of immense everyday detail, project a specific sense of people in the world. They embodied a philosophy that Bakhtin found immensely appealing. So do I.

\* \* \*

If Tolstoy is considered the supreme example of realism, then the realist novel suggests that the most important events in life are not the grand, dramatic, and striking ones. They are, instead, the prosaic, undramatic, and ordinary ones we often do not so much as notice. Those events include the "tiny alterations" of consciousness, the infinitesimally small and vanishingly brief mental gestures making us who we are. Taken together, they make life what it is. By bringing such events to our attention, novels can change our view of our world and our selves.

I coined the term *prosaics* to express two related ideas. First, as the word itself suggests, it indicates that what matters most—in history and individual lives, in ethics and aesthetics—are the details. As Tolstoy's greatest reader, Ludwig Wittgenstein, explained: "The aspects of things that are most important to us are hidden because of their simplicity and familiarity. (One is unable to notice something because it is always before one's eyes). ... And this means: we fail to be struck by what, once seen, is most striking and most powerful" (PI, 50e).

These details resist reduction to some overarching law. We would be mistaken to imagine that behind their inexhaustible variety lie some simple formulas, like Newton's laws of motion. The world, especially the social and psychological world, exhibits infinite and irreducible complexity. Instead of trying to explain away that complexity by ascribing everything to some social scientific principles, as thinkers as diverse as Bentham, Marx, Freud, Malinowski, Lévi-Strauss, the rational choice theorists, and countless others have tried to do, we would do better to follow Wittgenstein's repeated admonition: *Don't think, but look!* Or rather (and this what Wittgenstein meant), appreciate the complexity of things before imagining they can be made simple.

The form of thought that best represents the prosaic view of life is the realist novel, and so the second meaning of "prosaics" is an approach to literature that, unlike "poetics," focuses on prose generally and the realist novel in particular. As the term "poetics" implies, literary theory has seen prose as some sort of fallen poetry, literary only insofar as it can do what poetry does. That is why the word poetry often functions as a synonym for literature (not just verse) and why prose often means the opposite, whatever is unliterary. So we are told that poetry draws attention to the means of expression, but "prose" is indifferent to them. The phrase "prose literature" then seems paradoxical or oxymoronic.

If one approaches novels in terms defined by poetics, one will seek out metaphors, symbols, and other poetic devices, and thereby miss the distinctive features that make novels what they are. One needs instead to approach them, and everything else in culture one would like to understand, in their own terms.

* * *

I begin this book with an essay on prosaics, which can serve as a kind of overture to everything that follows. The four other chapters of this volume develop "prosaics" in different ways. In each case, some new concern approaches this concept from a new direction and so, I hope, results in something valuable.

The second chapter concerns open time. It develops a "prosaics of process."

I spent the academic year 1996-97 as a token humanist at the Center for Advanced Study in the Behavioral Sciences in order to develop ideas from my then-recently published book *Narrative and Freedom: The Shadows of Time* (Yale University Press, 1994). It was a year that had immense influence on my thinking. Hard-core Rational Choice theory dominated discussion. The methodology of economics, in its mathematicized form and most far-reaching ambitions, held sway.

Economics was conceived not as a subject matter but as an approach to human behavior that just happened to have been developed by economists but is universally applicable. Thus, as Nobel prize-winning economist Gary Becker has famously argued, "the economic approach does not draw conceptual distinctions between major and minor decisions, such as those involving life and death in contrast to the choice of a brand of coffee; or between decisions said to involve strong emotions and those with little emotional involvement, such as choosing a mate or the number of children in contrast to buying paint; or between decisions by persons with different incomes, education, or family backgrounds."[1]

In one conversation, a social scientist offered an argument I shall never forget. No real science, he explained, requires narrative.

---

[1]      EAHB, 8-9.

To the extent that one can account for phenomena by laws, one does not have to tell stories. Given Newton's laws of motion, there is no need to narrate the course of the planets. One can just derive their position at any chosen moment. When social science advances a bit more, with economics as its model, it too will dispense with narrative. Everything will be mathematicized. The only use for stories will be pedagogical, that is, as illustrative. But they will be superfluous for explanatory purposes.

It immediately struck me that if the world is *not* reducible to Newtonian formulae, then narrative *would* play an essential role. If open time exists, then predictability would be impossible and one would have to tell a story explaining how one outcome rather than another came about. The world would be characterized by *narrativeness*, that is, the indispensability of narrative for understanding. The first essay of chapter two, "Narrativeness," explicates this term.

The second essay of chapter two develops the concept of open time. The essay's first part, "The Vision of Poetics and Product," explicates closed time. When time is understood as closed, the world resembles a well-made literary work, a finished product described by poetics from Aristotle to the present. Such works create a sense of inevitability. Everything has to be just as it is: nothing in it is just there, and a sufficient reason accounts for each detail. Everything plays its part in a total structure. That is why, as we read a literary work, we can guess at its ending by imagining what an effective structure would require.

The essay's second part, "The Counter-Tradition: Presentness and Process," then explicates the alternative vision of a world in open time. In various forms, this vision has appeared in fields as diverse as biology, architecture, city planning, linguistics, and theology. Sometimes the traditional view of closed time is likely to prove more fruitful, as it did with Galileo, but at other times, the counter-traditional view fits the topic better, as it did for Darwin. I offer some rules of thumb for recognizing which situation is which. My overall point is that there is indeed a choice to be made. One cannot just presume the traditional view of closed time as if it were the only possible one.

If poetics and the works to which it best applies implicitly endorse closed time, are there literary masterpieces that poetics does not fit, works that exemplify open time? If so, how shall we describe their design?

In fact, there are many such works—including Tolstoy's *War and Peace*, Dostoevsky's *The Idiot*, Sterne's *Tristram Shandy*, Byron's *Don Juan*,

Burton's *Anatomy of Melancholy*, Montaigne's *Essays*, and, if approached in the right spirit, the Hebrew Bible. To be understood, they demand not a poetics of product but a prosaics of process. The third part of this essay outlines such a processual prosaics.

\* \* \*

My dear friend and pseudonym, Alicia Chudo, wrote the three essays constituting this volume's third chapter. Alicia is perhaps best known for her book *And Quiet Flows the Vodka, or When Pushkin Comes to Shove: The Curmudgeon's Guide to Russian Literature and Culture* (Evanston: Northwestern University Press, 2000), which succeeded in offending lovers of the Russian soul everywhere. People have often asked why I used a pseudonym for these works. The answer is, I found it helpful to think through a certain vision of the world in a forum in which I did not have to ask whether I believed all its implications. So I imagined a curmudgeonly personality whose view of human nature is decidedly bleak, and who invented a discipline she calls *misanthropology*, the study of the "cussedness of human nature."

Given such a view of humanity, Alicia despises all utopian visions. The worst suffering, she intones, has been caused by those who would abolish it forever. She prefers the great tradition of satire, from Swift and Pope to Voltaire and Gogol. Her favorite book of Freud's is *Civilization and Its Discontents*. Frequently quoting La Rochefoucauld, she sees history as Gibbon did. In her view, decline and fall is almost always far more likely than progress. She reminds us that there are no gains without losses, and that to soothe ourselves we usually underestimate the losses, especially if we would have to take responsibility for them. Original Sin, she remarks, is the one theological doctrine that has been empirically confirmed.

Noting that nineteenth-century thinkers typically envisaged the twentieth century as a time of great strides in human happiness, she points out that only Dostoevsky saw that it would witness the creation of totalitarianism and be the bloodiest century in human history. It gave birth to Auschwitz, the Final Solution, the Rwandan genocide, the Soviet Gulag, the Chinese Cultural Revolution, and the Khmer Rouge. If these events do not disprove an optimistic view of human nature, she asks, what would? Is it possible after these recent events to believe that History has an inevitable trajectory upward? And to believe that if only some set of reforms were adopted, we could rest easy?

Even if some reforms should help, new reformers would devote their zeal to reforming them away. Nothing can be relied on more thoroughly than human folly.

It is hardly surprising then, that she nods in agreement at the insights of Dostoevsky's Ivan Karamazov, even if she shakes her head in wonder that he could ever have been idealistic enough to be so disillusioned. That is the fate of misanthropes, from Shakespeare's Timon to Swift's Gulliver, and that is why Alicia thinks of herself not as a misanthrope but as a misanthropologist. Her first essay, "Misanthropology: Voyeurism and Human Nature" explains the difference.

Alicia has always been fascinated by the human taste for voyeurism, especially our delight in witnessing the suffering of others. Both Dostoevsky and Tolstoy developed the idea that looking is not mere passive observation but an action with moral value, and Alicia, with her taste for Dostoevsky, develops his insights. The old saw, "a cat can look at a king," with its implication that looking is entirely different from doing, is entirely mistaken. Her interest in voyeurism leads her to explore the delight humanity seems to take in cruelty. As she chuckles at the Kellogg-Briand Pact of 1928-29, in which fifty-four nations renounced war as a way to settle disputes, so she is amused by those who imagine they can legislate away the use of torture. In fact, she often alludes to the mentality she calls "Kellogg-Briandism" when giving her take on world affairs.

Alicia develops these views in this chapter's second essay, "Misanthropology, Continued: Disgust, Violence, and More on Voyeurism." Alicia believes that many of our characteristically human responses to the world have implied philosophical content. What we do presumes a world in which such responses make sense. Regret, for instance, suggests that, had we chosen differently, things might have worked out better. Thus, it suggests that time is open. It may also imply the possibility that future bad choices can be avoided, and so contains a measure of optimism. Regret is hope projected backward, sort of like one wit's definition of gratitude as a lively expectation of future favors. In the second essay of chapter three, Alicia explores the contrasting philosophical implications of laughter and disgust. Despite their underlying differences, both of these spontaneous reactions to the world tell us a great deal about ourselves.

Alicia made her debut with a poem that grew out of her work on translating Pushkin's novel in verse, *Eugene Onegin*. "An Onegin of Our

Times," written in the same stanzaic form as Pushkin's novel, depicts a contemporary literary "theorist," the intellectual world in which he lives, and the theories he develops to achieve its plaudits. Alicia did not expect this work, a sort of essay in verse like Pope's *Dunciad*, to win her any friends in the community of theorists.

\* \* \*

In Chapter Four, I respond to requests to explain how I manage to draw so many enthusiastic students (six hundred at a time) to take Russian literature courses without dumbing them down. I can't say I really know. But my experience of teaching and my conversations with students tentatively suggest some more broadly applicable insights.

Anyone who follows publications on higher education will have seen laments that fewer students want to take courses in, much less major in, literature. Usually, these analyses blame the students for their preprofessionalism and materialism, or fault technology for creating short attention spans. If all you care about is money, and you are comfortable with the length of a tweet, why read *War and Peace*? The problem lies with students and is, of course, ultimately the fault of "society."

And yet, I do teach *The Brothers Karamazov*, *Anna Karenina*, and *War and Peace* to large classes. I do not detect short attention spans. Nor is there any obvious material reward students can gain from reading, much less loving, these very long books.

When others do not appreciate what one offers, it is always more agreeable to blame their taste than one's offerings. But what if the problem lies not with the students but with us—that is, with how literature has been taught in recent years? After summarizing students' descriptions of their literature classes, I suggest that declining enrollments may testify to their good sense.

What does literature have to offer that cannot be learned, or learned equally well, elsewhere? If one cannot answer that question, one can hardly blame students for asking, why bother? After all, there are easier things to do than parse the syntax of *Paradise Lost*. And if one's answer is "nothing," because literature classes apply methods from theory or the social sciences to literature—literature is what one analyzes, not the source of insight—the question again arises, why bother? Why not apply those methods to something less mystifying?

There are good answers to students' questions. In the first place, great literature offers the richest psychological portraits of people we have. No other discipline or cultural artifact has come close. Matthew Arnold famously remarked that *Anna Karenina* is not a work of art but a piece of life, and countless writers, readers, and critics have endorsed the view that if life could write directly, it would write like Tolstoy.[2] Nobody ever said that about Jeremy Bentham, Gary Becker, or even Sigmund Freud.

Freud himself recognized the uncanny accuracy of "the poets" in general and of Dostoevsky in particular—he calls *Karamazov* "the most magnificent novel ever written"—but suggested that they result not from serious reflection but from the mystery of creative art.[3] In his view, the writers did not grasp what they were saying, so psychologists have to do it for them. This is an odd thing to say about Dostoevsky in particular, because his works contain long analyses of characters' unconscious motivations, conducted either by the author or, implausibly, by the characters themselves. So eager is Dostoevsky to explicate human complexity that he even gives remarkably insightful psychological arguments to that brawling officer, Dmitri Karamazov. Lack of explicitness is hardly Dostoevsky's problem.

One can also find explicit psychological analysis, as well as amazingly rich portraits of people, in the works of George Eliot, Tolstoy, and other novelists. Even when, as in Jane Austen, the analyses are left implicit, they are hardly outside the author's awareness. If these writers could describe people so well, isn't it possible they knew something?

This essay also argues that these writers offered especially rich descriptions of ethical dilemmas. Where philosopher's thought experiments tend to think away essential complexity, realist novels—which can be regarded as a special type of thought experiment—preserve it. So presented, these books command student recognition of their value. As much as they are concerned with their professional future, students care about themselves as ethical beings as well.

Most important, great novels invite us to identify with characters and, in so doing, offer *practice in empathy*. Philosophers, anthropologists, and historians may describe the importance of seeing the world from other points of view, but literature actually gives us the experience of

---

[2]    For a detailed account of critical responses, see chapters 2 and 3 of HIPV.

[3]    Sigmund Freud, "Dostoevsky and Parricide," in *Dostoevsky: a Collection of Critical Essays*, ed. René Wellek (Englewood Cliffs, NJ: Prentice -Hall, 1962), 98.

doing so. We feel from within what it is like to be a member of the opposite sex, another social class, or a different culture, and how personal choices and moral dilemmas might appear to other people. This essay describes the workings of novelistic empathy, its ethical implications, and how it might be taught.

By enabling students to place themselves in the position of others, literature in general and novels in particular offer a special sort of wisdom.

\* \* \*

I recognize how old-fashioned it is to view literature as a source of wisdom, but I have always done so. That is one reason I have long been fascinated with aphorisms, the shortest of literary genres. In chapter five, I explore the implicit philosophy of witticisms. I see this genre through the prism of games and play, which is also a favorite topic of mine and which I discuss in some detail. Faced with the contingency of the world, we invent a number of ways in which to control and cope with its challenge. We invent art, create the magical space of games, and stage confrontations of mind with social circumstance. Wit as I analyze it expresses the adequacy of mind to any challenge the social world may present. It can sometimes achieve real profundity and demonstrate impressive courage.

\* \* \*

As this summary suggests, these essays return time and again to a set of problems. Each essay approaches contingency from a different angle, all deal in one way or another with presentness and open time, and empathy is considered over and over again. So is the strength or weakness of our models of human experience. And I return time and again to the nature, meaning, and value of novels. I am not sure that, in viewing a topic in different contexts, I arrive at perfectly consistent conclusions, but I hope that one way or another, these explorations of accursed questions provoke the reader to respond with his or her own ideas.

Our greatest tool for understanding is dialogue, and the most important thing is to keep the conversation going.

Part One

---

# Overture

## Chapter One

## WHAT IS PROSAICS?

> be lowlie wise. . .
> . . . to know
> That which lies before us in daily life
> Is the prime Wisdom . . . .
> Therefore from this high pitch let us descend
> A lower flight, and speak of things at hand.
> —*Milton, Paradise Lost*[1]

### Prologue to Prosaics

Toward the end of *War and Peace,* Pierre realizes he has been looking for meaning in the wrong place. In everything near and familiar, he sees only "what was limited, petty, commonplace and meaningless." He scans the distance, as idealists tend to do. He at last finds what he has been seeking where he least expected, at his very feet.

In *Anna Karenina,* Levin also finds faith by appreciating the ordinary and familiar. "And I watched for miracles, complained that I did not see a miracle that would convince me. A material miracle would have persuaded me. And here is a miracle, the sole miracle possible, surrounding me on all sides, and I never noticed it" (AK, 829).

While working on Tolstoy, I thought to call this view of the world prosaics. Prosaics recognizes the importance and value of the ordinary, everyday, and undramatic, which we usually overlook precisely because of its familiarity. In fact, the familiar contains enormous richness and variety, if we could only learn to see it. "If we had a keen vision and feeling of all ordinary human life," writes George Eliot in *Middlemarch,* "it would be like hearing the grass grow and the squirrel's heart beat" (M, 189). We would come to appreciate the "unhistoric acts" that truly make the world a better place, not all at once, but by an "incalculably diffusive" process (M, 795).

---

[1]    Book 8, lines 173, 192-194, 198-199, in PL, 566-567.

Cloaked in their ordinariness, the truths we seek are hidden in plain view. The literary form best adapted to capturing those truths is the one that focuses on the tiny alterations of daily life: the realist novel.

The essay that follows combines my earliest statements on prosaics, written about twenty-five years ago. It adds a few more recent observations composed in their spirit. Take it as a sort of overture to the rest of this book. Like snatches of tunes woven together, it gives a brief taste of some key quotations discussed in later chapters. It also offers a first take on themes those chapters extend in different directions.

## Two Dogmatisms Debate

Sadly enough, humanist scholars have long been engaged in a series of futile debates. Two schools of thought stake out ever more extreme versions of their position, while responding to the other's proofs that it is untenable. Neither can conceive of any viable alternative.

Let us call one school the "semiotic totalists" and the other the "village relativists." The semiotic totalists presume that to understand any part of culture one must devise a system capable of grasping every part of it. All human experience must fit the system's iron-clad order. For these thinkers, nothing is innocent of meaning. All events, actions, and artifacts constitute *signs* that their system alone can decode. One or another version of semiotics—the study of signs—therefore offers a key to all mysteries. New and improved versions of Freud and Marx, seen as deciphering the psyche and the social world, are always in the making.

Like the proverbial "village atheists," who are mightily impressed with rather simplistic arguments against God, village relativists recycle familiar arguments to deny the very possibility of knowledge. They agree that explanations must be all-embracing systems but deny that such systems are possible. And they, too, invoke Freud and Marx, not as system-builders but as deconstructors of received belief systems.

As they understand things, other people hold their beliefs not because of evidence but because of unconscious drives or "false consciousness." Linguistics, the sociology of knowledge, "critical thinking," and whatever else comes to hand, demonstrate that truth, no less than beauty and goodness, is nothing more than a function of power. With jargon no less daunting than that of their totalist opponents', they repeatedly find ways to demonstrate a rather simple point—that one cannot know anything with certainty—and conclude, with sublime illogic, that one cannot know anything at all.

There is the old New York response to the assertion that we can't be absolutely certain of anything: so what else is new? And to the conclusion that one cannot know anything at all, the answer is that knowledge comes in degrees of certainty: and how much do you think you need?

Nonacademics often misunderstand the relativists' arguments as the healthy exposure of bias. It is wise (and uncontroversial) to recognize that our perceptions are shaped by our needs, preconceptions, and habits of thought. It is well to be suspicious when one finds oneself accepting arguments leading to conclusions one wants to believe; no one ever lost money persuading people they are right. But that is not the kind of reasonable skepticism that these humanists profess. Who could shock anyone with skepticism of that sort, and how could a profession justify its theories if they are nothing but common sense? Skepticism of the ordinary presumes that there *is* a truth of the matter, and the very notion of bias suggests an error that might be corrected or overcome.

The extreme relativists, by contrast, deny the very existence of facts. What we call facts are *entirely* the product of our individual and social interests, and any correction would simply be the product of some other set of interests. Ambrose Bierce once remarked that while conservatives are enamored of the evils of the past, liberals would replace them with new ones. There is no Archimedean point where one can view things objectively and without preconceptions.

Facts depend on systems of interpretation, and all systems, it is said, are "incommensurable." No common, objective standard can arbitrate among them. Each offers its own "narrative." Adopting this form of relativism, one thinker recommended that historians just invent whatever story best suits their political purposes, since there are no facts to violate anyway. If one is moved to reply that such an argument is illogical, because historical narratives by definition pertain to facts, the reply is easy enough: logic itself is just another form of rhetoric. The ease with which such arguments can be manufactured, along with the facile sense of superiority they convey, again suggests the link between this kind of relativism and cheap atheism.

Of course, these two schools talk past each other. One professes a positive dogmatism, the other a negative dogmatism. Since neither invites genuinely skeptical inquiry, or allows an external vantage point, each tries to outflank the other with its favorite rhetorical ploys. Semiotic totalists can always detect some form of bourgeois decadence or inner drive to repression in their opponents. Their nihilism simply reflects the condition and serves the interests of capitalist society. You can't make a revolution with no ground to stand on. For their part, the village relativists invariably discover incriminating evidence indicating that their opponents actually believe in something. They detect the falsity behind each ascription of false consciousness, or show the unconscious drives behind revelations of unconscious drives.

Each camp claims to win by virtue of being more radical: the totalists are politically "more radical than thou," and the relativists more nihilistic. In fact, both resemble a group of advanced thinkers in one of Dostoevsky's novels who claim to have "gone beyond nihilism" because they "deny more," including nihilism itself. We all know people who presume that in any given dispute truth probably lies somewhere in the middle. These two camps presume the opposite, that it lies on, or even beyond, an extreme. They share the spirit of Robespierre. Perhaps that is why Blake's maxims have become so popular: one way or another, one accepts that the road of excess leads to the palace of wisdom.

## Prosaics Defined

Let me offer an alternative to this endless oscillation of absolutes and absences. I call this alternative "prosaics." Coiners of a neologism enjoy a special freedom in defining it, so I will stipulate at the outset that "prosaics" has two distinct but closely related meanings. It is, first of all, a way of thinking about human events that focuses on the ordinary, messy, quotidian facts of daily life—in short, on the prosaic. As it happens, this form of thinking also offers a reason to take realist novels with renewed seriousness: of all literary forms, novels are best able to capture the messiness of the world. Thus the second meaning of "prosaics": whereas traditional *poetics* approaches literature that focuses on epics, lyrics, and tragedies, prosaics focuses on great prose and, especially, on novels.

Prosaic facts have been best represented in prosaic art.

### Essential Mess

Thinkers often presume that behind all apparent disorder there must lie a hidden order. One only needs to sort out the noise to discover the fundamental laws. When Galileo thought away the effects of friction, he was able to discover basic laws of motion. His example has inspired countless thinkers since.

Unfortunately, in the social and psychological spheres, such thinking typically fails. By thinking away the "noise" one thinks away the phenomenon itself. Though Galileo's method allowed him to supersede Aristotle's physics, Aristotle proves a better guide to the humanities. Here we must be content "to indicate the truth roughly and in outline, and in speaking of things which are only for the most part true and with premises of the same kind to reach conclusions that are no better.... It is equally foolish to accept probable reasoning from a mathematician and to demand from a rhetorician scientific proofs" (BWA, 936). By "rhetorician," Aristotle means someone who comments on human beings.

As a way of thinking about the cultural world, prosaics (in the first sense) does not presume, as semiotic totalism does, that order is fundamental and disorder an illusion. On the contrary, prosaics assumes that the natural state of the world—at least, the human world—is mess, and that it is order, not disorder, that requires an explanation. Order does exist, of course, but it is always the result of work. As the Russian thinker Mikhail Bakhtin liked to say, it is not given but made (*ne dan, a sozdan*).

The anthropologist Gregory Bateson captured this prosaic insight in one of his splendid dialogues with his daughter. Bateson called these dialogues "metalogues" because their shapes illustrate their themes, and in "Why Do Things Get in a Muddle?," father and daughter muddle and meander their way to a series of prosaic insights. "People spend a lot of time tidying things," the daughter observes, "but they never spend time muddling them. Things just seem to get in a muddle by themselves." If one pays no particular attention to what one is doing, tidy things get messy, but messy things never tidy themselves. Why?

Bateson at last arrives at an answer, which is disarmingly simple: there are an indefinitely numerous ways in which things can be messy, but very few that one would call tidy. His daughter expresses dissatisfaction with this explanation, because there must be a positive reason, some sort of active force, for disorder. Bateson replies that it is order, not disorder, that requires a reason:

> D[aughter]: Daddy, you didn't finish. Why do things get the way I say isn't tidy?
>
> F[ather]: But I *have* finished—it's just because there are more ways which you call "untidy" than there are ways which you call "tidy."
>
> D: But that isn't a reason why—
>
> F: But, yes, it is. And it is the real and only and very important reason.
>
> D: Oh, Daddy! Stop it.
>
> F: No, I'm not fooling. That is the reason, and *all of science is hooked up with that reason.* (SEM, 5)

Whether or not all of science is hooked up with that reason, all of prosaics is. The natural state of the world is mess.

By contrast, consider Freud's assumption that everything in the psyche operates according to a system in which no accidents whatsoever are possible. Slips of the tongue and the forgetting of facts, however trivial, are always "Freudian": they result from a disguised "intention to forget." Characteristically, Freud moves from the insight that some errors serve a purpose to the insistence that all do. "Since we overcame the error of supposing that the forgetting we are familiar with signified a destruction of the memory trace—that is, an annihilation," he writes in *Civilization and Its Discontents*, "we have been inclined to take the opposite view, that in mental life nothing which has once been formed can perish—that everything is somehow preserved and that in suitable circumstances ... it can be brought to light" (CAID, 17). Prosaics replies: why should we assume that the human mind is that efficient? After all, nothing else biological or social works perfectly. The laws of physics never fail, but organisms grow ill, machines break, and societies collapse. Can it really be that each and every act of forgetting must be purposeful and requires work?

If the natural state of the mind is mess, then forgetting and errors must often result from the simple inefficiency of all things human. The burden of proof goes the other way. Memory requires a reason, and perhaps the forgetting of some things requires a reason. But the mere fact that I cannot remember every speck of dust on the way to work does not mean I intend to forget it.

Here and elsewhere, Freud seems to be driven to such totalist reasoning by the assumption that a science—which he claims to be inventing—must resemble physics and admit of no exceptions. Hence his constant tendency to leap from a few cases to a claim that everything is just like them. He offers illustrations as if they were demonstrations. It is a habit that literary and cultural theorists today have readily adopted, but as the Yiddish proverb cautions, "'For example' is no proof.'"

The political analogue to Freudian logic is conspiracy theory. Such theorists hold that if you can identify a social problem, then you can find someone or some group that planned it; if no one can be proved to have planned it, that only shows how effectively the conspirators have suppressed the evidence. Or as we might say, absence reflects an "intention to conceal." In 1937, a trial in Switzerland established conclusively that the most influential modern conspiracy document, *The Protocols of the Elders of Zion*, was a forgery, but the proof did almost no good at all. Its Nazi circulators then and Middle Eastern ones now simply argue that the trial itself proves the extent of the Elders' influence. If one argues with a Marxist, one must be doing so from class interest; if one disputes a Freudian, it must be from a desire to avoid the painful truth. The idea that history doesn't fit a system is dismissed out of hand.

Any closed system can explain away objections to it. One has to stand outside it, and look at evidence without presuming the system's correctness, to test it. But testing is what believers in closed systems refuse to do. They prefer to *illustrate*.

## What We See We Do Not Notice

It was against such system-mongering that the greatest thinkers of the prosaic tradition rebelled. Contrary to received opinion, Leo Tolstoy, for instance, denied that history follows discoverable laws. "I see no reason whatsoever to seek out general laws of history, not to mention the impossibility of doing so," Tolstoy wrote.[2] He saw that the thought of his time, "from Hegel to Buckle," presumed a pattern behind the chaos of daily life, and he dedicated *War and Peace* to disputing that notion. He went so far as to include several

---

2      In "Progress and the Definition of Education," PSS 8:333.

essays on the logical fallacies typically committed by historical systematizers.

In the novel's councils of war, generals and rulers presume that a good plan will anticipate all contingencies. The wiser characters learn that battles, and all other historical events, are the product of "a hundred million diverse chances," the result of an indefinitely large number of causal lines reducible to no pattern whatsoever, even in principle (W&P, 930). Sometimes events happen for a specific reason, but sometimes they happen just "for some reason" (one of Tolstoy's favorite phrases). History is not a riddle with a hidden solution.

Tolstoy's wisest characters surrender the quest for certainty and instead seek ways to act effectively in a world of contingency. Kutuzov, the wisest general in *War and Peace*, sleeps through councils of war, not to show contempt for his fellow officers but because he knows that war is too unsystematic for late-night planning to be of much use. In fact, it might actually hurt, because in a world of uncertainty, the most valuable tool is *alertness*. The best preparation for a battle, Kutuzov advises, is not strategizing but "a good night's sleep" (W&P, 323).

*War and Peace* also teaches a prosaic lesson about perception. In contrast to most great systems, prosaics questions whether the most important events may not be the most ordinary and everyday ones—events we do not appreciate simply because they are so commonplace. Abe Lincoln supposedly quipped that God must have loved the common people, because he made so many of them. Tolstoy seems to add: He must have loved the ordinary events, because he made so many of them, too. Hidden by familiarity, the prosaic events that truly shape our lives—that truly *are* our lives—escape our notice.

The truths we seek lie unseen before us, and for that reason are all the more difficult to discern.

## Where Meaning Is

Historical thinkers tend to focus on the big events—wars, revolutions, dramatic incidents, critical choices, and decisive encounters. Individual people, too, tend to tell their life stories in terms of exceptional events and major decisions. But what if the important events are not the great ones but the infinitely numerous and apparently inconsequential ordinary ones, which, taken together, are far more effective and significant? Memorable events are memorable just because they are exceptional. To imagine they are important because they are memorable and noticeable, Tolstoy explains, would be like concluding that because only treetops are visible on a distant hill, nothing exists there but trees.

It is often the small items in the background of old photographs that most powerfully evoke elusive memories of the past. The things barely noticed at the time and included only by chance may best preserve the feeling of life as it was lived. The furniture long ago discarded, a spot on the wall, a picture we had long ignored but which now suggests the habitual life we lived beneath it—these small items remind us of how it felt to live in a room. The intended subject of a photograph can seem much less important in comparison with its background; and perhaps that is one reason that professional photographs without a background so often seem to miss the very point of photography.

Tolstoy's characters achieve wisdom when they learn not to seek the great and poetic but to appreciate the small and prosaic. In *War and Peace*, Pierre spends his life looking for a grand meaning far from the daily flux of events. And so Pierre equips himself "with a mental telescope and gazed into the distance" in the vain hope of finding the great and infinite (W&P, 1320). He oscillates between belief in utopian systems that will explain everything and despair at the impossibility of arriving at such a system—between totalism and relativism.

He eventually learns that meaning is not deep and distant but here and everywhere. He realizes that distant things seemed to him meaningful only because he could not clearly see them. No one is a prophet in his own country, and no events we see daily strike us as significant.

Freemasonry, philanthropies, and philosophies of history all tempt Pierre. Throughout the novel, he shifts between elation over his newest system for discovering the meaning of life and despair as each system proves to have a fatal flaw. But wisdom does eventually come to Pierre: "Now, however, he had learned to see the great, the eternal, the infinite in everything, and therefore ... he had naturally discarded the telescope through which he had till then been gazing over the heads of men, and joyfully he surveyed the ever-changing, eternally great, unfathomable, and infinite life around him." (W&P, 1320). The meaning Pierre has sought was always there before his eyes. Tolstoy's wisest characters, like Dolly Oblonskaya, know this lesson all along, but his questing heroes have to learn it over many years and hundreds of pages.

## Making a Self

Modern orthodoxy understands the self and meaning in the opposite way. In the shadow of Freud, Americans from Ann Landers to the most esoteric literary critic have tended to assume that selfhood, no less than history, is a riddle with a concealed solution: to know oneself is to know the hidden self deep within us. But what if there is no such central, core self? What if selfhood, like all forms of order and unity, is not discovered but made? That position was espoused by a remarkable minority of psychological thinkers. They rejected the Freudian model, and with it the notion of the self as essentially complete at a young age, hidden by layers of repression that only the analyst can probe.

Two Russian thinkers, Bakhtin and the psychologist Lev Vygotsky, extended prosaic premises. They denied that the self is a system, however complex. The self is something much looser, an aggregate of habits, contingent facts, and clusters of order that continually interact with one another and the hundred million diverse facts of daily life. Whatever wholeness we achieve requires enormous work, which is the effort of life; and that work is never complete. A self is not a gift, is not inborn and then distorted through socialization and repression. On the contrary, a child acquires a self as he or she is socialized. And that self, which can never achieve unity or fixity, changes throughout its lifetime.

Tolstoy emphatically rejected the idea of the self as a complete system, an idea associated (I think incorrectly) with that great inspirer of Freud, Dostoevsky. Tolstoy disliked the view that people are driven by a deep inner conflict leading either to salvation or catastrophe. Dostoevsky believed that lives are decided at critical moments. He structured his plots around crescendos of intense instants driven by sudden eruptions from the unconscious. By contrast, Tolstoy insisted that although we may imagine our lives are decided at important moments, our choices are in fact shaped by the whole climate of our minds, which itself results from countless small decisions made at ordinary moments.

## The Tiny Bit

Interestingly enough, Tolstoy chose to illustrate his thesis through an interpretation of *Crime and Punishment*, which he analyzes as if he had written it himself. The essay in which this analysis occurs—"Why Do Men Stupefy Themselves?"—might be taken as a central text of prosaics. Chapter 4 of the essay begins with an apparently minor point: even an occasional cigarette or glass of wine is harmful. People usually say that although drunkenness is surely to be avoided, surely "the trifling alterations of consciousness" produced by a cigarette or glass of wine at dinner are not. Arguing in this way, Tolstoy replies, is like supposing "that it may harm a watch to be struck against a stone, but that a little dirt introduced into it cannot be harmful" (R&E, 80).

Tolstoy then retells the story of the painter Bryullov, who corrected a student's sketch. "Why, you only touched it a tiny bit," the student exclaimed, "but it is quite a different thing." Bryullov replied: "Art begins where that tiny bit begins." Tolstoy then draws his prosaic moral: "That saying is strikingly true not only of art, but of all of life. One may say that true life begins where the tiny bit begins—where what seem to us minute and infinitely small alterations take place. True life is not lived where great external changes take place—where people move about, clash, fight, and slay one another—it is lived only where these tiny, tiny, infinitesimally small changes occur" (R&E, 81).

Tolstoy then turns to *Crime and Punishment*: "Raskolnikov did not live his true life when he murdered the old woman or her sister," nor did he decide to commit the murder at any single, "decisive" moment. That choice was made, and he lived his true life, neither when he entered the old woman's lodgings with a concealed ax, nor when he formulated plans for the perfect crime, nor when he worried about whether murder is morally permitted. No, it was made when he was just lying on his couch, thinking about the most everyday questions— whether he should take money from his mother or not, whether he should live in his present apartment or not, and other questions not at all related to the old woman. "That question was decided ... when he was doing nothing and only his consciousness was active; and in that consciousness, tiny, tiny alterations were taking place.... Tiny, tiny alterations—but on them depend the most important and terrible consequences" (R&E, 81-82).

Precisely because intentions are shaped continually, every moment of our lives has moral value. And because actions reflect the whole climate of our minds, everything that contributes to that climate—which means all of our thoughts and actions, however "inconsequential"—is potentially of great importance. In Anthony Trollope's novel *Can You Forgive Her?*—which is probably the novel that Anna Karenina reads on the train—one heroine tells another to refrain from saying unkind things about her husband even to herself, lest she teach herself to think that way by habit. In fact, Anna Karenina does teach herself to think badly of her husband, and later of Vronsky, in just this way. Her life is ruined, and lives generally are saved or ruined by innumerable prosaic moments, which together shape the self and all its subsequent actions. If we are honest, we must be so moment by moment; there are no unimportant moments. Or as Bakhtin liked to say, "there is no alibi for being."

### Prosaic Goodness

Tolstoy's most moral characters learn this truth. In *Father Sergius*, a novella written toward the end of Tolstoy's life, a proud man trains himself to attain sainthood by grand gestures and noticeable acts of self-sacrifice that imitate incidents in *The Lives of the Saints*. At times he bears a striking resemblance to Tolstoy himself, and the story doubtless reflects the author's skepticism of his own saintly pretensions. Sergius's quest fails, because no matter what he does to humble his pride he is still proud of his humility. When he at last meets a true saint, he discovers that she and everyone else is unaware of her exceptionality. She is a mother who supports her daughter and her daughter's neurasthenic husband while reproaching herself for not going to church. She lives a life of daily kindnesses that are entirely undramatic, undiscerned, and inimitable. Sergius learns that one cannot become a saint by imitating a model, and that true holiness, which never fits a pattern, grows out of the particular situations of daily life. Saints are prosaic and never recognizable as saints. Sergius draws a characteristically Tolstoyan lesson: if one is canonized, then one *cannot* be a saint.

The characters Tolstoy most truly admires are not the dramatic ones, like Prince Andrei, Natasha Rostova, or Anna Karenina, but the "mediocre" ones, like Nikolai Rostov or Dolly Oblonskaya. They live their prosaic lives rightly from moment to moment, and their stories unfold only as a background to the dramatic stories of the noticeable heroes and heroines. It could be no other way, because good lives don't make good stories, and that is because nothing especially narratable happens in them. That is the sense of Tolstoy's most famous sentence: "All happy families resemble each other; each unhappy family is unhappy in its own way." Happy families resemble each other because they are too prosaic to make a good story, but unhappy families have a story, and each story is different.

It follows for Tolstoy that the dramatic characters who provide plot—characters like Anna Karenina—misunderstand life and live badly. Tolstoy's real moral compass is the unromantic Dolly Oblonskaya. Once she accepts her husband's genial and habitual infidelity, nothing happens in her life worth narrating, except the undramatic flow of thoughts as she thinks through the details of her life and the lives of others. We catch glimpses of her struggling with her children's all-too-familiar illnesses and mischief, and talking with peasant women about women's daily cares. She always does the right thing moment by moment, and comes to understand that her life, however difficult it may be, is genuine and meaningful in a way that Anna's is not. By contrast, Dolly's philandering husband, Stiva, who would never deliberately harm anyone, stands as a symbol of prosaic evil, not because of any great sin or evil action but because he lives badly moment by moment. He has never trained himself to act responsibly and honestly in small ways.

## The Russian Idea of Evil

Most literature and most Western thought has described evil as something grand, terrifying, and Satanic, but Russian literature teaches that it is ordinary and banal. That great disciple of Tolstoy's prosaics, Anton Chekhov, attributes ruined lives to daily pettiness. As Elena Andreevna tells Uncle Vanya: "Ivan Petrovich, you are an educated, intelligent man, and I should think you would understand that the world is being destroyed not by crime and fire, but by … all these petty squabbles."[3] Dostoevsky advanced a prosaic theory of evil when he described the devil who haunts Ivan Karamazov as petty, commonplace, fashionably liberal, and politely skeptical. Hell, it turns out, is just like our world, and changes according to earthly intellectual fashions. It has adopted the metric system. The devil himself is, remarkably enough, an agnostic. Dostoevsky's point is that most evil is neither alien nor mysterious, but derives from our most common wishes and thoughts, and from our daily wishing of harm to others.

Tolstoy takes this prosaic insight one step further to a truly prosaic view. Most evil results neither from grand nor banal desires,

---

[3]     Anton Chekhov, *The Major Plays*, trans. Ann Dunnigan (New York: Signet, 1964).

but rather from something closer to criminal negligence. Evil happens not because we subconsciously wish it, but simply because we do not pay attention, because we fail to develop the habit of evaluating and correcting "the tiny alterations" of our thoughts. Dostoevsky seemed to cling to the idea that evil requires a principle, but Tolstoy knew that it is good that demands energy, like the moment-to-moment conscientiousness of a good mother.

### Love

Because they are suspicious of the grand gesture, prosaic thinkers tend to be debunkers. They are especially hostile to the ideology of romantic love, which regards ordinary marriage as uninteresting and grand passion as real life. That classic of twentieth-century criticism, Denis de Rougement's *Love in the Western World*, contends that Eros and romantic passion render impossible the truest and most important kind of love, family love. One cannot marry Iseult (Mrs. Tristran?), nor can one imagine Romeo and Juliet routinely sitting down to breakfast together.[4]

Romantic love comes complete with an ideology of transcendence and desire, along with a utopian contempt for prosaic marriage, which it finds hopelessly boring and middle-class. But in fact "to love in the sense of passion-love is the contrary of to live," de Rougement insists. "It is an impoverishment of one's being ... an inability to enjoy the present without imagining it as absent" (de Rougement, 285). Marriage cannot be based on passion, because marital love and romantic love are as contradictory as prose and poetry.

De Rougement's book reads like a gloss on the great prosaic novelists, by which I mean fiction writers who not only describe everyday details (as all realists do) but who also place the highest value on how those details are lived. The tradition includes Jane Austen, Anthony Trollope, George Eliot, Tolstoy, Chekhov, novels like George Orwell's *Keep the Aspidistra Flying*, and the works of Barbara Pym. One might say that Anna Karenina dies from a lack of prosaics, from her attempt to base her life with Vronsky entirely on passion and the excitement of desire. She refuses even to direct the household servants,

---

4    See Denis de Rougement, *Love in the Western World*, rev. ed., trans. Montgomery Belgion (New York: Harper and Row, 1974).

who are compelled to receive their orders from Vronsky, and, as Dolly notices with disapproval, she pays almost no attention to her daughter. Tolstoy contrasts Anna's rejection of the everyday world with Dolly's conversations with the peasant women and Kitty's involvement with her mother and the servants in making jam.

Tolstoy's wife related her husband's account of how the central idea of *Anna* came to him:

> I was sitting downstairs in my study and observing a very beautiful silk line on the sleeve of my robe. I was thinking about how people get the idea in their head to invent all these patterns and ornaments of embroidery, and that there exists a whole world of woman's work, fashions, ideas by which women live.... Anna is deprived of all these joys of occupying herself with the woman's side of life, because she is alone. All women have turned away from her, and she has nobody to talk with about all that which composes the everyday, purely feminine occupations.[5]

For Tolstoy, those "feminine occupations" are the truly important ones, and he usually described the world of men—Karenin's politics, Vronsky's military life, Koznyshev's sterile philosophizing, everything but working the land—as essentially meaningless by comparison. In all of these masculine occupations, he detected a contempt for the prosaic, and therefore falsity. Men's work becomes meaningful when it partakes of the spirit of women's work. At the end of *Emma*, Jane Austen makes much the same point when she has Knightley distinguish between the male world of "the great" and the prosaic stories describable only in "woman's language." Given that distinction, everything or almost everything important belongs to the woman's realm, including novels like *Emma*. Above all, anything that has positive moral value is to be found there.

### Moral Alertness

For Tolstoy, Bakhtin, and most prosaic thinkers, a special conception of ethics was of supreme importance. For it is above all in the realm

---

[5]     As cited in *The Norton Critical Edition of Anna Karenina*, ed. George Gibian (New York: Norton, 1970), 761.

of ethics that the systematic view of the world proves misleading and dangerous. Systematic ethics conceives of right and wrong as conformity or nonconformity to the abstract moral norms described by ethical philosophers. The alternative to such a view, it has often been stated, is one or another form of subjectivism, emotivism, or relativism, all of which ultimately make any true moral judgments impossible. Here again one is offered a choice between totalism and absolute relativism, both of which assume that without a system there is nothing. Tolstoy and Bakhtin believed that there is an alternative to these equally unacceptable positions.

If morality were a matter of rules, then the only work involved in making moral decisions would be in deciding which rules apply to a given situation. Moral agents, in such a view, come to resemble Tolstoy's Ivan Ilych, whose brilliance as a jurist arises from his adeptness at eliminating "all considerations irrelevant to the legal aspects of the case, and reducing even the most complicated case to a form in which it could be presented on paper only in its externals, excluding his personal opinion of the matter, while above all observing every prescribed formality."[6] Ivan Ilych is never led astray by irrelevant sympathies or particularities, and he judges every matter entirely according to abstract norms. For Tolstoy, thinking this way eliminates everything that makes a moral decision what it is. Or as Bakhtin puts it, one loses the very "oughtness" of moral decisions when they become mechanical and separated from the concerns of real people. For educators like Dickens's Gradgrind, all that matters are facts, and for jurists like Ivan Ilych, all that matter are rules. In a novel, such views could only be the object of parody.

If moral decision were simply a matter of applying rules, then a computer could be the most moral of agents. But this is monstrous. "If we concede that human life can be governed by reason," Tolstoy wrote, "then the possibility of life is destroyed" (W&P, 1354). But if morals are not a matter of rules, then what can be said about how they are and should be made?

Both Levin in *Anna Karenina* and Pierre in *War and Peace* learn after fruitless attempts to identify a guiding system that they do not need one. When Pierre lives wisely moment to moment and when the

---

6    *Great Short Works of Leo Tolstoy,* trans, Louise and Aylmer Maude (New York: Harper and Row, 1967), 258.

tiny alterations of his thoughts take place in the right way, he achieves a sensitivity to each situation that tells him what to do. Even though his actions conform to no rule, he becomes a good moral agent in much the same way as Nikolai Rostov becomes a good soldier and Dolly a good mother: by learning and practicing what Tolstoy calls "moral alertness."

Moral decisions require work in each case. Rules cannot substitute for presentness, for responsiveness to particular people at a particular moment. There is no alibi.

To be sure, rules, principles, and maxims can be, if not sufficient, then helpful. They can serve a pedagogic function, serve as a starting point for thought, or define a paradigm case. They can work not as commands but as rules of thumb. One can then see how a particular situation conforms or differs. One may sometimes arrive at a new rule, in a process that never ends as experience deepens.

### Novels

Such a view suggests the connection between prosaics as a view of life and prosaics as a view of literature focused on realist novels. For where are we to look for descriptions of situations rich enough to educate our moral sense? Surely we cannot look in philosophical texts, because even when philosophers talk in general terms about the irreducible importance of particulars, their observations are still too general to be of much use. We want life, and philosophers give us "being"; "praxis" is but a philosopher's notion of practice. In philosophers' examples or thought experiments, one lacks a rich sense of the psychological and social milieu of living people. Sociologists' case studies are no richer, and even in daily life, we do not see much of other people's thought processes. But the entire impulse of novels is to provide just such information.

Novels allow us to trace the process of thinking and feeling as the character experiences it, in a way we never could in life. We feel what it is like to be someone else, to see the world differently, not in the abstract but in the shifting alterations of quotidian experience. We live into the character, we empathize. No other kind of knowledge does that, and no other art form does it as well.

The entire impulse of novels is to provide the sort of detailed, "thick" experience that real moral action requires. Ethics is a matter of prosaics, and great novels develop our ethical sense.

## Prosaics and the Process of Reading

For these reasons, Bakhtin came to regard the novel as the highest art form—indeed, as the highest achievement of Western thought, more profound than all its abstract philosophy. In novels we see the texture of daily life rendered with a richness, depth, and attention to contingencies that no other form of thought offers. We see moral decisions made by inexhaustibly complex characters in unrepeatable social situations at particular historical times; and we appreciate that the value of these decisions cannot be entirely abstracted from these specifics.

Thus, for reasons both ethical and literary, Bakhtin became the champion of the novel and the opponent of traditional "poetics." From Aristotle to the present, "poetics" has identified the essence of literature with poetry (or with poetry and tragedy), which is why poetics has become a synonym for "theory of literature." Poetics recognizes in prose only those aspects it shares with poetry, like metaphor, and denies artistic significance to the rest. Prose turns out to be poetry without some poetic features, and with the addition of some unpoetic features. This is something like taking reptiles as the basic animal, and defining mammals as reptiles who lay eggs and have warm blood.

One needs to approach novels in their own terms if one is to grasp what makes them what they are, their novelness.

For Bakhtin, the greatness of prose art lies in what it does *not* share with poetry—its sense of the prosaic texture of life in all its richness and ordinariness. Consequently, to appreciate novels we need not poetics but prosaics, a theory recognizing that novels provide a special way of thinking about the world before our eyes and the ethical problems we constantly face.

This approach to novels differs from the one often taken in ethics classes that discuss novels. There students are encouraged to take the fiction as the instantiation of a norm, or an example from which to derive a norm. A good student learns to think away all those "irrelevancies" that conceal the "essential problem." But from the point of view of prosaics, the value of novels derives from these very "irrelevancies," from what Bakhtin called "the surplus of humanness," which cannot be transformed into norms. Where abstract philosophy ends, prosaic ethics begins.

The prosaic approach to novels departs from the method used in most literature classes today. Although most readers engage ethically with characters, moral approaches to literature have been essentially taboo in American universities for at least half a century. One can speak of moral themes in the same way one speaks of formal features—as elements the author has woven into a pattern—but real ethical engagement has long been a relic, a sign of philistinism. The New Criticism was hostile to ethical criticism, structuralism viewed ethics anthropologically, and cultural studies has substituted the political for the ethical as if they were the same. If they were, it would be impossible to judge politics ethically. To view the political as subsuming the ethical, as Lenin did, is itself unethical, from the point of view of prosaics. It also precludes real ethical engagement with works.

And this is very odd indeed. After all, one reason that people read literature is to understand other people and their moral decisions. Scholars look down on such vulgar concerns, but what if their students are the ones who see the matter correctly?

Tolstoy's *What Is Art?* has become proverbial for the narrow moralism that has given moral criticism a bad name, but that treatise also offers an approach to the ethics of reading that is anything but simplistic. Tolstoy argues that the explicit moral one may draw from a work may not be what is most important, even from an ethical point of view. What truly matters is how the work "infects" us with moral values *as* we read. To whom do we extend sympathy, when do we place ourselves in another's position? In one of his most interesting essays, Tolstoy argued that the overt moral of Chekhov's story "The Darling" is a bad one, but that nevertheless the story is a morally good one, because of what it does to us in the process of reading it. We extend sympathy unawares to a character we ostensibly condemn. The actual effect contradicts the message. Or, as Tolstoy puts the point: like the biblical Balaam, Chekhov blesses when he means to curse.

One might make the inverse point about television programs that ostensibly preach an uplifting moral—say, the evils of sexual abuse of children—but make such abuse interesting and titillating in the process. In pursuit of goodness, people become worse. We may regard a violent criminal as evil, but learn by experience a fascination with inflicting pain we had only known about abstractly before. What really matters most in reading fiction, and in having other experiences, are the tiny, tiny alterations of consciousness in process.

Perhaps the real education literature provides lies in the moment-to-moment decisions we make in the course of reading: where we desire a just punishment or feel another's suffering; when we are carried away and when we remain skeptical; when we recognize that we have unwittingly judged ourselves. Do we sense a twinge as we recognize we have made similar mistakes? When (to use a concept long banned from criticism) do we identify with a character? There are novels I find painful to read because some hero or heroine goes through a process of reasoning as I have—not once, but over a long period—to their own and others' eventual harm. Whatever explicit conclusions we may draw, we have *practiced* reactions to particular kinds of people and situations, and practice produces habits that may precede, preclude, or preform conscious moral judgments in daily life.

Of course, it is easier to remember the conclusion, summary, or interpretation of a work than the whole process of reading it. But if prosaics is right, the process itself affects us at least as much, for good or ill. When Tolstoy wrote that the only way he could tell what *Anna Karenina* was about would be to rewrite it, he was, I think, stressing not the formal intricacy of the text, but the complexity of reading as a series of small decisions and moment-to-moment judgments. This process is not just indispensable to the point of the book, it *is* the point of the book. Like true life, art begins where the tiny bit begins.

# Part Two

## WHAT IS OPEN TIME?

## Chapter Two

### NARRATIVENESS

## Prologue: Narration or Deduction

> If we concede that human life can be governed by reason, then the possibility of life is destroyed.
>
> —*Tolstoy (W&P, 1354)*

> All human actions will then, of course, be tabulated like tables of logarithms up to 108,000 ... everything will be so clearly calculated and designated that there will be no more incidents or adventures in the world.
>
> —*Dostoevsky's underground man (NFU, 22)*

Some disciplines explain things with stories; others do without them. Newtonian physics does not "take a history," the way doctors do, and the same may be said of Einsteinian physics. Mathematicians prove theorems by deduction, they don't watch to see how things happen to work out. Since the 1950s or so, economics has tried to do less and less history and more and more mathematical derivations. Other disciplines that use rational choice theory also aspire to overcome their need for narrative.

By contrast, some sciences, like evolutionary biology or geology, are by their nature historical. There is not a single formula in *The Origin of Species*, nor could any laws enable one to predict where evolution is going. Some historians avoid telling stories, but it is hard to see how the discipline could do without them.

Novels *are* stories. Is the world of real people more amenable to the sort of description economists prefer to use, or does it more closely resemble a novel?

## Theses

> The course of events? N.B. N.B. N.B.? The course of events.
> —*Dostoevsky, the notebooks to* The Idiot

Here are some theses I would like to advocate:

1. There is such a thing as narrativeness, which narratives may have in varying degrees. Some have no narrativeness at all.

2. Some views of the world by their nature require narrative whereas others try to overcome it. In the first case, only narrative can describe what is essential; in the second, the right theory and the requisite information make narrative dispensable. Its proper role is then at best illustratory. According to the second view, the need for narrative is a sign of temporary ignorance.

3. Since the time of Descartes, the history of Western thought has been increasingly dominated by the second, anti-narrativist view. One has a science when one no longer needs a story. The model of "science" so understood is classical physics. To this tradition belong Spinoza, Leibniz, Marx, and Einstein; the dominant traditions of theology, economics, anthropology, and city planning; and social science generally, when it is understood as a science. In the study of literature, Russian Formalism and structuralism reflect the spirit of this tradition with special intensity.

4. But there has always been a counter-tradition that regards the attempt to overcome narrative as a fundamental misunderstanding of the way things are. In the counter-traditional view, we live in a world where narrative is essential. To this tradition belong Darwin, Adam Smith, and Clausewitz; these three draw on earlier thinkers, from Aristotle and the casuists to Montaigne and numerous skeptics. The novel as a genre reflects a philosophical belief that the world requires narrative. It is essentially casuistical in its impulse; that is, it values particular *cases* irreducible to general laws.

5. I suspect we are at the beginning of a revival of narrativeness as a form of thought.

6. In literature, narrativeness characterizes different narrative genres in different ways and to different degrees. It is most palpably achieved in what I call the literature of process. Bakhtin's "polyphonic novel" would be, in this view, a subset of the literature of process.

7. The dominant tradition of poetics has been, like Leibniz's philosophy, an attempt to think narrativeness away. But here, too, there are alternatives.

## Essential Narrative

Narrativeness may be defined as the quality that makes narrative not merely present but essential. It comes in degrees.

One can have narrative without narrativeness. For example, in most contemporary economic theory, timeless equations dictate a specific and optimal result. In a commonly used metaphor, it's like placing a ball at the lip of a cup and letting it fall to the bottom. We know where the ball will end up, and the specific path doesn't matter. Of course, one could tell the story of how the ball fell from here to there until it reached the lowest point, but such a story would be entirely superfluous.

Such reasoning explains why the study of economic history, once essential to the education of economists, has now almost disappeared from the American PhD curriculum. What we have instead are occasional examples from economic events that illustrate, but do not explain, some general principle.

## Possible Futures

When is narrative needed? When is it impossible? When gratuitous?

Narratologists have repeatedly pointed out that narrative is impossible when no meaningful connection links a sequence of events. Think of all those medieval chronicles recording random events thought noteworthy: 1023: Prince Vasily began to rule in Tver. 1024: A two-headed calf was born. Later in 1024: Saint Pstislav of Perm cured a beggar of leprosy. These entries do not constitute a story. They are, at best, material for one or many stories. We see what they lack when we try to make a story out of them by ascribing meaningful connections. Perhaps Prince Vasily ruled badly, and so God warned the people with a two-headed calf, and then Saint Pstislav showed his holiness by curing a beggar in order to move the people to repentance....

Narratologists then proceed to offer a "minimal story," something like this: The queen grew ill, and so the king died of grief. "And so": there is a connection and so there is a story. The narratologists will go on to say that, of course, this isn't much of a story, but it is still a story. We have crossed a great divide from incidents into narrative.

True enough, but why isn't it much of a story? Answer: there is no *process* here. A process must have more than one step, because it involves tracing possible futures, but here, as soon as we are given the opportunity to do so, the story is over.

The sense of process, the activity of tracing possible futures from a given past, is essential to narrativeness, though not, as this example shows, to narrative. "The queen grew ill, so the king died of grief" is a narrative without narrativeness.

## The Romance of Mars

Here is a situation in which one could construct a sort of narrative, but it would be pointless. Imagine describing the orbit of Mars around the sun as a story. That orbit could be wholly specified by astronomical equations, but one could also say that in March, Mars was here, and then in May it was there, and in June, while my Uncle Toby watched my father wind the clock for the month, we saw Mars at yet another place, and so on. Such a story would be pointless because it adds nothing (or nothing about the life of Mars). One already knows where Mars is at any moment without the story. Time is just a parameter of the equation, and no specific moment makes any difference. We do not have to know where Mars was on October 10 to calculate where it will be on December 21.

What we learn from this example is that narrativeness requires *presentness*: the present moment must matter. It cannot be a mere derivative of early events or dictated by later events, that is, by the structure of the whole. It is not necessary that all moments have presentness, but some must, and it is from them that narrativeness derives.

## Open Time

What gives a moment presentness? In a phrase, open time. For a present moment to matter, to have real weight, more than one thing must be possible at the next moment. We may define open time as the excess of possibilities over actualities. For a determinist, one and only one thing can happen at any given moment; what did not happen could not have happened. In open time, at least one thing that did not happen could have.

Think of the incident in *War and Peace* when Rostov, with "his keen sportsman's eye," realizes that if he and his men charge the French at this moment, they will rout them, but if he waits, the configuration of the French troops climbing the hill will change and the opportunity will be lost. Rostov may charge or not, and his choice matters (W&P, 786).

Or consider Dmitri Karamazov holding a pestle over his father's head while trying to decide whether to kill him or let him live. He could do either—that's the whole point. If the situation could be repeated, he might choose differently.

The examples are endless.

## Contingency

For Aristotle, a contingent event is one that could either be or not be.[1] Contingency in this sense is what insures presentness, and therefore allows for narrativeness.

## The Species of Contingency

There are, so far as I know, three kinds of contingency. Since novels are about people, the one most often used is free will. Dmitri may either kill or not kill, and so he is morally responsible for what he chooses. Dostoevsky, whose project was to oppose determinism in the name of morality, provided especially intense descriptions of the agony of choice, of an intensified present in which something must be either done or not done.

To be sure, it is possible to argue that even the agony of choice is determined. But it is hard to believe that of oneself. Dostoevsky directs us to choose between the sort of metaphysical argument that often goes astray and our direct experience.

Contingency may also lack a human agent, in two ways. Absolute chance, if it really exists, presents events that come from

---

[1]     Aristotle insists that contingency in this sense genuinely exists. "In those things which are not continuously actual there is a potentiality in either direction. Such things may either be or not be; events also therefore may either take place or not take place." He rejects the idea that "nothing is or takes place fortuitously, whether in the present or in the future, and there are no real alternatives; everything takes place of necessity and is fixed." Aristotle, "On Interpretation," BWA, 46-47.

nowhere. Quantum physics appears to offer examples at the micro-level inasmuch as two identical systems can develop in different ways. Pure chance, however, provides weak material for narrative, precisely because it comes from nowhere and therefore seems to preclude the requirement that narratives offer meaningful connections. When it occurs in a novel or play, we usually attribute it to the overall design of the author. That is, if it is not occasioned internally by events in the narrated world, we take it as fulfilling some design of the whole. If it is occasioned entirely externally, we often call an incident a *deus ex machina*.

Sometimes the locus of open time may lie in events themselves, which in their complexity seem to have an impersonal agency of their own. We may call this subset of contingency "contingency in the narrow sense." Aristotle accepted this kind of contingency. Events themselves seem capable of working out in one way or the other, so that if a sequence were repeated, the outcome might be different. When critics of *War and Peace* objected that they could see why events could work out as they did but not why they had to, they were catching just what Tolstoy was up to.

The idea that events are themselves contingent was arguably Tolstoy's central idea in *War and Peace*. That is why no science of battle is possible. Neither is any other social science. Elie Halévy memorably called attempts to construct a social science modeled on Newtonian astronomy "moral Newtonianism" (GPR, 6). But if there is contingency in the narrow sense, then even without referring to free will, we may see why the idea of a social *science* is a chimera, as I think it is.

Contingency in the narrow sense differs from chance because the events do not come from nowhere. They come from earlier events, as in determinism. But in contrast to determinism, earlier events, though they limit options, do not reduce them to singularity. Given what happened before, only some things, but not every thing, can happen. And yet *more than one* thing can happen. Thus, Tolstoy frequently speaks of events taking place "for some reason"—not by pure chance, nor for no reason at all, but also not for any reason we could anticipate by any laws.

If there are contingent events in this sense, then predictability is out of the question. For if there is the slightest free play in the system—even if only between ten degrees of arc to ten degrees zero minutes and one tenth of a second—then the variation may concatenate from moment to moment until the possibilities are endless. Contingency ramifies. In chaos theory—and we may regard *War and Peace* as a sort of early treatise in chaos theory—that is why it is in principle impossible to predict the weather beyond about four days in the future. Besides, even a single minute difference can make a radical difference in outcome. Think of the difference that a fraction of a centimeter can make in the target of a bullet, another metaphor Tolstoy uses.

The generals believe that they have a science that in principle can "foresee all contingencies," but, as Andrei explains to Pierre before Borodino, "what are we facing tomorrow? A hundred million diverse chances, which will be decided on the instant by whether we run or they run, whether this man or that man is killed" (W&P, 930). By "chances," Prince Andrei has in mind what I have called contingency in the narrow sense: we typically use the word chance when we want to stress either the element of unpredictability in a contingent event or a great degree of uncertainty. Andrei's idea is that no science that could ever be developed will tell us such things, which really matter in determining the outcome of a battle and most other things in life. Andrei asks: "What science can there be in a matter in which, as in every practical matter, nothing can be determined and everything depends on innumerable circumstances, the significance of which becomes manifest at a particular moment and no one call tell when that moment will come?" (W&P, 775).

### Casuistry and Alertness

"On the instant," "at a particular moment": Andrei stresses the importance of presentness, and presentness depends on unpredictability and contingency. You have to pay attention to what is happening, what is taking place now, for *now* is not just yesterday plus one unit of time. After the fact, it will require narrative to explain. We were in this situation, which meant these things could have happened, and this one did, so we did that, which put us in that situation, where those other things could have happened, but what actually happened was that, and so…. That is what life is usually like, and what narrative is needed to describe.

For Andrei and for Kutuzov, recognition of contingency leads to a whole different kind of behavior, which requires wisdom more than knowledge and presence more than planning. To attend wisely to what is happening, you need two things. First, you need to be alert, which is why Kutuzov falls asleep at the council of war the night before

Austerlitz, and why Andrei at the end of his conversation with Pierre before Borodino explains that what matters most before a battle is a good night's sleep. If you rely simply on some general principles of battle, or whatever is equivalent in other practical matters, you will miss opportunities and dangers. Aristotle, a physician and the son of a physician, insisted that a good doctor does not just apply biology. You have to be there now.

Second, what you need is the sort of wisdom born of experience. You must have attended to many particular cases irreducible to some overarching law. In the root sense of the word, you must be a casuist. That is why Rostov knows when to charge: he has a "keen sportsman's eye," acquired during a great deal of hunting. Therefore you have to be alert for a second reason: to not only take in the shifting events, but also rapidly see them in terms set by earlier experiences.

The sense that events have narrativeness places one in a wholly different world.

## Wheels

A parable:

Nature has designed many highly complex structures. Just think of the eye, the liver, the brain. But why has it never designed an animal with wheels? Every time we get into a car, or even push a wheelbarrow, we know the advantage of wheels over legs. And they are much simpler to design than livers. After all, we have built a lot of wheels that work, but no liver that works.[2]

The answer is that the world is not paved. Wheels work on highways where the terrain is predictable. In a forest, or anywhere where the terrain is irregular, one may encounter an obstacle that wheels cannot negotiate, but which legs, which are more flexible than wheels, can. If the world were predictable, we would see a wheeled cheetah rolling after a wheeled antelope down the highway of the Serengeti. But animals have evolved to react to a world of radical contingency.

The fact that we have legs rather than wheels testifies to the world's contingency and the need for narrative.

In our hands is an inbuilt tremor, which is why we need tripods; our eyes are perpetually scanning the periphery of our vision; our

---

[2]     I owe this parable, which I have adapted, to the late Aron Katsenelinboigen.

attention continually moves unless we focus it, which is hard. All these actions of *scanning* the world also bespeak our design for facing contingency.

Perhaps consciousness itself is nature's most radical acknowledgment of the world's contingency. Only consciousness allows us both to do more than apply algorithms and to be alert.

### Lack of Fit

In mentioning evolution, I mean to invoke another thinker who, like Tolstoy, saw contingency as essential to the world and narrative as essential to its description: Darwin. When a social scientist refers to a process as "Darwinian," he usually means something like the ball that rolls to the bottom of the cup: everything tends inevitably to optimality, for anything less than optimal would be eliminated by competition. Such a view radically misunderstands Darwin.

Darwin explicitly and repeatedly denies that the world tends to optimality. There is no pre-given endpoint, like the bottom of the cup. It was natural theology that stressed the perfect design of organisms, which therefore testify to a divine creator working at a single moment of time. Precisely because Darwin insisted that the origin of species was historical, he described organisms as a hodgepodge of compromises layered on compromises, many of which come with other features that serve no purpose, or even cause harm, but have tagged along for the ride ("correlations of growth"). That would have to be the case, both because the environment in which each organism evolves, which crucially includes other organisms, is constantly shifting in unpredictable ways, and because one has to tinker with the tools at hand. Evolution cannot rewind the tape, go back in time, and choose a different path that only later shows its advantage. In short, it is the *im*perfect design of organisms, the features that no perfect creator designing at an instant would include, that testify to a historical process.

Darwin offers many examples, but my favorite, which he first noted in *The Voyage of the Beagle* and then explicated in *The Origin of Species*, concerns a certain species of mole, which has eyes but lives its entire life underground. Even if the mole were to surface, the eyes would be of no use because they are occluded with a thick membrane. Now, any organ requires energy to sustain, and so a useless organ hinders survival. What is more, those eyes are subject to infection. The mole is not optimally designed, so why does it have those eyes? The answer is simply that it is descended from earlier moles for whom the eyes were of some use. The explanation is historical; it requires narrative. Darwin observes:

> He who believes that each being has been created as we now see it must occasionally have felt surprised when he met an animal having habits and structures not at all in agreement. What could be plainer than that the webbed feet of geese are formed for swimming? Yet there are upland geese who never go near the water.... In such cases, and many others could be given, habits have changed without a corresponding change in structure (OoS, 185).

One needs story because the world is imperfect. One needs story because there is no goal. And one needs story because things do not fit.

### Sufficient Reason

Darwin offers us an example of a non-Newtonian science, one that requires narrative. In Darwin, the need for narrative derives from the essential messiness of the world, its lack of any pre-established harmony. By contrast, thinkers who seek to overcome narrative typically insist on the complete orderliness of the world. Though things may look messy, order lurks beneath, and the task of science or philosophy is to discover the order that will make the mess, and along with it the need for narrative, disappear. Things could not be different because then they would not all fit. There must be, as Leibniz put it, a "sufficient reason" for everything.

I think that Leibniz stands at the opposite pole from Darwin and Tolstoy, and that the dream of a social science is essentially Leibnizian. The idea that we live in the best of all possible worlds, and that no other was genuinely possible given the perfect goodness of God, is an unusually pure version of the anti-narrative view. For Leibniz, there are no events that could have been other. In the famous thirteenth chapter of the *Discourse on Metaphysics*, Leibniz contends that everything in the "concept" of any given person was there from the beginning of the universe. Whatever doubt Caesar may have felt, his crossing of the Rubicon was given in the nature of the universe, and was part and parcel of everything else, which has no loose play. The momentousness of the moment is entirely illusory, a product of our (and Caesar's) ignorance. The same holds with social science: alternatives are only apparent. To understand is to grasp why things had to be the way they are, because nothing is the least bit independent of other things, of the whole.

Events therefore lack what Bakhtin called *eventness*. In fact, Leibniz was far more extreme than Newton in this respect, and Halévy should probably have referred to moral Leibnizians. Unable to prove the stability of the solar system, Newton proposed that God occasionally intervenes to set things right. Leibniz was scandalized:[3] a perfect Being would design a perfectly harmonious world, in which there would be no need for events to possess eventness.

## Leibnizization and God Substitutes

Social scientists practice Leibnizism without God. Or to put it differently, they are natural theologians of a special sort. In natural theology, God created the laws and the laws run the world with perfect harmony. The social scientists accept the existence of such laws of perfection, but without a God who created them. The view of the world is identical, and entirely Leibnizian. Social scientists are, in effect, atheistic creationists.

Instead of God, they have given us God substitutes: principles that, without God, do what a perfect God would have done. And so natural selection, the invisible hand, and similar laws explain "in principle" all events, which could not have been otherwise and which are mere instantiations of the laws. I want to say that social science's claim to have broken with the dominant theological tradition is groundless.

And so whenever a thinker, like Darwin, seems too important to ignore, he is Leibnized. Economists have done the same with Adam Smith, who does not resemble the rational choice theorists invoking him. Anyone who has read *The Wealth of Nations* will recall that most of it is made up of narrative history of the economy and the social conditions shaping it. Narrative is at its core, all the more so when we reflect that Smith's most common explanation for why things happened the way they did is not rational choice, not some law insuring optimality, but what Smith calls "human folly."

---

3    See H. G. Alexander, ed., *The Leibniz-Clarke Correspondence* (Manchester: Manchester University Press, 1956).

For Smith, the invisible hand, and for Darwin, natural selection, are but one of several loose organizing principles operating in a world of contingency (in the broad sense). They operate in a world requiring narrative.

## Suspense

Here then are factors contributing to narrativeness: presentness, contingency, eventness, messiness, unpredictability, the need for alertness, and possibilities in excess of actualities. What all of these provide is one more factor, a sign of narrativeness: suspense.

Children like to tell the following "story." Once there was an ant who moved a grain of sand. Then another ant moved another grain of sand. Then another ant, etc.

Imagine interrupting to ask excitedly: Wow! And what happened next? Well, then another ant moved another grain of sand. And *then*?

To use Bakhtin's term again, these events lack eventness. The reason there is no eventness is that there is no possibility of being surprised. "Surprisingness," as Bakhtin calls it, can be present only when something unexpected is added to what came before. In the dead world of the determinist and the perfectly ordered world of the structuralist, everything is given, "ready-made" (*uzhe gotov*). Thus we have Bakhtin's acid summary of structuralism:

> An object is ready-made, the linguistic means for its description are ready-made, the artist himself is ready-made, and his world view is ready-made. And here with ready-made means, in light of ready-made world view, the ready-made poet reflects a ready-made object. But in fact the object is created in the process of creativity, as are the poet himself, his world view, and his means of expression.[4]

But in fact, the making of art is not making in the Formalist or structuralist sense, fabrication by predictable rules. Creativity uses the ready-made as material and then, going surprisingly beyond, produces

---

4     Mikhail Bakhtin, "The Problem of the Text in Linguistics, Philology, and the Human Sciences: An Experiment in Philosophical Analysis," *Speech Genres and Other Late Essays*, ed. Caryl Emerson and Michael Holquist, trans. Vern McGee (Austin: University of Texas Press, 1986), 120.

something unpredictably new. Otherwise, it is not really creative at all. It does so, crucially, because of a process with numerable unpredictable events, events with real eventness and presentness. There is a story to be told about it.

The creation of narrative art, like the narratives themselves, has real suspense.

No suspense, no narrativeness.

## Eventness Is Not Narrativeness

Eventness pertains to specific events, narrativeness to the entire sequence.

Bakhtin interpreted the extreme moments of suspense in Dostoevsky as an attempt to maximalize eventness, but in Bakhtin's view Dostoevsky does not achieve very well what the realist novel does. His novels do not show small moments of open time following each other and concatenating into a real process of continuous, gradual development, with each moment a causal nexus. Dostoevsky for Bakhtin is all "suddenly." I think Bakhtin exaggerates, but in the terms I am using he is saying that Dostoevsky displays maximal eventness but limited narrativeness.

## Virtual History

We can also see the difference between eventness and narrativeness if we consider the recent school of virtual history as practiced and explicated by Niall Ferguson and others.[5] These historians deeply value narrativeness and appreciate the openness of time, and so what they strive to do is "what-if" history, a project that presents problems beyond the obvious lack of documentation.

---

[5]  See VH. See also Robert Cowley, ed., *What If: The World's Foremost Historians Imagine What Might Have Been* (New York: G. P. Putnam's Sons, 1999); Robert Cowley, ed., *More What If?: Eminent Historians Imagine What Might Have Been* (New York: G. P. Putnam's Sons; 2001); Gardner Dozois and Stanley Schmidt, eds., *Roads Not Taken: Tales of Alternate History* (New York: Ballantine, 1998); Andrew Roberts, ed., *What Might Have Been: Leading Historians on Twelve "What Ifs" of History* (London: Orion, 2004); and Harry Turtledove, ed., with Martin H. Greenberg, *The Best Alternate History Stories of the 20th Century*, (New York: Random House, 2001).

One may easily imagine the first step. If Halifax, rather than the new prime minister Churchill, had won the debate in the cabinet in May 1940, England would have sued for peace and Hitler would have won. And then?

After the first step, the tendency is to imagine the future by drawing straight lines from the imagined situation. But if one is going to do that, one could just as well draw straight lines from the situation that did take place and show that what actually happened was entirely predictable, which no one could do. If they could, if the future were predictable from the present, what is the point of a what-if exercise in the first place?

The problem with what-if history is that there is only *one* moment of eventness, which is singularly odd, for there is nothing unique about the moment chosen. If contingencies ramify and if choices constantly present themselves, then there are no straight lines to draw. Of course, one might imagine, in great richness, the evolving fictive situation, and specify moments of choice, and then follow one of them, again and again, thus repeating the initial what-if. But then one would have something resembling a novel.

Perhaps a better alternative, one much more consonant with the thinking of Tolstoy, Dostoevsky, and Bakhtin, would be to imagine the what-ifs—several of them, most likely—and then follow the choice that was actually made; and at the next moment of choice, do the same, repeatedly. In that case, one would have a sense of history as constantly presenting alternatives and the history we know as one possibility among legions.

## An Occupational Hazard of Literary Critics

Suppose that you have read a suspenseful story and then discovered the outcome was entirely predictable. Or imagine reading a detective story where you can easily guess the criminal. Or that you are re-reading a novel with foreshadowing and see all the signs and know where they are leading. In such cases, suspense is decidedly reduced, because the possibilities that might be projected are barely possibilities at all. They are mere possibilities of possibilities.

Re-reading almost inevitably diminishes suspense. The more re-readings, and the better our memories, the more we focus at each juncture less on what might happen and more on how what did happen relates to the outcome and overall structure.

Literary critics are by necessity re-readers. Almost all their methods presuppose a firm grasp of the whole and all details. They are therefore naturally inclined to overlook possibilities of what might have happened. The occupational hazard of narrative critics is reading the narrativeness out of narrative. In structuralism, this tendency reaches its apogee.

## Great Expectations

When we understand a work as a whole, and contemplate its design or structure, we see it as a pattern in which everything fits. It is, so to speak, visible at a glance. Process exists only within the narrated world, not in the artifact taken as a whole. A radical divide typically separates the characters from the author, critic, or re-reader. The characters experience open time and process, but the critic has overcome it. As in the social sciences, suspense and contingency merely reflect ignorance.

Imagine Pip having read the novel he is in; what would happen to his great expectations? Interestingly enough, the devil in *The Brothers Karamazov* does seem to have read *Faust* (and perhaps *Paradise Lost*).

First readers, and re-readers whose memory is imperfect, have a double experience. Insofar as they identify with the characters, they experience suspense, open time, narrativeness; but when they pause to contemplate the artifact, these experiences are overcome. Whenever a reader asks what an apparently contingent event (giving a pie to a convict) must lead to if the novel is successful; whenever he or she counts up all the unmarried males and females and anticipates how they will be paired off at the end; whenever, in short, the reader uses knowledge that the artifact *is* an artifact of a given sort, suspense and narrativeness are diminished.

Structuralism by its nature contemplates the whole, for that is where structure lies. It therefore follows that structuralist readings of narratives, insofar as they do not go beyond the method, can only illuminate those elements that lack narrativeness, for much the same reason that social sciences deal poorly with spontaneous actions. By its very nature, structuralism denarratizes narrative. We need something entirely different to understand narrativeness. I believe the same observation holds, in varying degrees, for all current schools, especially those which, like new historicism and deconstruction, are formed from structuralist debris. They have not transcended its assumptions.

## "The Real Present of the Creative Process"

The sort of work that maximizes narrativeness and eventness is what I call the literature of process. Its essential feature is that the author places himself within the narrated world, on a level with his characters, in the sense that there is no overall structure or end-point toward which the narrative aims. When Tolstoy began to publish *War and Peace*, he recognized that having an overall plan or structure in mind would make it impossible to represent contingency, his central theme, because then the demands of a whole would guide events. Events would be pulled forward in just the right way to complete the plan. They could not be contingent, and the work would become Leibnizian. And so, as Tolstoy explains in his draft prefaces and in his published essay on his book, he did without a structure. In each serially-published installment, he simply set up a series of potentials that could develop in many directions, and, writing from scene to scene, chose one of the rich possibilities available. He was entirely guided by the characters' present, not their pregiven future or some need to harmonize the whole. Tolstoy explained:

> In printing the beginning of my proposed work, I promise neither a continuation nor a conclusion for it.... this proposed work can least of all be called a novel—with a plot that has constantly growing complexity, and a happy or unhappy denouement, with which interest in the narration ceases. In order to explain to the reader what this present work is, I find it most convenient to describe how I began to write it. (PSS 13:54)

Narrativeness is eternally present in the world and so a truly realist work must never have a point at which narrativeness ceases: there can be no denouement, no closure. Tolstoy seems to be indicting the genre of the realist novel for being neither realistic nor novelistic enough, for yielding to the desire to overcome narrative, and for providing a teleological pull to events that takes the presentness out of them.

In stressing that his book is best explained by the process of writing it, Tolstoy suggests that the creative process has the same presentness, contingency, and eventness as the events in the narrated world. Like the characters, he has no idea what will happen to them next. He will guide the characters through different epochs, but "I do not foresee the outcome of these characters' relationships in even a single one of these epochs" (PSS 13:55). The result is that we sense that whatever should happened, something else might have; and that the *War and Peace* we have is only one of many possible books that could have emerged. Narrativeness is intensified, or as Tolstoy put it: "I strove so that each part of the work would have an independent interest, which would consist not in the development of events but in development [itself]" (PSS 13:55-56). *Development itself*: this is Tolstoy's term for narrativeness.

Bakhtin described the polyphonic novel, which I regard as one type of literature of process, as a work in which the author achieves eventness by surrendering the "essential surplus of meaning" provided by knowledge of the work's structure, and placing himself on a level of ignorance with the characters (PDP, 73).[6] Characters do not choose and act in execution of a plan of which they know nothing, like Milton's Satan, because the author knows what they will do only when they do it. The events take place "right now, in the *real present* of the creative process" (PDP. 63).

## Process and Poetics

And what have critics done with *War and Peace, The Idiot,* and other process works? Why—you guessed it—they have imposed a structure on them, read the narrativeness out of them, treated all events as if they could not be other. Mess turns into fit. The works have, like those of Darwin and Smith, been Leibnized. Poetics, after all, gives us almost no other tools, and the Leibnization of these works is itself testimony to the power of what I take to be an essentially mystical impulse: to seek to overcome the world of events and escape into a purely Platonic realm of the eternal and stable.

I end with a plea: find the alternative. Reenter the world in which we actually live, the world of eventness, in which narrative is essential and in which some authors have produced works that take narrativeness to its extreme.

We live in a world of everlasting and perpetual process, and to embrace process is to embrace life itself.

---

6    For an account of polyphony as a theory of the creative process (differing from most presentations), see MB: CP, chapter 6, 231-268.

## Chapter Three

## THE PROSAICS OF PROCESS

The dominant tradition of poetics has tended to reflect a view of the world that banishes contingency. But some works reflect a different vision, a counter-vision, in which contingency plays an essential role. These works demand a different poetics. The first two parts of this essay outline vision and counter-vision, while the third develops the alternative poetics, what I shall henceforth call a prosaics of process. Poetics describes works with a strong sense of product, prosaics (as I shall use the term in this essay) describes works of process. Works of process manifest an alternative to structure. They are governed by a different sense of intentionality.

The world of processual works is one in which time is open, there are more possibilities than actualities, and the moment is truly momentous. Whatever does happen, something else might have. Because each moment has multiple potentials, not everything is already given at the beginning. Time matters, and the present is not a mere derivative of the past. In the processual vision, and the works that correspond to them, more than one moment has independent causal power.

Each of these types of work reflects a tradition of Western thought. As poetics has dominated literary criticism and theory, so the vision to which it corresponds has dominated Western thought. My purpose is to revive the counter-tradition of thought as an alternative to be considered. Rather than presume the correctness of the tradition, we should, in each case, recognize that we have a choice of visions. Sometimes the tradition is to be preferred, and sometimes the counter-tradition.

By the same token, some literary works are best analyzed in terms of poetics of product, and some in terms of the prosaics of process.

Each of these visions has both a theological and a secular variant, but for my purposes the difference made by the presence or absence of God is not important. What matters is the difference between the two visions.

# 1 / The Vision of Poetics and Product

### Foreknowledge of the Free

In Lorenzo Valla's dialogue on free will, Antonio poses a problem that, despite frequent claims to the contrary, theologians have never managed to resolve: either God lacks certain knowledge of the future, in which case he is imperfect and there is no providence, or else we have only the illusion of free will. For free will meaningfully to exist, he reasons, the future must contain more than one possibility:

> If it were possible for things to go differently from what is foreseen, providence would be out of the picture; if instead, we admit that it was impossible, out goes freedom of the will, and this would be a thing no less unworthy to God than if we should deny His providence.[1]

"If it were possible for things to go differently"—if the tape were played over again—could the result be different? To be or to be something else: that is the question. Omar Khayyam posed essentially the same question from a Muslim perspective:

> Oh, Thou, who didst with Pitfall and with Gin
> Beset the Road I was to wander in,
> Thou wilt not with Predestination round
> Enmesh me, and impute my Fall to Sin? (QOK, 12).

If I am predestined, if I was made so that I could not do otherwise, how can I be responsible? No alternative, no sin.

In Valla's dialogue, Lorenzo answers, as theologians and philosophers often have, that to foreknow something is not to cause it, because foreknowledge need have no effect on the action. In *Paradise Lost*, Milton's God insists that

---

[1]     Lorenzo Valla, "On Free Will" in *Renaissance Philosophy*, vol. 1, *The Italian Philosophers: Selected Readings from Petrarch to Bruno*, ed. and trans.Arturo B. Fallico and Herman Shapiro (New York: Modern Library, 1967), 52.

> . . . if I foreknew,
> Foreknowledge had no influence on their fault,
> Which had no less proved certain unforeknown.[2]

Of course, God is not just the observer but also the Creator of the world, and so in making it he did not just foreknow what people would do, He also made them knowing for certain what they would do. In creating them, He knowingly created their entire lives. It is not as if He were calculating something in which He had no part.

In its various forms, this argument reconciling foreknowledge and closed time with freedom proceeds first by defining freedom not as the ability to act unpredictably but as the ability to do what one wills—sometimes called the freedom of spontaneity. Since the will makes choices on the basis of knowable factors and preferences, its choices are in principle predictable; and God has such knowledge. Therefore no contradiction exists between freedom and the sort of time in which at any moment one and only one state of affairs is possible.

Notice what this position does to the concept of contingency. Aristotle defined a contingent event as one that can either be or not be, and he insisted that contingency so defined exists. Some events can either happen or not happen, and we just have to wait for the moment to see. Until it happens or doesn't happen, a sea battle, for instance, can either be or not be.

But for Valla and the Christian tradition generally, such a position would infringe on the omniscience of God. To reconcile freedom with closed time, medieval and Renaissance thinkers repeatedly resorted to redefining freedom, omniscience, foreknowledge, necessity, contingency, and other key terms. I recommend the method: If a problem seems unsolvable, try redefining its terms.

Leibniz thus defined a contingent event not as one that might actually happen if the tape were played over again, but merely as one that implies no logical contradiction. Contingent events in this sense remain impossible—not for logical reasons, since they have no logical problem, but for the quite different reason that God created the world providentially, as the best of all possible worlds. Any alternative state of affairs would necessarily lead to a worse world. Thus Leibniz's

---

[2]     PL, Book III, ll 117-19, p. 419.

"contingency," unlike Aristotle's, allows for no alternatives that might actually happen.

We may imagine the world as a novel we are rereading or a drama we are watching. The characters go on responding to circumstances according to their will, choosing actions on the basis of their limited knowledge. But we, who can see the whole pattern, who may even have read the work before and can in any case guess what a good author would do, know what they will choose. The characters freely choose what the structure predestines them to choose. Othello will not rise above his jealousy and Macbeth will not resist his wife. A tragedy cannot have a happy ending because it would then not be a tragedy. By the same token, no matter how many confusing twists and turns, deceits and disguises, create an apparently unresolvable tangle, a Shakespearean comedy will culminate in the right marriages.

Structure is the literary counterpart of providence. If the work is well made, readers know that any alternative sequence would lessen the perfection of the whole. That is why they experience a sense of rightness, that, yes, it had to happen just this way.

In short, a kind of causality pertaining to the whole story from without, in addition to whatever specific causes operate from within, ensures the outcome. This *double causation* may be figured in the work as the gods deciding what characters will choose, but what is really double is the causation operating within the work to fulfill the demands of the structure operating on the whole.

Recognizing such doubleness requires no special training in literary criticism. All but the very youngest readers are aware of it. And so as novels draw to a close we may begin counting up the unmarried males and females and anticipate the final pairings. We rule out certain endings as incompatible with the genre we are reading. Others are impossible simply because they would lead to an inferior work. We guess in this way because we have a sense of what overall structure demands, and we know that if the author has done his or her job right, the choices of the characters will produce just what the perfect structure requires. Otherwise it would not be the best of all possible works.

In God's world and the literary masterpiece, optimality—the best state of affairs or the best structure—reconciles free will and providence.

## *Afterthoughts*

> His prospect high,
> Wherein past, present, future he beholds.
> —Milton, *Paradise Lost*[3]

If God is perfect, he cannot be affected by events in the world, a point made by Aristotle and accepted by almost all Christian theologians. Only an imperfect being can be changed, or change his mind because of events. A world made by a perfect God runs like clockwork—no, better, because clocks require resetting.

Recall that Isaac Newton allowed for God to intervene in the world, while Leibniz regarded such a view as blasphemy. Is God, he asks, "an inferior watchmaker," who must stand and wait to see if his work needs correcting? Is he affected by events, and therefore a being in time rather out of it? A being outside of time operates by one and only one will that takes into account everything that will result. A succession of wills would necessarily mean He had not foreseen something and had not made the perfect choice to begin with. Where there is adjustment, there is imperfection. Leibniz's view resembles that of modern scientific determinism in seeing the world as a system entirely governed by its own flawless laws.

Holding such views, it is not surprising that Leibniz rejected miracles in the usual sense of an intervention that violates the laws of nature. If God had to intervene in this way, then with each miracle he would add a new act of will to correct his initial dispensation. He would be imperfect, short of omniscient, and a tinkerer with his own less-than-ideal artifact.

Leibniz could not very well deny the existence of miracles—since the Bible described them—without incurring a charge of heresy. So he resorted again to redefinition. Although miracles in the usual vulgar sense do not exist, events that from the human perspective work like miracles, and which the Bible therefore presents as miracles of a sort, do happen. To us, they look like violations of the law of nature, but in fact the laws of nature God established at the outset led inexorably to these apparent violations of them. When the sun stopped for Joshua and the sea parted for Moses, God was not actually intervening to

---

[3]     PL, Book III, ll, 77-78, p. 418.

suspend his laws of nature. Those laws led inevitably to just these special occurrences whose necessity God in his omniscience had foreseen. These miracles did not change his design, but revealed it in all its wisdom.

Despite appearances, what we call a miracle is really a rare effect of natural law, something like snow in the tropics. Saharan snow might seem a miracle, but it would just be a freak occurrence. This was not an idea Leibniz invented. Augustine explains that a miracle happens "not contrary to nature, but contrary to what we know of nature," and would excite no more wonder than ordinary processes "if men were not accustomed to admire nothing but what is rare."[4] Only the vulgar think that God is a being in time who must step in to correct things that have gone astray. His will is singular from all eternity.

Literary works offer a direct analogy to this problematic. From Aristotle on, it has been recognized that to be successful a work must unfold by its own inner logic. The author must not be seen intervening to secure a desired outcome, as if the plan got away from him; that would be a *deus ex machina*, a term always used as a criticism. Nor must the author be seen intervening in thin disguise, tipping the scales to produce events that are less than necessary given the logic of the whole. A gratuitous ending provokes our contempt of the author's skill.

We sometimes hear such criticisms: Turgenev killed off Bazarov; Tolstoy punished Anna. When are such criticisms uttered? I think it is when readers feel that the inner logic of the work does not lead to its conclusion. The idea is that Bazarov's illness too obviously helps the author conclude his work as he wants, but there is insufficient reason within the story for such a death. We do not feel it was necessary within the novelistic world but only for external reasons. Those who, on the contrary, find Turgenev's ending appropriate contend that given who Bazarov was, such a death makes good sense. I do not wish to take sides in this debate, or the similar one about the epilogue to *Crime and Punishment*. I am concerned with the debate's logic and terms: both sides argue that if Bazarov's death or Dostoevsky's epilogue is successful, it can be shown not to be an afterthought but to flow from the structure of the whole.

---

[4]  Cited in Jones, *The Medieval Mind: A History of Western Philosophy*, second edition (New York: Harcourt Brace, 1969), 133 (from *The City of God*).

The successful author, like God in Leibniz's theology, *has no afterthoughts*, which would mean a change in will and deign. There is one design, and so there is only forethought. As God is not affected by events in the world he made, so the author does not have to adjust his plan—in effect make a new plan—when he sees how things are working out. To be sure, in the course of writing he may have altered his plan many times, but those alterations are not visible in the finished work. In literature, we assume that all such adjustment has taken place before the work is published, in the drafts, so that the work, once arrived at, is wholly present in its forethought—or as we say, it is governed by its design or structure. If changes are made in the process of writing after the design is achieved, as they sometimes are, they must conform to it, or we speak of a flaw.

The idea of a literary work as such a structure informs almost every school of literary criticism ever devised. Schools may differ on the kind of structure, or the proper way to understand it, or what term to use for it, or on countless other questions, but structure is there, and ideally explains everything in the work as a coherent whole.

This view of literature is a theology.

### Theology without God

> I [Wisdom] was set up from everlasting, from the beginning, or ever the earth was. . . . When he [God] prepared the heavens, I was there: when he set a compass upon the face of the depth.
>
> —*Proverbs 8:23-27*

The vision of the world as a perfect, if partially hidden, structure has dominated Western thought, especially since the seventeenth century. The entire tradition of "natural theology" presumed that God wrote two books, Scripture and Nature, and that we can discern his will by studying either. Both Scripture and Nature reveal design, and both the sacred books (the Bible for Christians, the Torah for the Jews, the Quran for the Muslims) and natural laws are a divine blueprint to the universe. The Book of Proverbs personifies this blueprint as Wisdom, and the goal of the sage, philosopher, or scientist was to understand Wisdom. The idea that scientists were hostile to religion is a later myth, a much later development projected anachronistically backward.

Newton, who spent many years interpreting the book of Revelation, was no atheist.

God made the laws of nature, and they reveal the divine mind as surely as the laws of Moses. Our quasi-sacred view of the scientist reflects this way of thinking.

As Sir Thomas Browne observed, "There are two Books from which I collect my Divinity, besides that written one of God, another of His servant Nature, that universal and public Manuscript that lies expans'd unto the Eyes of all: those that never saw Him in the one, have discovered Him in the other."[5]

If God can be read through nature, then we can guess that as the book of nature becomes more intelligible, it will surpass scripture with its dark obscurities. Spinoza was far from the only thinker who verified part of scripture by reason and dispensed with the rest as a primitive historical record. Einstein invoked this way of thinking when he explained: "I believe in Spinoza's God who reveals Himself in the orderly harmony of what exists, not in a God who concerns himself with fates and actions of human beings" (YBQ, 230). It did not take long after Spinoza for thinkers to ask: if one could understand God through nature, who requires Scripture at all?

A perfect being needs to exert will only once. God at the outset brought into being secondary causes, laws of nature, and they on their own determine all. It soon became apparent that nothing but pious sentiment is added by saying that those laws are of God's creation, since if the laws were all there were, the world would operate the same way. This insight transformed natural theology into natural science as we know it. Deism represented a sort of intermediate step to the banishment of God from explanation of nature.

By the principles of Ockham's razor—do not multiply entities needlessly and of two explanations of equal power prefer the simpler—God became at best optional, at worst a consolation for the weak-minded. As Laplace famously replied to Napoleon when that ruler asked about the role of God in his astronomical system: "I don't need that hypothesis."

---

[5]    As cited in Basil Willey, *The Seventeenth Century Background: Studies in the Thought of the Age in Relation to Poetry and Religion* (Garden City: Doubleday, 1953), 58 (from the *Religio Medici,* first appeared in 1642).

Even though God disappeared from new theories, the world created by a perfect being remained. It was a world in which everything fit and nothing is contingent, a world governed by laws of symmetry and optimality. If anything, the triumph of secular thinking strengthened this originally theologically justified view. I would like to stress that *modern atheists are haunted by a theology they do not recognize as such*. Instead of God, thinkers appealed to numerous God substitutes: principles that, without God, do what God would do.

Events were no longer known in advance by a divine being, but they were in principle knowable. There is still a sufficient, if not divine, reason for everything. Neither God nor his Substitutes play dice with the universe.

That applies to the social universe as well.

### Social Science

We have become so used to the term "social science" that we often do not pause to consider how strange it is. Auguste Comte coined the term "sociology," but his original name for the new discipline was "social physics." Economics self-consciously based itself on astronomy (see RtR, 47-66). But what is the justification for presuming that society, the economy, the individual psyche, and many other social phenomena can have the predictability of Newtonian mechanics? Certainly no actual results justify such faith, which Tolstoy called "superstition." Dostoevsky liked to point out that while atoms cannot know the laws that govern them and alter their behavior accordingly, people can.

What haunts social scientists—I mean the ones who take seriously the idea that their discipline can resemble classical physics—is an image of what the world must be like and what real knowledge would have to look like. Both must resemble their counterparts in natural theology.

We might say that each claimant to the status of a new social science needed to establish its own God substitute, a principle of optimality and sufficient reason, governing the particular domain to be accounted for.

Without a principle of optimality, what is to insure predictability, and without predictability how can there be a real science? If agents maximize utility and competition insures maximal efficiency; if external disruptions to a system factor out as a new equilibrium is attained; if all society's institutions pay their way by contibuting to its survival;

if institutions or practices that are mere relics of the past are always driven to extinction; if equations lead to a single solution and time is simply the interval by which that solution is reached; if a principle of minimizing expenditure of energy or anxiety governs unconscious behavior—if these or many analogous mechanisms work, then the social scientist can, at least in principle, predict the result. (Failing that, he can at least account for it after the fact as inevitable.)

By contrast, if multiple equilibria are possible; if events can tend not only to a point where a resource is maximized but also to other points; if some institutions serve a function well, some poorly, and some not at all; if the mind sometimes behaves efficiently according to some law and sometimes does not—in all these cases, there can be more than one outcome, and so the outcome actually reached lacks a sufficient reason. It remains unpredictable.

What drew Freud to claim not that sometimes slips of the tongue, acts of forgetting, or other errors can be meaningful and result from a concealed intention—a point that today few would dispute—but that they always and necessarily do? Could not other causes—such as the dynamics of attention; the ease of automatically doing the wrong thing; poor mental funcioning due to illness, sleepiness, or age; reactions inbuilt in our remote ancestors, or habits developed decades ago— could not any of these sometimes cause errors without a concealed intention at work? All Freud had was evidence that some errors work this way, and he simply asserted that others must. Why the leap?

In his early work *The Psychopathology of Everyday Life* (1901), Freud insists absolutely that there is no such thing as chance in the mind. All errors are meaningful—by meaningful he means intended— and "nothing in the mind is arbitrary and undetermined."[6] Nothing at all: "Every change in the clothing usually worn, every small sign of carelessness—such as an unfastened button—every piece of exposure, is intended to express something which the wearer of the clothes does not want to say straight out and for which he is for the most part unaware."[7]

---

[6]    Sigmund Freud, *The Psychopathology of Everyday Life*, ed. James Strachey, trans. Alan Tyson (New York: Norton, 1965), 242.

[7]    Cited from *The Psychopathology of Everyday* Life in the Standard Edition of Freud's works, SE:256-265, in John Farrell, *Freud's Paranoid Quest: Psychoanalysis and Modern Suspicion* (New York: New York University Press,

Freud even maintains that paranoid people are correct—at least, more correct than normal people—when they regard nothing as the result of mere chance. They err only in rejecting chance in the external, instead of the internal, world. Freud reminds us that supersititious, as well as paranoid, people discover in the external world the meaningfulness that is in fact always present within. And they too are, except for confusing internal and external, more realistic than the supposed realists: "I believe in real (external) chance, it is true, but not in internal (psychical) accidental events. With the supersititous person it is the other way around" (Freud, *Psychopathology*, 257).

In his last book, *Civilization and Its Discontents* (1930), Freud again insists that—in the absence of direct traumas to the brain—memory is perfectly efficient. All apparent forgetting results from effort, from the intention to forget: "Since we overcame the error of supposing that the forgetting we are familiar with signified a destruction of the memory-trace—that is, its annihilation—we have been inclined to take the opposite view, that in mental life nothing which has once been formed can perish—that everything is somehow preserved and that in suitable circumstances … it can once more be brought to light" (CAID, 17). *Everything, nothing, all*: Freud's rhetoric is categorical when the evidence obviously could be only partial.

Why would a putative scientist go so far beyond the evidence? The answer, I think, is that, like so many founders of social sciences, Freud had in mind a model of what a science looked like. For him as for so many others, it looked like Newtonian physics, and just as the law of gravity does not work "on the whole and for the most part," so the laws governing the mind must admit of no exceptions or they are not really scientific laws at all. Behind Freud's exaggerated claims lay a metaphysics, and, his atheism not withstanding, that metaphysics was essentially theological.

We need only add that what Freud regards as a superstition— denying chance to the external world—has been regarded as the basis

---

1996), 47. For Farrell, Freud exemplifies, as well as describes, the paranoid style of modern thought, with its cultivated suspicion that everything has a hidden, and unpleasant, meanng. I would describe this sort of suspicion as appealing because it gives the unmasker a supposedly scientific way to decode the behavior of others; and the heady feeling of such superiority partly explains why the promise of a social science has been so hard to resist.

of science by the founders of other disciplines, from anthropology to economics and political science. Again, such thinkers have been guided by the model of what a science must be. Whether we look within or without, someone has found perfect order.

Superstition is the social science of others.

### Laplace as a Model Modern Thinker

Laplace claimed to have perfected Newton's solar mechanics to meet Leibniz's exacting specifications. He apparently proved the stability of the solar system, as Newton could not, without appealing to any outside interventions. More precisely, Laplace thought he did, for, as Poincaré later pointed out, for good mathematical reasons not only was such stability unproved but it was also unprovable, as is the case to this day: the three-body problem remains unsolvable.[8]

Laplace was also the inventor of an especially compelling image for modern thought: a calculating demon or "intelligence" who, if he knew the position of every particle in the universe today, could calculate exactly what would happen, and had happened, at every other moment of the universe. For such an intelligence, he wrote, "nothing would be uncertain and the future, as the past, would be present to his eyes. The human mind offers, in the perfection which it has been able to give to astronomy, a feeble idea of this intelligence."[9] Nothing is uncertain, not even the smallest thing:

> All events, even those that on account of their insignificance do not seem to follow the great laws of nature, are a result of it just as necessarily as the revolution of the sun.... Present events are connected with preceding ones by a tie based upon the evident principle that a thing cannot occur without a cause which produces it. This axiom known by the name of *the principle of sufficient reason*, extends even to actions which are considered indifferent (Laplace, 3; italics in original).

The "evident principle": things just have to be this way. Leibniz's God has become Laplace's God substitute.

---

[8]    See RtR, 47-66.

[9]    Pierre Simon, Marquis de Laplace, *A Philosophical Essay on Probabilities* (New York: Dover, 1951), 4.

Laplace in effect believed in divine foreknowledge without the divine: the universe behaves as if an omniscient God foreknew it. We live under the rule of an absent God, an as-if God, a God-substitute called Laws of Nature. As for free will, it is already included in the calculations, for, as Laplace insists, "the freest will is unable without a determinative motive to give them [actions] birth" (Laplace, 3), and the motives that guide the will are part of the chain of calculable events. It should be obvious that this formulation—the will does what it wills, but cannot will what it wills—repeats Lorenzo Valla's argument that freedom and foreknowledge do not conflict.

Of course, human history and society exhibit too many causes for Newtonian formulae to be easily apparent. But Laplace's mathematics of probability theory is designed to close the gap. It is crucial to recognize that Laplace does not ascribe probability to events themselves. Events are absolutely certain, and the principle of sufficient reason precludes any other events. No, when Laplace speaks of the probability of an event, as he carefully explains, he means the probability that our guess, based on imperfect knowledge, should prove correct. We are right to ascribe a probability of one in two to a coin flip, but if we had all the relevant facts, we would know in advance with perfect certainty whether to call heads or tails. There is providence in the fall of a sparrow.

As we have seen, Laplace was by no means the only thinker to assume that what Newton had done for astronomy could be done for all the social sciences. Elie Halévy famously referred to this style of thinking as "moral Newtonianism" (GPR, 6). The social and its laws lie hid in night;/ Come Newton Two, and all will soon be light.

Indeed, for most of the nineteenth century, it seemed palpably absurd to oppose social science in this sense; it was like arguing that effects may not have causes or that twice two equals five. Dostoevsky's underground man, in opposing this vision, knows that his views must seem deeply perverse, and himself doubts whether the "advanced" gentlemen in their crystal palace might not be right, damn them the more for that!

### Take No Survivals!

Two centuries after Laplace, this vision has remained surprisingly robust. The "new atheists," as they are called, somehow seem to think that it is only benighted religious folk who believe in chance, contingency, open time, or free will. So far as I can determine, they remain ignorant of the fact that their own view derives from, and covertly affirms, the West's dominant theological tradition. And they do not seem to realize that their picture seems compelling for reasons essentially metaphysical—how could there be an event without a cause?—rather than scientific or evidentiary.

Only by thinking in terms of contingency, open time, and genuine process can we break from the grip of the dominant theological tradition.

What evidence do we have that the social world is governed by iron-clad deterministic laws? Like second marriages, social sciences represent the triumph of hope over experience. Consider, for instance, the twentieth century's predominant trend in cultural anthropology. This discipline conventionally traces its status as a discipline to Bronislaw Malinowski, who argued that an anthropology worthy of its name would resemble physics. Above all, Malinowski insisted, it would banish the concept of "adventitious and fortuitous happenings." If it couldn't, it was no science at all. All social facts and events fit into a larger system that in principle, and soon in practice, allows for "prediction of the future."[10]

Malinowski argued that culture always exhibits the features that literary critics would recognize as characteristic of great poems. Nothing is just there; there are no accidents; everything serves a function in a perfectly harmonious whole whose structure is in principle visible at a glance. As in Leibniz's universe, or an Aristotelian tragedy, there is a sufficient reason for everything. What else could such a view represent than a translation of divine providence?

But is it not possible that some things exist in a culture simply because of inertia? Perhaps they are there for no particular reason at all, or perhaps they once served a function, and now no longer do? Think of a dead staircase in an old building leading to a wing that no longer exists; or Britain's House of Lords.

Malinowski reacts to this suggestion with all the vehemence of an English professor answering an undergraduate who explains an event in a novel as "just interesting." He argues, categorically, that it is impossible for something to exist for no particular reason and to

---

10      Bronislaw Malinowski, *A Scientific Theory of Culture and Other Essays* (Chapel Hill: University of North Carolina Press, 1944), 8.

serve no particular function. A sufficient reason accounts for every last feature of a culture, and that reason is a present function. There are no mere "vestiges" or "survivals" from earlier stages, nor could there ever be. To accept their existence would be to give in to the "anti-scientific concept of 'dead-weights' or cultural fossils in human culture" (Malinowski, 27-28). Not evidence but an *a priori* sense of what a science requires dictates Malinowski's rejection of survivals and all apparent evidence to the contrary.

What's more, everything serves its function with "full efficiency" (Malinowski, 143); otherwise "the group ... would not survive." He knows this, too, by an *a priori*. Culture is not only a machine, but also a perfect one with no friction. Though a human product, it has the characteristics we normally associate with the divine.

The strength of Malinowski's rhetoric—the unqualified nature of the claim and the denomination of opponents as unscientific—clearly cannot be justified by the evidence. The reasoning is entirely circular: if anthropology is to be a social science, everything must fit; and we know that everything fits because anthropology is a science and that is the scientific view.

Malinowski claims that every time something looks like a mere survival without a present function, or a function not in harmony with the rest of the culture, we simply do not see the function it really serves. Thus, horse-drawn carriages persist not as a means of transportation but to serve another function, namely romantic rides. But how does Malinowski know that this is always and necessarily the case? He presumes that if a contrary case should present itself, a function will eventually be discovered, much as Freud believes that, if we look hard enough, we can find a disguised intention behind every error. The method guarantees we will succeed. But where there are guarantees given in advance, when no conceivable evidence can demonstrate the falsity of a tenet, we are dealing not with science but with metaphysical faith.

I wish social scientists (and humanists) could be instructed to repeat daily: to offer an example is not to disprove the impossibility of counter-examples.

An ideology of what both science and culture must be has replaced what science itself demands.

Dostoevsky's underground man understood this fallacy well. In arguing against Benthamite psychology and laws of history, he repeatedly brings up counter-examples: the educated man with a toothache, Cleopatra's pleasure in sticking pins into her slave girls' breasts. But no evidence can prevail against systems with a ready-made answer to everything that might happen. Whatever is unexplained is unexpained yet. The systems are "mere logical exercises.... But man is so fond of systems and abstract deductions that he is ready to distort the truth intentionally, he is ready to deny what he can see and hear, to justify his logic" (NFU, 21). The underground man repeatedly drives his opponents into assertions that there must be an explanation that will save their theory; he forces them into revealing their unscientific apriorism. Like medieval scholastics, their theories treat evidence by "saving the appearances."

By turning the tables in this way, the underground man and Dostoevsky draw on a well-worn device in the history of satire. A man who claims to know something infallibly derives more and more absurd explanations to save the appearances. For Dostoevsky, the prime example was Don Quixote, whose spirit lives on in the Benthams and Bernards. Dostoevsky also knew of Tolstoy's portrait of General Pfühl in *War and Peace*; Tolstoy, in turn, would have had in mind Walter Shandy, that greatest of all systematizers; and Sterne was obviously drawing on a tradition that also included Dr. Pangloss in *Candide*. In creating Pangloss, Voltaire mocked not only Leibniz but also all thinkers who Leibnizize the world. What must be so triumphs over what plainly is so.

### Enchanted by Mendeleev

The idea of survivals or vestiges, so derided by Malinowski and the functional school, derives from a historical understanding of social change, in which things do not alter simultaneously. Because there is no invisible hand, no author ensuring that everything fits, things change at different rates and move in different directions. Therefore some things are bound to persist from an earlier period. Culture exhibits no Leibnizian "pre-established harmony." Malinowski, and those who replaced his functionalism with structuralism, remained true to the spirit of Leibniz (and Pangloss), and consequently insisted that all things do change in tandem. Malinowski contended that cultures change only when needs force them to, but that then they engage in a "complete remolding" of all institutions. For the functionalists, if something could not be remolded, it would die, because there would be no reason to keep it.

Anyone who has glanced at the federal budget, studied the institutions of government, or reflected on his own bad habits will recognize that this reasoning puts the cart before the horse. Most often, it takes great energy *not* to keep an institution, just as it is usually much harder to break a bad habit than to persist in it. The economy of effort favors not complete remolding but, at best, one small change at a time. Of course, sometimes people do amend bad habits, but how many can one change at a time? There are bound to be survivals. I leave aside the idea of "full efficiency," since I imagine no one knows an institution that works that way.

Although important exceptions exist, the general trend towards such a crypto-theological view of society is clear. Malinowski was far from the only anthroplogist who believed in "prediction of the future." Claude Lévi-Strauss enthused about the ability of social scientists to formulate a table of human possibilities "that would be comparable to the table of elements which Mendeleieff introduced into modern chemistry." Looking at such a table, we would "discover the place of languages that have disappeared or are unknown, yet to come, or simply possible."[11]

The vision of society as a series of perfectly harmonized structures in which everything fits necessarily does away with messy transition periods. History becomes a series of leaps. We move from box to box in the periodic table. Why then is periodization so disputed and why so different from field to field?

If everything in a period harmonizes with everything else, and changes with everything else, what force keeps time? It is as if the social world, like a poem, was governed from without by an author. A single, advance design makes sure that nothing just happens and that everything fits.

So much in our experience is inharmonious that it takes the most strenuous efforts to preserve minimal order. Indeed, if that were not the case, no one could have gained credit as a founder of a social science for having discovered the putative ordering principle.

And what if we did not presume a single causal moment imposing a poetic design? What if there are many causal moments,

---

[11]    Claude Lévi-Strauss, *Structural Anthropology*, trans. Claire Jacobson and Brooke Grundfest Schoepf (New York: Basic, 1963), 58.

unharmonized with each other, giving real meaining to presentness and open time?

To grasp such a world, we need to think differently.

## 2 / The Counter-Tradition. Presentness and Process

### *Actors versus Spectators*

As Leibniz may stand for one pole of an opposition, Tolstoy stands for the other: the counter-tradition of Western thought.

Tolstoy may be regarded as the name of an idea, and that idea is contingency, along with its close relatives, unpredictability and the importance of each present moment. "What are we facing tomorrow?," Prince Andrei asks Pierre before Borodino. "A hundred million diverse chances that will be decided on the instant by whether we run or they run, whether this man or that man is killed" (W&P, 930). On the instant: the present moment matters. It is not a mere product of the past state of the universe according to Laplacian laws. Presentness has real weight because something else might have happened and, if it had, it might have had concatenating effects.

In the view of the tradition, time is simply t in an equation. As d'Alembert remarked in 1754, it is a mere "geometrical parameter."[12] Newton's equations can be run equally well in both directions. We can just as easily retrodict the position of Mars as predict it. The directedness of time is illusory.

In the mind of God, all is simultaneous, and the future is consequently no less irrevocable than the past. It follows, as Peter Damian pointed out in the eleventh century, that if God can change the future, he can just as well change the past. "God has that power after Rome was founded, that it be not-founded." Anselm agreed: "it is not right to say that it is impossible for God to make what is past not to be past. For it is not ... the impossibility of acting that has effect in this case but only the will of God." The strangeness we sense

---

[12]  As cited in Ilya Prigogine, *From Being to Becoming: Time and Complexity in the Physican Sciences* (San Francisco: Freeman, 1980), xi.

at this conclusion testifies to our sense that future and past really are different. [13]

But we can appreciate Damian's and Anselm's point if we recall that a novelist can just as well change the beginning of his work as the end. From the outside, all is part of a simultaneous structure. God views history in just this way.

From this perspective, the present moment is simply the one where we happen to be located. It is like the page of a novel we happen to have reached. What happens later is already determined, indeed, already accomplished. The present moment has no presentness.

If by pastness we mean this sort of irrevocability—something unchangeable because it is already accomplished—then each moment, including those to come, has pastness. It is already contained in, and contains, every other moment. The future is simply the past-to-be. Einstein once famously consoled the children of a friend who had died by denying that death means absolute non-existence: "This signifies nothing. For us believing physicists, the distinction between past, present, and future is only an illusion, if a stuboorn one."[14] The dead person exists in an inaccessible time, which is no different from existing in an inaccesible place.

By contrast, the counter-traditional view regards time not as a parameter but as an "operator" (Prigogine, xvi). Time is genuinely asymmetrical and has an inherent directedness. The past is given, but the future is what we, or sheer contingency, make it. The present has more than one possibility hidden in its womb, and some possible futures are never born while others come to be only because of what we do or what chances to happen.[15] No moment has pastness until it is past.

---

13    See Peter Remnant, "Peter Damian: Could God Change the Past?" *Canadian Journal of Philosophy* VIII, no. 2 (June 1978): 259-268. Citations from 266.

14    As cited in Paul J. Nahin, *Time Machines: Time Travel in Physics, Metaphysics, and Science Fiction* (New York: American Institute of Physics, 1993), 74.

15    Prigogine insisted that this was as true of physics as of the social sciences: "The future is not included in the past. Even in physics, as in sociology, only various 'scenarios' can be predicted. But it is for this very reason that we are participating in a fascinating advenure in which, in the words of Niels Bohr, we are 'both spectators and actors'" (Prigogine, xvii).

Human effort can affect the future in a way that it cannot affect the past. We are, as Niels Bohr remarked, actors as well as spectators. For that matter, it is entirely conceivable that God could alter the future in a way that he cannot alter the past. Perhaps he too is an actor. If God chose to create a world with presentness, then he does not know what will happen until it does. He can be affected by events. Things happen to him. He exists in time.

### What Is Process?

The counter-traditional view makes room for genuine *process*. Let me define this key term as I shall use it.

By process I mean not just a sequence of events extending over time but a sequence in which multiple paths are open at multiple moments. If one moment—say, an initial one—determines all that follow, the sequence is a process in some sense of the word but not in the sense in which I am using it. In my sense of process, no moment already contains all the rest. If the very same circumstances leading up to an event were repeated, something else might well result.

In a genuine process, *more than one moment has causal efficacy*. If we are thinking of conscious beings, we can say that a process requires independent acts of will, each of which chooses one possibility rather than others.

Where there is genuine process, presentness matters. To grasp what happens one needs narrative. Conversely, narrativeness demands process.

### The Spectrum of Sufficiency

Is the world genuinely processual? In contrast to Laplace, processualists do not regard our inability to predict all events as the result only of ignorance. They do not believe, as Laplace did, that a being who knew all circumstances at any moment along with the timeless laws governing them could know for sure what happened or would happen at all other moments. Rather, *events themselves have probability*.

Part of what God detects in a given state of affairs is its *likeliness*.

As Bakhtin expressed the point, the world at its root manifests *surprisingness*. If so, there are events lacking a sufficient reason—not that there is no reason at all, but that the reasons do not necessarily determine a single outcome. Or we may say that there is a *spectrum of sufficiency*, from complete sufficiency of the sort Leibniz imagined to radical chanciness, and everything in between.

The world contains three kinds of events: as for the Leibnizian and the determinist, some are actual and others impossible. But there is also a third class of events—genuine possibilities that might have been actualized but were not; and which, if given another chance, might well happen. Possibilities compete for actuality. They must, so to speak, exert effort to come to be; as the idiom has it, events *take* place. They do not just *have* a place. This competition for being lacks a predetermined outcome. Suspense belongs to the nature of the world.

### *Something Else: The Detour*

As events can be more or less likely, moments contain a field of possibilities. Whichever possibility happens to become actual may not have been the most likely. As Aristotle remarks, given enough chances, the improbable is highly probable. To understand any historical event is to ask what else might have happened.

Indeed, to say that one event caused another is to say that, without it, something else might have taken place. If A caused B, then without A there would have been no B.

If so, then the very project of historical explanation suggests sideshadows or, as it is now common to say, counter-factuals. As Hugh Trevor-Roper explained:

> At any given moment in history there are real alternatives …
> How can we *"explain* what happened and *why"* if we only look at
> what happened and never consider the alternatives…. It is only
> if we place ourselves before the alternatives of the past…, only if
> we live for a moment, as the men of the time lived, in its still fluid
> context and among its still unresolved problems, if we see those
> problems coming upon us,… that we can draw useful lessons
> from history.[16]

To understand why things happen is to ask "what if" the sequence had developed differently.

To understand a past time historically is to recreate it when it still had presentness. To treat it as if what followed was somehow already

---

[16]     As cited in VH, 85.

given is not to think historically. Soviet historiography, in fact, treated the future as already irrevocable.[17] From a processual perspective, that is a way of seeing history without historicity.

We must instead place outselves at the time when what happened subsequently not only had not yet happened but also did not have to happen. To understand a moment is to understand the possible futures it contains, and historical explanation must sketch them in even though they did not happen. Those unactualized possibilities were genuinely real — real in the form of possibilites that, at that earlier present moment, could be.

Sometimes what does happen results from the attempt to avoid what was most likely to happen. Historians who presume the main road overlook the possibility that it detoured.

Placing ourselves at the moment with multipe potentials allows us to survey its broad temporal horizon. "What is" is intimately tied to — is partly constituted by — "what if."[18]


### Someone Else

Much as understanding a historical event includes imagining alternative happenings, so understanding a person includes intimating who he or she might have become. Part of me is the other character I could have developed, the other habits I might have cultivated, the other deeds I could have performed, the other professions I might have followed, the other loves I might have fallen into, and the other sins I might have committed. My unborn children call out to me. Thomas Gray's "Elegy in a Country Churchyard" famously discovers graves of shadow persons — "Hands that the might of empire might have swayed,/Or waked to ecstasy the living lyre" — the possible lives of

---

[17]    Or as Arthur Danto puts the point, Marxists tend to make *historical* statemens about the future. See chapter one ("Substantive and Analytical Philosophies of History") of Arthur C. Danto, *Analytical Philosophy of History* (Cambridge: Cambridge University Press, 1968), 1-16.

[18]    Gerald Prince has coined the term "the disnarrated" for authorial comments indicating that while something could have happened, it did not. See Gerald Prince, *Narrative as Theme: Studies in French Fiction* (Nebraska: University of Nebraska Press, 1992), 28-28.

people who never lived them: "Some mute inglorious Milton here may rest,/ Some Cromwell, guiltless of his country's blood."[19]

Perhaps one reason we are so fascinated by stories about twins, or even siblings, is that they allow us to ask what else a person might have become? Stories about changelings or look-alikes (*A Tale of Two Cities*, *The Prince and the Pauper*) satisfy the same curiosity, as do the many tales about doubles. The reader may come to ask whether he might be his own imposter, the mere double of his true self.

We cannot help interpreting dreams as adumbrations of possibilities. We indulge in daydreams to entertain realities desired and perhaps just barely possible. Historical fiction works only if it is not pure fantasy but includes the sense that something like this might very well—or at least might possibly—have happened.

We cry over the death of novelistic heroines who do what we might have done or might still do. Dangers narrowly avoided make us wince, as they would not unless we sensed them as genuinely possible. Perhaps, indeed, circumvented threats still linger, as our very dread of them even when they are past suggests. So do hopes no longer realizable.

Perhaps the dead regret most the lack of potential futures. In the *Odyssey*, the shade of Achilles longs for possibility, any possibility: "Don't try to sell me on death, Odysseus. / I'd rather be a hired hand back up on earth,/ Slaving away for some poor farmer,/ Than lord it over all these withered dead."[20]

Or, quite the contrary, we may imagine that ghosts "embody" the dead person's other possibilities, regretted tragedies, and thwarted hopes. Like a criminal wanting to undo a deed, they return to the scene. So viewed, ghosts give shape, if not weight,to alternatives, a person's might-be (or might-have-been) self, as do ideas of reincarnation. Perhaps the very idea of a soul separable from the body derived not only from the desire for immortality but also from the predilection to imagine an alternative life.

---

[19]   Thomas Gray, "Elegy Written in a Country Churchyard," in *English Prose and Poetry, 1660-1800: A Selection*, ed. Frank Brady and Martin Price (New York: Holt, 1961), 224-225.

[20]   Homer, *Odyssey*, trans. Stanley Lombardo (Indianapolis: Hackett, 2000), 172, ll. 510-513.

### Shadows of What Must Be or May Be?

Interestingly enough, Christmas stories as a genre allow us to explore who else a person might have become. That is the question posed so dramatically by the classic film *It's a Wonderful Life* and the story on which it is based, Philip van Doren Stern's "The Greatest Gift." The hero must learn that his life has mattered when he sees the world without him. And of course, Dickens's Scrooge changes his life after the Ghost allows him to see his end if he remains the person he has made himself.

Scrooge begs the Ghost for an alternative, a might-have-been that might still be. At first the Ghost refuses, but at last relents:

> "Before I draw nearer to that stone to which you point," said Scrooge, "answer me one question. Are these the shadows of the things that Will be, or are they the shadows of the things that May be, only?"
>
> Still the Ghost pointed downward to the grave by which it stood.
>
> "Men's courses will foreshadow certain ends, to which, if persevered in, they must lead," said Scrooge. "But if the courses be departed from, the ends will change. Say it is thus with what you show me."
>
> The Spirit was immovable as ever.
>
> . . .
>
> "Good Spirit," he pursued, as down upon the ground he fell before it. "Your nature intercedes for me, and pities me. Assure me that I may yet change these shadows you have shown me by an altered life."
>
> The kind hand trembled.[21]

Scrooge asks for a "may be" different from a "must be" and, in place of the foreshadow, a sideshadow. Dickens's story instructs the reader in the possibility of altering one's life, and figures Christmas as a time when such a decision can be made. Did not God give Himself a second life and, along with it, the possibility of a salvation we could not have earned?

Dickens's Christmas teaches us to regard life as having more than one possibility. It insists on our freedom.

---

[21]    Charles Dickens, *Christmas Books* (Oxford: Oxford University Press, 1987), 69-70.

### *Empathy*

The sigh of relief, the wince, pinching onself to make sure one is not dreaming: all these gestures testify to our sense that we are close to a might-be. The experience of choice and responsibility persuades us, in a way no argument could, that regardless of what we may profess, we live in a world of the morally significant alternative.

When we consider the significance of our decisions or of the chances that have befallen us, we wonder how things might have turned out otherwise. Morality begins with such wonder. The more one cultivates the sense that one might easily have experienced another person's bad fortune, or committed his evil deed, the more one is likely to empathize with others.

Empathy performs an as-if ensoulment into the life of another. Through compassion (etymologically, "suffering-with"), our sense of right and wrong develops. In Russian, the etymology of that word (*sostradanie*) stands on the surface, as if the English word were "cosuffering." When we are compassionate, we feel as if we were two people at once. We self-consciously imagine being another.

La Rochefoucauld famously remarked that we all have sufficient fortitude to endure the misfortunes of others. No matter what we piously profess, others are alien. Perhaps so, but we may teach ourselves to make their misfortunes something between alien and our own.

Morality starts from the sense that *there but for the grace of God go I.*[22] We forgive others more readily for deeds we feel could easily have been our own. Conversely, we excuse our lapses by persuading ourselves that they had to be, that they couldn't be helped, and that anyone would have done the same thing. Sinners love fatalism.

Even people who never think about philosophical questions concerning fate often say that an event was somehow "meant to be."

### *Thou Art the Man!*

When we condemn others, we may tacitly presume that we could in no circumstances have done what they did. We often deceive ourselves.

---

22    See YBQ, 98, WoO, 7, and the discussion of this line in chapter 4 of the present study.

That is the lesson Nathan the prophet teaches King David when he narrates the story of the rich man with many flocks who, to feed a guest, takes a poor man's only ewe. "And David's anger was greatly kindled against the [rich] man; and he said to Nathan, As the Lord liveth, the man that hath done this thing shall surely die" (2 Samuel 12:5). Nathan replies: "Thou art the man.... Wherefore has thou despised the commandment of the Lord, to do evil in his sight? Thou has killed Uriah the Hittite with the sword, and hast taken his wife to be thy wife.... Now therefore the sword shall never depart from thy house" (2 Samuel 12:7-11).

We must all learn to do on our own what Nathan teaches: to ask, before condemning another, whether we have ever done something essentially similar. If so, then we could, in other circumstances, have done exactly what we are about to condemn. Indeed, if we ever even contemplated something similar, we could have done what might prompt a prophet to say: Thou art the man!

Rejecting the rationalist, "scientific" premises of detective stories as a genre, G. K. Chesterton's detective Father Brown adopts this biblical wisdom to solve crimes. As Dostoevsky's Porfiry Petrovich also knows, a good detective is aware of himself as a might-be criminal. Porfiry Petrovich traps Raskolnikov not by logic or evidence but by empathy.[23] So, too, Father Brown categorically rejects the possibility of a scientific method, like that of "Dupin, Lecoq, Holmes, and Carter," which presumes that iron-clad laws govern behavior. He believes not in social science but in Christian original sin and freedom, which taken together mean we are all capable both of committing and refraining from crime. If so, a person can gain insight by imagining himself as someone who made the other choice.

Father Brown solves crime by *empathy*, which allows him to reconstruct the circumstances in which he himself might have committed a given crime.[24] He explains that "no man's really any good until he knows how bad he is" (Chesterton, 427). And so he has taught himself to consider from within "how a man might come to be like that, until I realized that I really was like that, in everything except the

---

[23]  I once heard Richard Strier remark that Porfiry Petrovich was Russian literature's most empathetic character.

[24]  G. K. Chesteron, *The Father Brown Omnibus* (New York: Dodd, Mead, 1951), 425

actual final consent to the [criminal] action.... And when I was quite sure that I felt exactly like the murderer myself, of course, I knew who he was" (Chesterton, 426).

When viewed as a mere product of scientific laws, people do what they must do. But from within, each of us senses his freedom. Father Brown explains:

> Science is a grand thing when you can have it.... But what do these men mean, nine times out of ten, when they use it nowadays.... They mean getting *outside* a man and studying him as if he were a giant insect; in what they call a dry impartial light.... When the scientist talks about a type, he never means himself, but always his neighbor. (Chesterton, 426-427)

By contrast, empathy means getting *inside* a man.

The moral sense instructs: there but for the grace of God go I; thou art the other man! In *The Brothers Karamazov*, Father Zossima takes the point as far as possible: everyone is responsible, he says, for everyone and everything.

Each of us takes the road not taken, and it makes all the difference.

Father Brown identifies an essential inconsistency: one can never apply to oneself the causal laws and closed time one might ascribe to people in general. That is because while one is choosing one experiences oneself from within. No one makes a difficult decision from without: just imagine saying to oneself, "Well, I am a determinist, so I will just wait and see what I do!"

Chesterton and Dostoevsky touch upon a problem of belief: does one really believe a proposition that applies to everyone but which one cannot apply to oneself? The sociology of knowledge is always the sociology of other people's knowledge.

For the processualists, the preferred view of human events is from within: within oneself, and within another.

### Theography

Leibniz and the natural theologians notwithstanding, God in the Hebrew Bible does not resemble the God of the dominant tradition's theologians.

Far from being outside time, God, as the Hebrew Bible describes Him, participates in events and—again, contrary to the theologians, both Jewish and Christian—*is affected by them*. When, at the beginning of the Noah story, God sees the wickedness of humanity, "it repented the Lord that he had made man on the earth, and it grieved him at his heart" (Genesis 6:6).[25] After the deluge subsides, God establishes the rainbow to remind himself of his promise never to bring another such flood: "And the bow shall be in the cloud; and I will look upon it, that I may remember the everlasting covenant between God and every living creature" (Genesis 9:16).

God regrets, is grieved to the heart, needs reminders: this is not a God outside time. If he regrets that he did something, then he did not foresee the full result; if he grieves, then he is affected by events; if he can forget, then he knows at one moment what he does not at another. He must be in time.

Skip some seven hundred years to the Book of Judges, which begins by establishing its recurrent pattern: "Whenever the Lord raised up judges for them, the Lord was with the judge … for the Lord would be moved to pity for their groaning. But whenever the judge died, they would relapse and behave worse than their ancestors…. So the anger of the Lord was kindled against Israel."[26] At first God intended for all the Canaanites to be destroyed, but He changes His mind: "In order to test Israel, whether or not they would take care to walk in the way of the Lord as their ancestors did, the Lord had left these other nations, not driving them out at once, and had not handed them over to Joshua," as originally planned.[27]

God changes his mind; he is repeatedly disappointed; and events move him to pity and anger. Here, as elsewhere, He constructs a test, and a test demands uncertainty of outcome. To take the most remarkable example, when God tests Abraham by ordering him to sacrifice Isaac, it is not just Abraham who does not know until the last instant what he will do. God Himself remains in suspense. Only when

---

[25]   Robert Alter's translation gives: "And the lord regretted having made the human on earth and was grieved to the heart." Robert Alter, *Genesis: Translation and Commentary* (New York: Norton, 1996), 28. Other versions give "was sorry" or "repented." All versions carry the sense that God did not foresee what would happen and was affected by the outcome.

[26]   Judges 2:18-20 in HC, 372. As the editors of HC observe, "Repeated covenantal failure on Israel's part at last brings a change in the Lord's strategy to Israel."

[27]   Judges 2:22-23 in HC.

Abraham at last "stretched forth his hand, and took the knife to slay his son"—when he at last makes up his mind—does God intervene. "And he said, Lay not thine hand upon the lad, neither do any thing unto him: for now I know that thou fearest God, seeing thou has not withheld thy son, thy only son, from me" (Genesis 22:11-12). *Now I know*: I do not see any other plausible way to interpret God's words except as a statement that he, too, did not know in advance what would happen.

This is not Leibniz's God, not a God unaffected by events and knowing the entire future from outside time. Jewish and Christian commentators were, of course, aware of such passages, but interpreted them away as figures of speech or concessions to the ignorance of the people. But if the question to be asked is whether God exists outside of time, then such an explanation only begs it.

Suppose one were to take seriously the idea that God lives in time and that everything, including the Creator, is in process, a process including eventness and surprisingness. Why, one could even attempt a biography, rather than just a theology, of God—an account of how God changes over time in response to His choices and those of others. Carl Jung did as much in his *Answer to Job*, and, more recently, Jack Miles's *God: A Biography* offers what Miles calls a theography, tracing God's development through the Hebrew Bible. Miles explains:

> A medieval mystic once wrote, "God cancels the successiveness of men," meaning that while human beings experience their lives one day at a time, God sees their lives' time as a portrait on a wall, every moment visible to him at once. But human beings have returned the favor with a vengeance, canceling the successiveness of the protagonist of the Bible by a tradition of Bible reading that regards the entirety of the text as simultaneous to itself, so that any verse may be read as the commentary on any other verse and any statement true of God at one point is taken to be true of God at all points.... [But] there is virtually no warrant in the New Testament for any claim that God is immutable, and there is equally little in the Hebrew Bible.[28]

This "immutable" and "simultaneous" approach, Miles suggests, probably derives from Aristotle's idea of the unmoved mover existing

---

28      Jack Miles, *God: A Biography* (New York: Vintage, 1995), 12.

at a single and eternal moment. We might add that this "tradition of Bible reading" follows the traditions of poetics. It makes the Bible a certain sort of work, one governed by an overall structure. Earlier and later moments belong equally to a text that we take as a whole, as a pattern which, viewed from the outside, is simultaneous to itself.

This tradition of Bible reading deprives its narrative of genuine narrativeness. Miles proposes instead to take it as a record of events unfolding without an overall plan, the story of God as a hero developing in time. In this story, Miles discovers, God "enters time and is changed by experience. Were it not so, he could not be surprised; and he is endlessly and often most unpleasantly surprised" (Miles, 12).

### God in Time

In the twentieth century, more than one school of theologians has challenged the dominant tradition's idea of an impassive God wholly out of time. As its name suggests, the school usually called "process theology" sees process (not as I have defined that term) as constitutive of actuality itself. The world is not only Creation, but also creative, as is God Himself. Past moments limit possibilities for the present but do not exhaustively determine a single state of affairs. Or as process theologians like to say, each actuality is partially "self-creative" and "self-determinative" (C&G, 25).

This view of time tries to give real substance to concepts like gratitude and responsibility by making it possible for us not to do what we do. In process theology, God tries to influence—or, as they say, to "persuade"—us to follow the best aims, but He does not force us. His purposes can, and often do, go unfulfilled, which is one reason there is evil in the world. Theodicy is not a difficult problem in process theology.

In the course of history and individual lives, genuinely "novel elements" appear. "One aspect of God is a primordial envisagement of pure possibilities.... This means that the divine reality is understood to be the ground of novelty." Without God, the world could produce nothing new, but with God "as the organ of novelty," genuine self-creativity becomes possible (C&G, 26).

Process theology defends God's omniscience at the cost of radically redefining that term: it means that at any given moment God knows whatever it is *possible* to know. But since the genuinely new constantly takes place, God's knowledge constantly changes. Such omniscience does not constrain the openness of time, and it makes God's knowledge "dependent."

So is God's emotional state. For the dominant tradition, God does not actually experience emotions, or He would be affected by events in the world. Commentators have described references to emotions as translations into our terms, concessions to what Philo of Alexandria called "duller folk." Anselm, for example, argued that by God's "compassion" we must understand what he does for us, not what he experiences: "When thou beholdest us in our wretchedness, we experience the effect of compassion, but thou does not experience the feeling." As Aquinas concludes: "to sorrow, therefore, over the misery of others belongs not to God, but it does most properly belong to Him to dispel that misery." By the same token, God loves us in the sense that he does good to us, but not in such a way that he the unmovable Being is "moved."[29]

For process theologians, the world is what Alfred North Whitehead calls an "adventure," as is God's own life (C&G, 25).

Process theology did not go far enough for a more recent group of thinkers, sometimes called "open theists" or "free-will theists."[30] Open theists ground themselves firmly in a reading of scripture, which to them must be more authoritative than abstract philosophy. They insist we take at face value the many biblical passages in which God repents, relents, is moved to anger, loves, pities, changes his mind, and tests. Such passages are not mere anthropomorphisms or "anthropopathisms" (mistaken attribution of human feelings).

God *could* have made the world of classical theism and so could have foreknown from the outset everything that would ever happen. But he chose rather to make people free in the strong sense, which means he could not know what they would choose until they chose it. In such a world, not all agency is his, and so history is a co-creation.

---

29      Citations from Anselm and Aquinas as given in C&G, 45.

30      On open theism, see the essays in Clark Pinnock, Richard Rice, John Sanders, William Hasker, and David Basinger, *The Openness of God: A Biblical Challenge to the Traditional Understanding of God* (Downers Grove, IL: InterVarsity, 1994); Millard J. Erickson, *What Does God Know and When Does He Know It?: The Current Controversy Over Divine Foreknowledge* (Grand Rapids, MI: Zondervan, 2003); and John Sanders, *The God Who Risks: A Theology of Providence* (Downers Grove, IL: InterVarsity, 1998).

Contrary to classical theists, God genuinely loves, suffers, and cares. And contrary to process theologians, God does a lot more than persuade: he actively intervenes. There are genuine miracles. In response to people, he changes his mind. In short, God wills more than once, and that is why petitionary prayer can make a difference. His agreements and covenants with people are genuinely two-sided.

From this perspective, we can understand Jesus's plea "oh, my Father, *if it be possible,* let this cup pass from me" (Matthew 26:39): the world consists of genuine possibilities. For Jesus, there is an *if.* God chose to be incarnated as a person because his experience is in some important respects similar to ours. When Jesus is tempted, the result is a genuine triumph, not a foregone conclusion.

Open theists are keenly aware that biblical testimony does not unambiguously support their argument. To be sure, they can readily take at face value Jeremiah 32:34-35, where God exclaims: "But they set their abominations in the house, which is called by my name, to defile it..... Neither came it into my mind, that they should do this abomination."[31] God has to learn something from experience.

But other passages seem to fit the traditional view. The Psalmist declares: "My frame was not hidden from You, when I was made in a secret place, knitted in the utmost depths. My unformed shape Your eyes did see, and in Your book all was written down" (Psalms 139:16).[32] In Isaiah, God proclaims: "I am God, and there is none like me, Declaring the end from the beginning, and from ancient times the things that are not yet come" (Isaiah 46:9-10). In Romans, Paul famously states: "For who he did foreknow, he also did predestinate.... Moreover whom he did predestinate, them also he called; and whom he called, them also he justified; and whom he justified, he also glorified" (Romans 8:20-30). Most obviously, countless prophetic passages show God knowing the future in advance, sometimes in great detail.

The open theists reply by distinguishing extratemporal knowledge of the classical sort from mere prediction, which can be and sometimes is mistaken; from conditional statements stating what will happen if people choose in a particular way, as they may or may not;

---

[31]    Another favorite passage is Hosea 11:8-9, in which God "recoils" from his intentions against Israel.

[32]    Robert Alter, *The Book of Psalms; a Translation with Commentary* (New York: Norton, 2007), 481-482.

and from statements of what God is sure will happen only because he will himself make sure it happens one way or another. Some troubling passages can indeed be explained in these ways, but with others, the open theists, no less than their classical opponents, seem to be straining to justify at all costs conclusions given in advance.

They need not do so. If they were to take a truly processual view of the Bible—view it as a processual work of the type I describe below—the inconsistencies would not be so troubling and might even count as what one should expect. At the conclusion of this essay, I shall indicate how.

### Dialogic Theology

Most theorists have agreed that Bakhtin, as a Russian Orthodox believer of a sort, intended some of his literary theories as encoded theologies.[33] He followed the Russian tradition of using "Aesopian language" when direct speech was impossible. In his exposition of Dostoevsky's "polyphonic novel," Bakhtin offered a theology that is, in its basic elements, very similar to "free-will theism."

God's relation to the world resembles the polyphonic author's relation to the novelistic world he creates. In both cases, the author could have created a universe in which he would know in advance everything his characters would do, but he chose not to do so. In Bakhtin's terms, God and the polyphonic author chose instead to surrender their "essential surplus of meaning." They surrendered the superiority derived from knowing in advance the pattern of the whole, and therefore the sufficient reason determining each event and each detail. Whatever harmony the essential surplus provides, it does so at the cost of genuine freedom on the part of the people God or the author creates.

Published in the Soviet Union, Bakhtin's book on Dostoevsky obviously could not theorize directly about the Christian God. So Bakhtin analogized to Greek mythology, which no one could accuse him of believing: "Dostoevsky, like Goethe's Prometheus, creates not voiceless slaves (as does Zeus) but *free* people, capable of standing

---

33      See, for instance, *Bakhtin and Religion: A Feeling for Faith,* ed. Susan M. Felch and Paul J. Contino (Evanston: Northwesten University Press, 2001).

*alongside* their creator, capable of not agreeing with him and even of rebelling against him" (PDP, 6). In his notebooks, Bakhtin does invoke the Christian God: "This is, so to speak, the activity of God in his relation to man, a relation allowing man to reveal himself utterly (in his immanent development), to judge himself, to refute himself. This is activity of a higher quality. It surmounts not the resistance of dead material, but the resistance of another's consciousness, another's truth" (PDP, 285-286).

God creates a world in which there are many independent agents, but in surrendering his power to control everything he in no sense remains passive. On the contrary, he, and the polyphonic author, are active in two ways: first, they create the basic setting in which action takes place; and second, they engage "alongside" their charcters in genuine, "unfinalized" dialogues. The essence of dialogue lies in its openendedness: participants genuinely respond to each other in unforeseen ways.

In entering into dialogue with people, God treats people as genuine others capable of surprising him. They affect Him, as He affects them. He addresses them as other agents or, as Bakhtin prefers to say, as independent voices. "It is one thing to be active in relation to a dead thing, to voiceless material that can be molded and formed as one wishes, and another to be active *in relation to someone else's living consciousness*. This is questioning, provoking, answering, agreeing, objecting activity" (PDP, 285). Everyone has his say.

The Bible uses dialogues not just for technical reasons but because it conceives of the relation of man to God as dialogic. If for Plato, existence is participating in the Idea, for the Bible and Dostoevsky it means participating in dialogue. "The influence on Dostoevsky of Job's dialogue and several evangelical dialogues is indisputable, while Platonic dialogues simply lay outside the sphere of his interest. In its structure Job's dialogue is internally endless, for the opposition of the soul to God—whether the opposition be hostile or humble—is conceived to be endless" (PDP, 280).

The world itself is dialogic. We must conceive of it not as something "ready-made" but as always in the making, "not as a given but as a task." Indeed, to understand the fundamental truth about the world, we must stop thinking of truth as the sort of thing that can be expressed in propositions belonging to no one in particular. Rather, truth is essentially dialogic, an interaction of embodied points of view. It requires two or more independent voices. "The entire ideological culture" we have inherited takes for granted that truth is impersonal, a series of "separate thoughts" assembled into a system (PDP). What else could truth be?:

> It is quite possible to imagine and postulate a unified truth that requires a plurality of consciousnesses, one that cannot in principle be fitted into the bounds of a single consciousness, one that is, so to speak, by its very nature full of event potential and is born at a point of contact among various consciousness. (PDP, 81)

Truth, like life, possesses "event potential" ("eventness"). Biblical dialogues are not an inferior systematic theology. No, theology as usually practiced is but a distillation of dialogues.

Bakhtin's early version of "free-will theism" leads to a special sense of what it is to be human. One becomes a genuine "personality," rather than a thing, when one is not just the sum of one's experiences and qualities. A personality retains the capacity to surprise. He or she can render untrue anything that might be said about him or her by anyone—be he as well-informed as God himself—from outside. Or as Bakhtin likes to say, personalities are "unfinalizable" and "noncoincident with themselves":

> A person never coincides with himself…. The genuine life of the personality takes place at the point of noncoincidence between a person and himself, at his point of departure beyond the limits of all that he is as a material being, a being that can be spied on, defined, predicted apart from its own will, "at second hand."… The truth about a person in the mouths of others, not directed to him dialogically and therefore a secondhand truth, becomes a lie degrading and deadening him, if it touches upon his "holy of holies," that is, "the man in man." (PDP, 59)

A fundamental ethical principle immediately follows: one must never treat another as a nonpersonality, that is, as someone utterly predictable from without. One must treat another as unfinalizable, as capable of surprise and of genuine dialogue.

Theology and philosophy need to reorient themselves around the idea Bakhtin claims is implicit in the very form of Dostoevsky's works: "Nothing conclusive has yet taken place in the world, the ultimate word of the world and about the world has not yet been spoken, the world is open and free, everything is still in the future and will always be in the future" (PDP, 166). And that is true not only of the world, but also of each person and of God himself.

### The London Principle and the Test of Symmetry

If God acts in time, and if many human agents can act in ways He cannot foresee, then the world they jointly create must be less than perfect. This imperfection testifies to process.

Laws of optimality, equilibrium, symmetry, and perfect fit all derive from a faith in perfection. But where contingency plays a role, nothing guarantees the best or maximal result; and when independent decisions operate over long periods, asymmetry results. Symmetry demands coordination.

A single will can produce a harmonious design, but a series of independent moments of cause or agency has no way to do so, except by sheer and highly remote chance.

If you found yourself in a city with streets at right angles, with circular roads whose radii were evenly spaced from a center, and with a perfect symmetry of broad to narrow avenues in each quarter, you would probably guess that the city had been laid out according to an initial plan. Would such symmetrical order have arisen by chance? But if you found yourself in a city with roads that curved unexpectedly, emerged from each other at odd angles, defied all rules of symmetry, and changed their names frequently according to no discernible pattern, the possibility of an initial plan would never occur to you.

Symmetry serves as an excellent, if not infallible, test of overall or advance design.

The grid of Center City, Philadelphia, or the map of any town where roads follow geometrical principles, shows it to have been laid out according to an advance design. One needs no biography of William Penn to guess that the original part of the city was planned. By contrast, London's streets go off in all directions, follow irregular terrain, and seem to have been laid down according to a series of whims. It is hard not to suspect that fleeting economic opportunities, now undiscoverable, account for some odd shapes, while aesthetic tastes of bygone eras or newcomers reproducing some distant village gave rise to others.

By the same test of symmetry it is easy to discern where the planned part of Philadelphia ends: at the point where the streets cease to follow the principles of geometry and go off according to the exigencies and demands of the moment: what I shall call *the London principle*.

Of course, logically speaking, your guess might be wrong: it is just possible that sheer chance would produce perfect geometry, and a planner who had attended the Monty Python School of City Planning might lay out a city like London at a stroke. But the chance of either is vanishingly small. If not logically airtight, the test of symmetry works remarkably well.

The test presumes that symmetry and perfection indicate either a single overarching design or a force that mimics it. Asymmetry and imperfection bear witness to multiple distinct moments of agency. They show not design but historicity, a genuine process.

### Narrativeness and Architecture

The same test applies to buildings. A gleaming structure with a complex perfect symmetry was doubtless the creation of an inspired architect. By contrast, imagine happening upon a house where staircases lead to rooms now blocked off, where a new wing does not match an old, where some parts have been gutted and remodeled in one way and others in another, where materials differ depending on their ages, and where temporary fixes were later adapted into a new aesthetic. One would guess that the building as it now stands resulted from a historical process over a succession of generations with changing tastes and needs. Many different people made independent decisions at different times.

Whoever first built the structure could not possibly have known the uses to which it would be put. As Stewart Brand has argued, "All buildings are predictions. All predictions are wrong."[34]

When buildings survive long enough, they may even retain vestiges of changes prepared for but barely begun. In such cases, one limns unrealized possibilities—the architectural "sideshadows." One can see where a porch was meant to be. An unfinished side door may lead to someone's dream of a garage. Sometimes a "what if" becomes palpable.

---

[34]    See Stewart Brand, *How Buildings Learn: What Happens After They're Built* (New York: Penguin, 1994), 178.

Such buildings embody narrativeness. One can explain them only historically. They respond to a series of shifting presents. In so doing, they may achieve their own kind of beauty very different from that of buildings planned by an architect determing every detail and doing his utmost to prevent occupants from introducing changes.

What we might call *contingent buildings*—buildings following the London principle—are "time-drenched" (Brand, 63). Over eight hundred years, Brand explains, Venice "celebrated duration in its buildings by swirling together over time a kaleidoscope of periods and cultural styles all patched together in layers of mismatched fragments" (Brand, 63).

### Darwin and Process

After the voyage of the *Beagle*, Darwin saw organisms in this time-drenched way. His proof of evolution was what I have called the test of symmetry. He delighted in pointing out parts of organisms that do not quite fit, that serve their function badly, or that are adapted to a function the organism does not need. A function not needed may have been needed by a remote ancestor. An organ may fulfill its function less than optimally if already existing organs precluded solutions that were superior. These less than perfect organisms, with adaptations layered imperfectly on each other, testify not to a single design according to an advance plan but to a series of tinkerings and adaptations over a long period.

In short, the proof of evolution is imperfection. Darwin recognized the temporal significance of jury-rigged structures that no good engineer would have chosen from the outset.

This view of Darwin as the theorist of imperfection may sound odd, because when social scientists (or sociobiologists) refer to a process as "Darwinian," they almost always mean that natural selection ensures an optimal solution. They take natural selection as they take the "invisible hand," as a God-substitute. The blind watchmaker designs a perfect watch. But to read Darwin this way is to miss his central point.

Perhaps Darwin's greatest insight was not natural selection but his demonstration of historicity. We have long grasped the significance of the first but have barely begun to think in terms of the second. If we did, we might truly escape the prison house of natural theology. We might begin to think of a world not only without the traditional God but also without His substitutes.

As Darwin saw things, the biological world testifies to a long historical process, with causation happening at many different times, and contingency repeatedly playing a role. Its imperfections, strangenesses, and layerings of just-workable solutions all testify to history.

I think Stephen Jay Gould understood this point when he objected to the way "our textbooks like to illustrate evolution with examples of optimal design—nearly perfect mimicry of a dead leaf by a butterfly or of a poisonous species by a palatable relative. But ideal design is a lousy argument for evolution, for it mimics the postulated action of an omnipotent creator. Odd arrangements and funny solutions are the proof of evolution—paths that a sensible God would never tread but that a natural process, constrained by history, follows perforce."[35]

To be sure, if a God substitute operates, then evolution might produce optimal results, and sometimes does. But in that case the result looks exactly as if a divine creator had operated from a single advance design. There is no way to tell the difference between the work of a perfect God and a perfect God substitute. "You cannot demonstrate evolution with perfection because perfection need not have a history" (Gould, 28).

What is needed is some equivalent to the London principle, some sign that agency was operable independently at distinct moments: genuine process. Is there asymmetry?

Darwin recognized that imperfection would be the best evidence that the world was created not by a single act of divine will, but by a succession of independent changes, which is to say by a historical process irreducible to advance design. In fact, if we are to believe Darwin's account in *The Voyage of the Beagle*, it was meditation on striking examples of imperfections that led to his evolutionary convictions. Properly understood, Darwinism testifies to life's narrativeness.

A theology like Miles's or Bakhtin's might be reconciled with Darwinism, but not one like Leibniz's or Milton's.

Darwin offers numerous examples of structures and organs that do not harmonize with the rest of the organism or its surroundings, structures that no rule of optimality—whether divine or mechanical—

---

[35]     Stephen Jay Gould, *The Panda's Thumb: More Reflections in Natural History* (New York: Norton, 1982), 20-21.

would have produced. Let me turn to a key passage, which I have considered in earlier essays, to draw a new conclusion:

> He who believes that each being has been created as we now see it, must occasionally have felt surprise when he has met with *an animal having habits and structure not at all in agreement*. What can be plainer than that the webbed feet of ducks and geese are formed for swimming? Yet there are upland geese with webbed feet which rarely or never go near the water.... In such cases, and many others could be given, *habits have changed without a corresponding change in structure*. The webbed feet of the upland goose may be said to have become rudimentary in function, though not in structure. (OoS, 185)

Web-footed geese that do not go near the water suggest that the geese's ancestors did live a maritime life. Habits have changed faster than structure, and that is why the two do not harmonize. These geese must have developed features at distinct moments. They do not reflect the unfolding of a perfect initial plan. A genuine process took place.

Darwin challenges not only Divine Creation but also As-if divine creation.

### The Atheist's Providence

The real radicalism of Darwin's vision disappears from many supposedly Darwinian accounts of human evolution. It has become distressingly common to read descriptions of human culture and behavior as so many optimal adaptations made in our Pleistocene ancestors.[36] These just-so stories—"How the Human Got His Taste for

---

[36] See, for instance, Charles Matthewes' review of Nicholas Wade's book *The Faith Instinct*. Matthewes observes that Wade takes evolution as a source for just-so stories in which an old problem reached its ideal present solution, a form of thinking that "baptizes the way things happen to be as the way they ... of necessity *must be*. This loses one of the great insights of evolutionary theory itself, namely contingency: If we understand anything about evolution, it is that things are heavily dependent on small accidental changes, or on the context of development itself." Charles Mathewes, "The Evolution of Religion," *The American Interest*, July/August 2012, http://www.the-american-interest.com/article.cfm?piece=1270. For a more substantial critique of this approach, see Raymond Tallis, *Aping Mankind: Neuromania,*

Beauty," "How People Learned to Cooperate"—posit a story in the Pleistocene to show why just such a feature was needed. Such accounts leave no room for imperfection, contingency, and narrativeness.

Their evidence that the feature arose from a Pleistocene need—indeed the evidence that such a need existed—is that it is good at satisfying that need. Are structures designed for one purpose never co-opted to serve another? Do institutions never develop to fill one need fairly well when they would serve another, absent, need even better? Do we never discover a new use for a tool long after its invention? In short, might not some human behaviors be mere by-products, or conditioned by a historical process that could and in some places did unfold differently?

These stories have only two moments: the presumed origin and the present. Then they draw a straight line. But why could there not have been many causal moments and many divergences into different directions before the present moment was reached? After all, no matter how many new causal moments, shifts, adjustments, misdirections, and reorientations one experiences, one has to wind up somewhere, and so after the fact one can always draw a straight line back to the origin!

And are there no imperfections to explain? Children need happy endings, but do sociobiologists? So far as I know, they never tell a story about how a behavior that was and is not terribly successful came about in the Pleistocene. And I know no proposed story about how, given what evolution had to work with at a given moment, rather unimpressive adaptations just had to do, which is why we are the ill-formed, maladapted creatures that we are. Take a look at human history, especially over the past century, and you may ask, as atheists have about evil, why does so much seem to have gone wrong?

Where is the sociobiologists' theodicy, justifying the ways of human evolution? Human history might suggest that to explain our origins we also need an anthology of *misanthropic* just-so stories.

Recall that Malinowski utterly rejects the possibility of societies with practices that do not pay their way in insuring survival. He denies the possibility that habits and structures, institutions and functions, may not be in perfect agreement. In so doing he too seems to presume

---

*Darwinitis and the Misrepresentation of Humanity* (Durham, UK: Acumen, 2011).

a force as providential as the traditional God. Reading Darwin, one wants to ask: Did Malinowski lack an appendix?

If Darwin categorically denied that natural selection drives organisms to optimal solutions, why is he so often understood otherwise? Evidently, it is a lot easier to do without God than to do without a divinely created world.

The providence of the God-substitute must be vindicated. God lives in disguise in the new atheism and survives posthumously in social science.

### Prosaics and Economics: Lock-In

When in the 1990s I first wrote the essays that I have here combined and adapted, I was fascinated by what to many economists was then a shocking new idea: path dependency. What shocked *me* was that anyone found this idea shocking.

Our suboptimal QWERTY keyboard, the VHS recording system, and several other examples seemed to show that, even in a market economy where rational choice operates, optimality is not necessarily reached. A small initial advantage, combined with a positive feedback mechanism, can lead to "lock-in" of a suboptimal situation. No matter how many keyboards prove superior to QWERTY, the fact that people have invested so much time in learning it preserves it. Even if someone could prove Esperanto superior to English or Chinese, native speakers will not switch to it.

Imagine that you are in a valley trying to climb to the highest point, and have to choose between two fog-covered hills. Since you cannot see which hill is higher, you might rationally go by what in retrospect proves to be a misleading sign—which one starts out steeper?—and wind up on the lower hill. You might not realize your mistake until it no longer paid to climb down and start over.

Recall that in a standard illustration of optimality, a ball released at the cup's rim is bound to reach the lowest point: the precise route does not affect the result. This is another way of saying that *process* as I have defined it in this essay is irrelevant.

But if one instead imagines a bowl pitted with multiple depressions of different depths, the route does make a difference. Once a ball is lodged in one depression, it cannot somehow get to a lower one. Gravity will not agree to move it briefly up so it can ultimately descend further, or cisterns would not work. Because there are multiple stable equilibria, and because unknowable contingent factors can lead to one equilibrium rather than another, predictability is severely limited even in principle.[37]

In that case, as they say, "history matters," and it was this proposition that was felt to be shocking. An author of the original QWERTY articles, Paul David, describes critics as "strenuously resisting" the very possibility of path depndence. As he remarks, opponents viewed QWERTY as a "Trojan horse" designed to undermine the core assumptions of economics as a discipline,[38] a threat to this very approach to social science.[39] Two defenders of the traditional view concluded, "Some path dependence theorists have argued that past decisions might have locked-in certain inferior outcomes.... Upon investigation, [all] such claims have been found to be without empirical support (in private markets) and based on fairly narrow theoretical assumptions."[40]

To a non-economist like myself, it was not obvious why so much was at stake. Do economists really doubt that contingent factors in a culture's history may exert an important influence on its social, cultural, historical, and material development? Can they truly believe that economic laws operate flawlessly? How often do we see anything human designed beyond the reach of improvement? Who, examining his or her own psyche, would conclude that it is optimally designed for productivity, goodness, or any other value? How many of our bad habits would qualify as path-dependent lock-ins? But these are the objections of prosaics.

---

[37]    On path dependency, lock-in, and related concepts, see W. Brian Arthur, *Increasing Returns and Path Dependence in the Economy* (Ann Arbor, MI: University of Michigan Press, 1994) and Pierre Garrouste and Stavros Ioannides, eds., *Evolution and Path Dependence in Economic Ideas: Past and Present* (Cheltenham, UK: Elgar, 2001).

[38]    Citations are from Paul A. David, "Path Dependence and the Quest for Historical Economics: One More Chorus of the Ballad of QWERTY" (1997), http://www.utdallas.edu/~liebowit/knowledge_goods/david2.htm. "Strenuously resisting" is from part 8, "Trojan horse" from Part 1.

[39]    See S. J. Leibowitz and Stephen E. Margolis, "Path Dependence, Lock-In, and History," https://www.ekatetra.com/downloads/liebowitz_econ_pathdependence.pdf.

[40]    See Stan J. Leibowitz and Stephen E. Margolis, "Path Dependence," http://encyclo.findlaw.com/0770book.pdf.

In fact, numerous authors, both specialist and popular, have defended economics precisely as a universal, in principle flawless method that can be applied equally well to all, not just economic, behavior.

For example, Gary Becker famously defined his discipline not by subject matter but by approach. "The combined assumptions of maximizing behavior, market equilibrium, and stable preferences, used relentlessly and unflinchingly, form the heart of the economic approach as I see it."[41] Becker is nothing if not relentless and unflinching. He insists that "the economic approach is a comprehensive one that is applicable to all human behavior, be it behavior involving money prices or imputed shadow prices, repeated or infrequent decisions, large or minor decisions, emotional or mechanical ends ... patients or therapists, businessmen or politicians, teachers or students" (EAHB, 8).

To be sure, Becker remarks, when timid economists cannot explain something they call it irrational, or appeal to luck, chance, ignorance, ad hoc shifts in values, and similar dodges, but that is like physicists resorting to miracles. For that matter, when other putative social sciences appeal to culture, tradition, or psychological factors, they are either speaking nonsense or failing to ask whether those factors may themselves be resolvable in terms of the economic approach, as they surely can be. The best other disciplines can do is describe the stable preferences with which economic analysis begins, but that analysis

> provides a valuable unified framework for understanding all human behavior... The heart of my argument is that human behavior is not compartmentalized, sometimes based on maximizing, sometimes not, sometimes motivated by stable preferences, sometimes by volatile ones, sometimes resulting in an optimal accumulation of information, sometimes not. Rather, all human behavior can be viewed as involving participants who maximize their utility from a stable set of preferences and

---

[41] EAHB, 5. See also Gary S. Becker, *A Treatise on the Family: Enlarged Edition* (Cambridge, MA: Harvard University Press, 1991), 5. Best-sellers popularizing this approach applied broadly are the two books by Steven D. Levitt and Stephen J. Dubner, *Freakonomics: A Rogue Economist Explores the Hidden Side of Everything* (New York: HarperCollins, 2005) and *Superfreakonomics: Global Cooling, Patriotic Prostitutes, and Why Suicide Bombers Should Buy Life Insurance* (New York: HarperCollins, 2009).

> accumulate an optimal amount of information and other inputs
> in a variety of markets. (EAHB, 14)

There can be no "sometimes." While not all economists extend the reach of the model as far as Becker, those committed to it have traditionally presumed it applies without fail to its proper domain. That is why the idea of lock-in, which applies both to economic phenomena and to human behavior more generally, posed such a threat. If true, then an optimal equilibrium is reached only "sometimes."

To grasp this approach is to recognize how modern economics developed (as David puts it) "as an ahistorical system of thought," a model to which economists have devoted so much effort and training that it constitutes its own kind of lock-in:

> They thus have a "learned incapacity" (in Thorstein Veblen's apt phrase) to see how historical events could exert a causal influence upon subsequent outcomes that would be economically important. Perhaps unknowingly, such folk have fully internalized Aristotle's teleological principle of causation, which rejected the method of reference to antecedents ... by subsituting forward looking functionalism.... Mainstream economics is not alone among the social sciences in providing a way to explain an existing state of the world by reference to the end (telos) that it serves.... (David, part 9)

"Mainstream economics" is indeed not alone: as we have seen, both functionalist and structuralist anthropology also work by presuming a tendency to a harmonious state that covers its historical traces.

### Jared Diamond's History without Historicity

Interestingly enough, the urge to create a social science—one that will eliminate contingency, mark out a single path, and show that history does not matter—applies even when the model for a science is not physics but a historical science, like geology! Apparently, the whole point of "science" is to take the historicity out of history, to eliminate the need for narrativeness in narrative, and to reduce process to mere unfolding of what is already given.

Such dehistoricizing of history, which obviously afflicted Soviet historical materialism, more recently served as Jared Diamond's goal in his celebrated *Guns, Germs, and Steel*.[42] Diamond's "geographical determinism" endeavors to "develop human history as a science, on a par with acknowledged historical sciences such as astronomy, geology and evolutionary biology" (Diamond, 408).

If Diamond had been content to point out that geography makes much more of a difference than we usually recognize, he would have proven his point, at least to my satisfaction. But as the dream of a science led Freud to make untenable claims about errors, so Diamond insists that only geography matters.

Diamond explains that, of course, it may seem as if culture, specific histories, individual efforts, or accident sometimes make a difference. But then one needs to look beyond these "proximate" causes to the "ultimate" ones, which are always geographical (Diamond, 410). For example, some historians have argued for the importance of institutions in the development of Western power, but they fail to notice that institutions are themselves the consequence of geography. Accidents doubtless occur and individual geniuses exist, but over time all such factors "average out" (Diamond, 424).

Diamond believes that he has already established these ultimate principles on the broad scale and that the next step "will be to smaller geographical scales and shorter time scales than those of this book" (Diamond, 409). The shorter and the smaller they are, the less "history matters"—if "history" is understood to include the contingent, the processual, and the excess of possibilities over actualities. Ultimately, once the starting point—our species and the earth's geography—is given, so too is the present. It's like that ball and cup.

Like mainstream economists, Diamond considers the arguments for lock-in and multiple equilibria only to deny they matter (Diamond, 418-19). What locks in averages out.

### Predictably "Irrational"

What is striking, if far from unique, about the economics literature is how deep is its sense that only one sort of explanation could possibly be right. Even the recent movement known as behavioral economics, which discovers ways in which economic decisions are made

---

42      Jared Diamond, *Guns, Germs, and Steel: The Fates of Human Societies* (New York: Norton, 1999).

"irrationally," conforms in its essentials to the same style of thinking. I shall consider behavioral economics in more detail in chapter four, but for now it would be useful to note that, despite its promise of a break from traditional economics, it retains the same sense of a science and the same rejection of contingency.

For one thing, "irrational" turns out to mean anything different from what is predicted by standard economic theory. What is "rational" is just what standard economics says it is, except that people do not do it.

For behavioral economists, the reasons people do not behave "rationally" are all intensely simple. They do not involve culture, tradition, or anything too complex to model in an elementary experiment. The subjects who make decisions in behavioral economics are no closer to resembling real people than are the subjects of traditional economics.

Nor is any more room given to historical contingencies. Behavioral economics apparently requires narrative no more than do the rational choice models of Gary Becker. After all, where narrativeness is needed, there are no simple experiments to perform. Nor do any simple laws ensure predictability.

Human behavior as described by this school is not just irrational, but also (to use the title of the most popular summary of the movement) *Predictably Irrational* (see PI). If cultural differences, individual biographies, and historical contingencies irreducible to a timeless mathematical model were taken into account, would the irrationality be as predictable?

And strangely enough, for all the critique of mainstream economics, an optimality model of a sort still operates. To be sure, the market no longer necessarily reaches the best possible state on its own, but a wise official can lead it there, if guided by the insights of behavioral economics. And they stand ready to help. To paraphrase Paul David, we move from nirvana economics to nirvana political economy (David, part 5).

### Exogenous or Endogenous? Economic History

To the extent that influences come from outside a domain—are *exogenous*—no investigation of the domain can be sufficient to predict its course. From the perspective of the domain itself, an exogenous cause cannot be distinguished from a pure accident. Only if causes are *endogenous* (internal) can the model of the domain aspire to prediction.

It follows that would-be social sciences try, as much as possible, to diminish the attention that must be paid to the exogenous. Perhaps, as Becker would have it, exogenous influences merely set the preferences, which then remain stable and can be taken as givens. Or perhaps such influences are not really so influential. Or perhaps they somehow cancel each other ("average out"). Or they may not be exogenous at all.

As Diamond regards cultural factors as determined by geography, so Marxists traditionally assign them to the "superstructure," which is in turn determined by the economic "base." Joel Mokyr remarks of most market economists that they, too, "ironically enough, share with Marx a historical materialism which holds that ideology is basically endogenous to economic environments and does not shape them."[43]

Examining why he feels that Britain played the pivotal role in industrializing the world, Mokyr insists not only that beliefs mattered but also that one cannot reduce beliefs to some more solid cause. What's more, he continues, the same may be said of "persuasion" and rhetoric to make beliefs attractive. Indeed, many other factors were involved which did not have to be there.

For all these reasons and more, beliefs and actions interacted in a way that was "historically contigent. By this I mean that it was the result of a confluence of circumstances that was in no way inevitable.... Some ideas will succeed when the 'circumstances' are right, and at other times the circustances seem propitious but the ideas are not forthcoming or fail. Just as in evolutionary biology we can never know precisely why some highly fit species emerged and others, just as fit, did not, there is a baffling indeterminacy in history" (Mokyr, 2). Events that do not have to happen sometimes do, and then they make all the difference (Mokyr, 2-3).

### Prosaics, or the Extraordinary Origin of Ordinary Things

Is the development of technology determined to evolve in a single direction? Does competition drive the artifact to its perfect form,

---

43    Joel Mokyr, *The Enlightened Economy: An Economic History of Britain 1700-1850* (New Haven: Yale University Press, 2009), 1.

according to the maxim "form follows function"? Numerous thinkers in recent years have argued that it does not.

In *The Evolution of Useful Things,* Henry Petroski pointedly asks whether forks or chopsticks represent a superior way to convey food to the mouth.[44] As soon as one appreciates that the question has no answer, one recognizes that the evolution of artifacts is not constrained to a single path.

There are always tradeoffs. A shape that serves one function conflicts with another; a solution may be preferable but cost more; aesthetic criteria may matter more or less; and cultural norms may make a big difference. Eating is not just conveying food to the mouth, but is intimately involved with a civilization's basic rituals. Prosaics matters.

As David Pye observes, "nothing we design or make ever really works [flawlessly].... Our dinner table ought to be variable in size [for different numbers of guests] and height [for children and adults], removable altogether, impervious to scratches, self-cleaning, and having no legs [or legs in different places].... Every thing we design and make is an improvisation, a lash-up, something inept and provisional" (cited in Petroski, 26-27). What drives innovation is "ubiquitous imperfection," but the result is not perfection but a variety of new solutions with their own tradeoffs. "It is quite impossible for any design to be 'the logical outcome of the requirements simply because, the requirements being in conflict, their logical outcome is an impossibility" (cited Petroski, 27-28).

As with the evolution of species, an innovation that arises to satisfy one purpose often suggests others; or the serendipitous joining of two changes, neither made with the other in mind, may produce yet another new possibility. These and other reasons demolish "any overly deterministic argument, for clearly there is no unique solution.... Different innovators in different places, starting with rudimetary solutions to the same basic problem, focused on culture-specific artifacts that are daily reminders that even so primitive a function as eating imposes no single form" (Petroski, 20).

---

44      Henry Petroski, *The Evolution of Useful Things* (New York: Random House, 1994).

### The Process of Languages

I have before me a chart of the Indo-European languages.[45] At the top, Proto-Indo-European, the presumed origin language, produces some thirteen branches, some familiar (Germanic, Italic, Indo-Iranian), some much less so (Anatolian, Phrygian). There are branches which have died out (Tocharian). Some have divided into subbranches, which have in turn divided and redivided; the Indic branch of Indo-Iranian begot Sanskrit, which begot eleven languages. Others, like Armenian and Albanian, seem not to have bifurcated.

Of course, just as Darwin insisted that there are no clear criteria for distinguishing a variety from a species, so too there are none for distinguishing a language from a dialect. (Do Norwegian, Danish, and Swedish really differ enough to qualify as separate languages, as the chart represents them?). That old saw that the difference between a dialect and a language is that a lannguage has an army, suggests that the very identity of "a language" depends on nonlinguistic (exogenous) criteria.

The chart shows what I called "the London principle" in action. Nothing about Proto-Indo-European ensured that it would beget these and only these languages. What made West Slavic languages branch off from South Slavic ones? The answer is not linguistic: it is the invasion of the Hungarians who settled between them.

This map presents the operation of genuinely exogenous forces. It shows contingency in operation. It could not be more asymmetrical. A narrative would be required to explain what we see, and there were obviously other possibilities. Many moments of cause in many places operated independently.

This is what the world as process looks like.

---

[45] Inside back cover and last page *of The American Heritage Dictionary of the English Language* (Boston: Houghton Mifflin, 1975).

## 3 / Outlining a Prosaics of Process

### Prosaics and Aesthetic Necessity

Poetics has usually described the successful literary work as one in which a single comprehensive design governs the whole. As Aristotle observed, we sense "a structural union of the parts such that, if any one of them is displaced or removed, the whole will be disjointed and disturbed. For a thing whose presence or absence makes no visible difference, is not an organic part of the whole" (AP, 55). The work's end must be not just a stopping point but the achievement of closure, the sense of a completed design to which everything has been tending, and that includes all details. All apparent contingencies have been shown to fit the design.

Indeed, we often equate explaining a given feature of a work with showing its place in the overall plan of the whole. To understand it is to grasp why it has to be there. Everything has a sufficient reason. Even when different critical schools posit different kinds of structural unity, they usually agree that some such unity must be present.

In classical theology, actions are doubly determined, within time by human choice and from outside time by God. By the same token, in a literary work characters freely choose what the work's structure demands. They are governed by what Bakhtin calls "aesthetic necessity" (AA, 119). Bakhtin means by this term that, by reason of the work's design, what happens is what had to happen.

But real freedom demands surprisingness. It must be impossible to know what a person will do. "In this sense," Bakhtin elucidates, "ethical freedom ('freedom of the will') is not only freedom from cognitive necessity (causal necessity), but also freedom from aesthetic necessity" (AA, 119). Process theology and open time theism picture how people could be surprising to God, but how can a character surpise an author? Hasn't the author invented the character and chosen his actions? And if the work allows for more than one alternative path, how could it function as a succesful aesthetic whole?

Authors' experience answers the first question. Numerous writers testify that a convincing character seems to take on a life of its own and do what the author did not expect. Upon reflection, that is not so odd because, after all, we surprise even ourselves. Actors also know the phenomenon well. What usually happens in literature, however, is that when an author is surprised by a character, he redesigns the work to give the newly discovered action a fitting place. Then the action seems not only right from within but also from without, psychologically convincing and guided by aesthetic necessity. The initial surprise remains in the notebooks.

A character could escape aesthetic necessity only if the author's surprise could survive in the published work, which must somehow retain the rough draft's palpable spontaneities. Then some actions would be singly, not doubly, determined. Such a work could represent human freedom or sheer contingency. But how could it be aesthetically successful?

The answer is, it would have to rely on an alternative to structure. Such an alternative exists. To be understood, it demands not a poetics of structure but a prosaics of process.

### "Outsideness"

Interpreting the story of the creation, Saint Augustine took great pains to deny what the text seems to say, that in creating the world God first planned a day's work and then, having completed it, judged it. He "saw that it was good." In that case, God would have been working in sequence and creation would involve a series of independent acts of will.

But surely God must foreknow the outcome of all actions. He must have known as he created something that it would be good, or he wouldn't have created it. "For not in our fashion does He look forward to what is future, nor at what is present, nor back upon what is past ... for those variations of time, past, present, and future, though they alter our knowledge, do not affect his.... He knows all things with a knowledge time cannot measure."[46]

Poetics trains us to make an Augustinian assumption about the authors of masterpieces. Only in the notebooks does the author write a scene and then judge it good or bad. In the finished work, unless it is flawed, the author lies beyond sequence. His single intention, unmodified by the narrated events, embraces the whole.

---

[46]   Saint Augustine, *The City of God*, trans. Marcus Dodd, 2 volumes (New York: Hafner, 1948), I, 460 (Book 9, chapter 21).

After all, if the author had reread a passage and judged it bad, he would already have gone back and changed it.

Thus, presentness as experienced by the characters proves illusory. That is because author and reader possess what Bakhtin called radical outsideness (*vnenakhodimost'*): they occupy a position qualitatively "outside" the time of the characters. No human being knows his future or can envisage the moment of his death. But an author knows these things of a character. He knows the *whole* of a person as no person can know himself.

Outsideness ensures that events can be doubly caused: by past and future, by prior causes and telos, by characters' choices and the pattern to which they conform. For Augustine as for Leibniz, a person's choices, no matter how agonizing, have been given from all eternity to fit optimally the world's overall design. Poetics posits the same of literary characters.

Sophisticated readers recongize this double causation. When, in perusing a Dickens novel, we guess at how some minor incident, character, or apparent loose end will figure in an overall plan, we are expressing faith in a design inaccessible to the characters but known to an author outside their time.

### The Multi-Plot Novel

Consider the classic multiplot novel. Readers know that the different stories illuminate each other and display parallels in theme and plot. After all, there must be some reason that the author has placed these stories together. The stories of Anna Karenina and Levin must say something about each other. In Anthony Trollope's *Can You Forgive Her?* we read three narratives about heroines who must choose between "a wild man" and "a worthy man." Each story's incidents beg comparison with those of the others. But the three heroines cannot know that.

In life, none of us presumes that there is some other person whose story runs parallel with our own, and Trollope's heroines view the world as we do. The perception of such parallels as anything more than arbitrary is available only from outside the world of the characters.

Heroes and heroines could not know that they decide to do something because their counterpart has decided not to. And yet, over their heads, aesthetic necessity makes sure that each moment of the story shapes their actions in just this way, fulfilling a structure and tending to an already given outcome.

### Escaping the *A Priori* of Poetics

Let us suppose that an author discovered how to eliminate aesthetic necessity by discovering a processual alternative to structure. What would the response of the critics be?

They would Leibnizize. Trained to think in terms of structure, they would find one. Ignoring incoherence, they would point to all coherence as signs of advance planning, force some loose ends to fit, and ignore the rest.

In many cases, of course, apparent loose ends, properly understood, really can be shown to fit a structure. But why must that necessarily and always be true? We accept the *a priori* of poetics on essentially theological grounds. In the work as in the world, everything simply must have a sufficient reason.

### *The Literature of Process, Examples and Kinds*

How is it possible to design a work with causation operating only within the created world? How can a successful work contain parts that have a reason, but not a sufficient reason, for being there?

In such works, the author would participate in the created world and be affected by it as it unfolds. He would resemble not the theologian's but the Hebrew Bible's God. Characters' sense of presentness would not be illusory.

If such works are not to be entirely haphazard, they must be governed by some principle. If not structure, some alternative design must operate. How?

Such works exist. They require not a poetics of product but a prosaics of process.

Some processual works are narrative, while others are not. Despite their "loose and baggy" shape, many are acknowledged, if with a sign of wonder, as supreme masterpieces. Processual works include Dostoevsky's *The Idiot*, *A Writer's Diary*, and perhaps *The Possessed*; Tolstoy's *War and Peace* and perhaps *Anna Karenina*; Sterne's *Tristram Shandy*; two other works inspired by Sterne, Byron's *Don Juan* and Pushkin's *Eugene Onegin*; and perhaps Samuel Butler's mock-epic *Hudibras*, which surprised with new parts. Although most Dickens novels are perfectly structured, *The Pickwick Papers* exemplifies processuality. *A Writer's Diary*, indeed, is indebted to Dickens' similar effort, *Master Humphrey's Clock*.[47] Both *War and Peace* and *A Writer's Diary* follow the lead (as Dostoevsky makes explicit) of Alexander Herzen's *From the Other Shore*, which looks forward to Herzen's ungainly masterpiece, *The Past and Recollections*.

It is also possible to read processually some compositions written over centuries, such as the Hebrew Bible. Instead of treating extended authorship by many hands as the mere revelation of a single advance plan, one would need to read the Bible's parts as distinct acts of creation, none composed with a final structure in mind. No book was completed with a later book already given. The David story does not implicitly contain the Book of Esther. The Bible so read would have an integrity different from a predetermined plan. The unity would be one of a consistent process.

Once one sees how the Bible could be read processually, one discovers similar layered compositions, both narrative and non-narrative. In Ghent, I was fascinated by the town hall, which had been built and rebuilt over the centuries. With distinct parts made from different materials and in different styles, it produced a unified impression that did not depend on thinking away the fact of sequential additions. It did not involve imagining a single architect creating the building as we see it. On the contrary, one wondered at the earlier unified impressions made when the building was one or two parts smaller, or when it had a wing now demolished; and imagined what it would look like when someone should dream up some new addition or subtraction. With the same spirit of innovation animating distinct moments of creation, the building's peculiar aesthetic unity was one of process.

One can also discover many verbal compositions to which several authors contributed at different times. If A. C. Spearing is correct, an appreciation of such works as sequential better accords with their governing aesthetic than today's literary theories, based as they are on masterpieces with a single author and "narrator."[48]

---

[47]    See BoG, 26-27.

[48]    See A. C. Spearing, *Textual Subjectivity: The Encoding of Subjectivity in Medieval Narratives and Lyrics* (Oxford: Oxford University Press, 2005).

Yet another type of processual work, typically non-narrative, expands from within. Instead of adding parts to the end, these compositions generate new editions with burgeonings and expansions at many points. They bud. We expect still more changes, and never imagine we at last have a perfect Aristotelian structure tolerating neither additions nor subtractions. On the contrary, we experience the joyful sense that these works may sprout anywhere.

Encyclopedic books like Burton's *Anatomy of Melancholy* grow in this way, as do works that take the form of anthologies or reference books, like Erasmus's *Adages* or Bierce's *The Devil's Dictionary*. Whenever the principle of organization is essentially arbitrary, like the alphabet, or has no natural termination, like a calendar, the work can advertise its potentially unlimited expandability.

Anthologizing a potentially endless set can serve a similar purpose. Necessarily partial, the collection can always grow. The Bible's Book of Proverbs flaunts its status as an anthology of anthologies that have already expanded many times. Wisdom, after all, is unlimited. This and other such collections of sayings served as models for Erasmus. Montaigne's essays also expand in this way, as their many quotations suggest still more, *ad infinitum*. We may speak of an *aesthetic of expandability* that goes well with an aesthetic of spontaneity.[49]

Burton, Montaigne, and others refer to their works as always in the making. Montaigne's "essays" advertise themselves as just that, "tryings out." In this case, processual composition dramatizes the endless mutability of all things, including of the self at work composing the essays. How can a work be finished when the author alters from moment to moment?: "I aim here only at revealing myself, who will perhaps be different tomorrow, if I learn something new that changes me," as he always does, either from life or the very writing of the essays.[50]

Sometimes this sort of work invites a sort of reading as roaming. One does not have to read Burton, or any other "anatomy," in a specific order, while Montaigne seems to invite picking up his essays, or even parts of an essay, at any of several points and continuing in a haphazard manner. Erasmus encourages us to jump around. When

---

[49]    See WoO, 221-280.

[50]    *The Complete Essays of Montaigne,* ed. Donald M. Frame (Stanford: Stanford University Press, 1965), 109.

literature takes the form of a commonplace book (Auden's *A Certain World*, Kronenberger's *Animal, Vegetable, and Mineral*, E. M. Forster's *Commonplace Book*), they almost always insist that there can be no right order of reading and that an indefinitely large number of experiences may be generated as one chooses.

Whether narrative or not, processual works must be carefully distinguished from those which, like Gogol's "Ivan Fyodorovich Shponka and His Auntie" and Dostoevsky's *Notes from Underground*, really are product works in which denial of structure is itself part of the structure. Metaliterature that creates a careful whole out of an apparent fragment is hardly unusual. An anti-design is still a design, but a processual succession of wills is not. One can sometimes make a case for reading a work in either way.

My concern here is not to defend the assignment of specific works to one of these classes. If you agree that what I say applies to *The Idiot* and *War and Peace* but not to *Anna Karenina* or *The Possessed*, I am content, because my purpose is to establish the need for a processual appreciation of some works. If that is once conceded, then the *a priori* of poetics dies. If it is possibe for a work to be governed either by structure or by process, then structure can no longer be presumed. One must make a case for one's classification.[51]

### Processual Intentionality

A special intentionality defines a processual work. The intention governing it is not located at a moment but spread out over time. It is not the last moment of a process but itself a process. There is never a single moment when it is complete. This *temporally extensive intention* consists of many acts of willing.

With his keen interest in psychology, Dostoevsky distinguished two types of intentionality. The first—let us call it Lockean—is assumed by the law courts, and so Dostoevsky confronts it in his crime writing. It is also presumed by poetics.

In the *Essay on Human Understanding*, Locke traces all actions to a prior complete intention. Intentions may of course be changed, and we may "hold our wills undetermined until we have examined" the

---

51      Jerome McGann encouraged me to make explicit that some works combine structural and processual designs.

relevant circumstances. But if we are to act at all, at some point we must arrive at an intention. If no external obstacles intervene, "what follows after that, follows in a chain of consequences, linked one to another, all depending on the *last* determination of the will."[52] The literary analogy would be the final plan of a work—the last determination of the will— as distinguished from experiments in the notebooks.

For Dostoevsky, the Lockean view is naïve. To be sure, some intentions are of this sort, but others are genuinely processual and always incomplete. Consider Dostoevsky's discussion of the Kairova case: this woman, accused of attempted murder, had learned that her lover was betraying her with his wife. Kairova discovered the couple asleep in her own bed and attacked the wife with a razor. Awakened, they prevented Kairova from continuing the attack. The jury was asked to determine her prior intention—whether she had intended to kill the wife and would have done so if not restrained. What was the last determination of her will on which she had acted?

Dostoevsky argues that this question is unanswerable, not, as we might suppose, because of a lack of information about her inner state, but because of a mistaken assumption about the nature of intentions. In asking about Kairova's completed prior intention, the question presumes that there must have been one.

In this case, Dostoevsky argues, there was most likely no such prior intention, either to kill or not to kill. At no moment was a determination of the will complete; Kairova never came to a decision; at every instant, her evolving intentionality allowed for many actions at the next. The actions she took did not follow from a prior intention but were part of the process by which an incomplete intention continued to develop.

Dostoevsky is not arguing that Kairova did not know what she was doing. Quite the contrary, at each instant "when slashing her rival *she knew what she was doing*" but she did not know what she would do at the next moment. She took each step without an intention as to what she would do next. She would decide each action by the results of the previous one.

It would also be mistaken to ascribe an unconscious intention. Sometimes there is one, but to assert that a missing conscious intention

---

52      John Locke, *An Essay Concerning Human Understanding*, ed. Alexander Campbell Fraser (New York: Dover, 1959), vol. 1, 349.

necessarily indicates an unconscious one is to presume that intentions must be complete if we are to act at all. In fact, people sometimes act on an incomplete intention in process.

At no moment was it *certain* what Kairova would do if not restrained. If the identical situation could be repeated, Dostoevsky states boldly, each time the result might be different. Perhaps Kairova would have passed the razor over her rival's throat, "and then cried out, shuddered, and ran away as fast as she could." Or she might have "made a slash and then took fright and turned the razor on herself" or even have "killed herself right there." Or she might have "flown into a frenzy when she felt the first spurts of hot blood and not only murdered Velikanova [the wife] but even begun to abuse the body" (AWD1, 477). All these possibilities are consistent with *her developing and processual intention*.

Here nothing is inevitable. Kairova's many possible actions "all could have happened and could have been done by this very same woman and sprung from the very same soul, in the very same mood and under the very same circumstances" (AWD1, 477). If identical circumstances can lead to different outcomes, then by definition time is open. There is no sufficient reason for the outcome. What happens depends on presentness, in fact, on a succession of presentnesses.

Dostoevsky depicted this intentionality in his next novel, *Karamazov*. Murderously angry with his father, Dmitri grabs a pestle and goes to his father's house. The prosecutor at Dmitri's trial claims that this action proves prior intent and regards as absurd Dmitri's statement that in picking up the pestle he had no clear idea what he would do with it. And yet Dmitri was telling the truth. He was angry, and picked up a weapon, but had not determined when, how, or whether he would use it. One understands the prosecutor's skepticism, and, I think, one might easily grasp why critics have usually read the scene as evidence that Dmitri *changed* his intention. But in fact he did not have a fully formed intention to begin with. The moment with the pestle was just one in an evolving sequence of decisions. As with Kairova and the razor, it might have led to a different outcome.

This is the sort of intentionality governing works of process. At each moment we sense that whatever happens is not inevitable. The work seems to be perpetually in process. The author tries out a possibility leading he is not sure where. He adjusts his writing in response to what he has written or, perhaps, to the judgment of readers. He may double back, leaving untouched the record of false starts. The work resembles a published notebook for itself. The entire process of forming it—moment by incomplete moment—defines the work.

### War and Presentness

While *War and Peace* was being published in installments, Tolstoy wrote some draft prefaces for it and published an essay about it. In "Some Words About the Book *War and Peace*," he insisted that his odd "book" could not be called a "novel" because it departed from that form's essential characteristics. Novels have a structure, a planned story with a "denouement," and an ending after which nothing could appropriately be added, but *War and Peace* would not. With no structure to complete, the book could always grow another part. Some "principle of expandability" typifies processual works.

Tolstoy explained that the shape of traditional novels misrepresents history, which is shaped by events that might very well not have happened. Contingency operates all the time. Decisions not possible, or even foreseeable, a moment before are constantly made in response to other unforeseeable decisions. As a result, history can lead in different directions and lacks a neat shape. It exists at a continual present. Neat endings can only be imposed from outside, by historians selecting events to make a good story, but any selection is arbitary. Each is false to history as a continuum.

Life does not tie up loose ends. Nothing ever manifests completeness. There are no endings. All that was to be true of *War and Peace* as well.

Professing only the vaguest of plans—to guide characters "through the historical events of 1805, 1807, 1825, and 1856"—Tolstoy declared that "I do not foresee the outcome of these characters' relationships in a single one of the epochs" (PSS 13:55). He would write and publish each section with no idea where it might lead, or even whether it would be the last. Foreshadowing, which presumes a pregiven future sending signs backward, would be out of the question. In writing each part, Tolstoy would just see how things developed under his pen. He would let characters surprise him. Exploiting some potentials left from previous parts, he would leave others undeveloped. Some might be developed in future sections, and some might remain unexploited.

Readers guessing what would happen based on their intuitions of a good structure found themselves repeatedly disappointed, and many faulted the work for its supposed formlessness. Characters like Dolokhov, who appeared to be major, disappeared for hundreds of pages only to reappear as minor figures. We now assume that Prince Andrei is a (if not the) major character, but if Tolstoy had continued his story until 1856, as he once had considered, Andrei would have been no more important in that version than Dolokhov is in the one we have. His centrality depends on the accident of where Toltstoy chose to provide no more installments.

Some critics complained that although they could see why Prine Andrei could have developed as he did, they did not see why he *had* to. That was precisiely Tolstoy's point: he did not have to. For Andrei and for *War and Peace*, time is open and, unlike a traditional novel, lacks a predetermined ending.[53]

### "No Libretto"

Herzen's *From the Other Shore* combines fiction, journalism, speeches, and, most famously, dialogues between a skeptic and an idealist. The parts of this work orginally appeared separately, with Herzen combining them differently in various editions. Like history, which the work describes as unkempt processes going in no particular direction, this work offers a series of odd shapes and surprises.

The skeptic of one dialogue explains that people who discover a plot in history "are misled by categories not fitted to catch the flow of life" (FTOS, 35). Events do not fit a pattern because

> the path is not determined.... Nature has hinted only vaguely, in the most general terms, at her intentions, and has left all the details to the will of man, circumstances, climate, and a thousand conflicts. The struggle, the reciprocal action of natural forces and the forces of will, the consequences of which one cannot know in advance, give an overwhelming interest to every historical epoch. If mankind marched straight towards some kind of result, then there would be no history, only logic; humanity would have come to rest, a finished article, in an absolute *status quo* like animals. (FTOS, 38-39)

---

[53]     On these features of *War and Peace*, see HIPV

For Herzen, history is open, shaped by unforeseeable contingencies and acts of will, while people are ever unfinished and always remaking themselves in innovative ways. In history "there is no *libretto*. If there were a libretto, history would lose all interest, become unnecessary.... In history all is improvisation, all is will, all is *ex tempore*" (FTOS, 39). And the same is true of this work.

Dostoevsky's essays on processual intentionality appeared in *A Writer's Diary: A Monthly Publication*, which is itself a processual work. As Dostoevsky explains, this "new genre" would be guided by a *unity of procedure* applied to material the author could not foresee. Each month he would select a theme, showing Russia's changing spiritual state, from "all I have seen, heard, and read" in the periodical press or his own observation. He would then create a dialogue of genres, teasing out the theme's implications. Viewed through the glass of short story, sketch, feuilleton, reminiscence, crime reporting, communication with his readers, plans for possible fiction, dreams, and many other genres, the chosen theme would reveal unexpected complexity. Like an *improvisatore* who offers to make up a poem on the spot about any subject the audience might suggest, the author would be forced by his deadline to publish work rapidly and without the possibility of later revision. As a result, some monthly issues would have to succeed more than others.

Each month the author would be able to develop ideas from previous issues, but not to anticipate future ones. He could no more do that than he could foresee the future. As with *War and Peace*, there was no possibility of foreshadowing. The author would know as little as his readers or recurrent characters what might happen. If he offered predictions, they might—and often did—prove false.

### Literature as Algorithm

One might say that these books create literature by algorithm or heuristic: they apply a more or less consistent method to whatever might present itself.[54] "You ask me for the plan of Donny Johnny," wrote Byron. "I *have* no plan ... but I had or have materials."[55] If that

---

[54] Robert Belknap offered me the phrase "literature as algorithm" after he was kind enough to read my first book more than three decades ago.

[55] Byron's comments as cited in Leslie A. Marchand's "Introduction" to DJ, v-xiv.

seems too free and unstructured, "Why, Man, the Soul of such writing is its license" (DJ, vi).

I say that these works apply a method that is "more or less" consistent because the method itself gradually evolves as the work proceeds. We watch the author learning, from the process of improvisation, ever-new ways of improvising. The comparison with art improvised on the spot comes readily:

> I don't know that there may be much ability
>     Shown in this sort of desultory rhyme;
> But there's a conversational facility,
>     Which may round off an hour upon a time;
> Of this I'm sure at least, there's no servility
>     In mine irregularity of chime,
> Which rings what's uppermost of new or hoary,
> Just as I feel the *improvisatore* (DJ, vii).

Byron adapted this technique from Sterne's *Tristram Shandy*, and neither author upon setting out had any idea how long their work might be. Length would depend not only on how long inspiration might last but also on what the public would think. "To how many cantos this may extend, I know not," Byron explained. He published two cantos in 1819, three more in 1821, and over the next three years published up to Canto XVI (part of seventeen exists as well), with no sign of an ending. Sterne, Byron, and Dostoevsky allowed us to sense their writing at a continuous present, experimenting with material and with methods of experimenting.

### Writing Like Roulette

When Dostoevsky sent his publisher the opening chapters of *The Idiot*, he had literally no idea what would follow or how the plot would develop. Desperately in need of money, he had been working on a novel about an evil man who would eventually find God, but could not make it convincing. He at last decided to begin with a perfectly good man and pillage his notebooks if possible.

"I turned things over in my mind from December 4 to December 18 [1867]," he explained in a letter to his friend Maikov. "I would say that on the average I came up with six plans a day (at least that)." The new idea would be "to portray a perfectly beautiful man ... the idea used to flash through my my mind in somewhat artistic form, but only *somewhat* ... I took a chance as at roulette: 'Maybe it will develop as I write it!'"[56] If we follow the notebooks to this novel, we see what we sense when reading it: the author wrote from scene to scene, with no idea what would come next. He developed earlier possibilities, while planting potentials for the future, each of which could be developed in different directions or be left entirely undeveloped. Lots of shoes don't drop. *The Idiot* is written forwards, not backwards, and even the novel's powerful ending did not so much as occur to the author until he was working on the third of four parts. Even then, it remained but one of several possibilities he was considering until he chose it. There is no possibility of foreshadowing here, and yet the critics have detected it!

It was only after he had published a significant portion of the novel—probably when he was was writing Part Two—that he realized that he could make a virtue of necessity. What if he make this a work about experience as presentness, the openness of time, and life as process? He did, and from that point on, the work and its writing illustrated its key theme.

### Necessary Flaws

The flaws that result from process design acquire a unique status. They become indications that the challenge the author has set himself is not too easy. Their presence makes the triumphs all the more impressive.

The reader watches the author grapple with problems whose solution is not guaranteed. Real suspense pertains here both to characters and to the author at work.

It follows that loose ends and false starts are not something to be edited out. As we saw with Darwinian organisms, when design is perfect, it covers its traces. History is erased, and the organism appears the same as if it had been designed at an instant. But imperfections readily testify to a process. The work demanded some—if not these, some other ones. With processual design they indicate how the work is to be read.

Byron commented that he would be pleased if half of *Don Juan* turned out to be good, but that willingness to fail made his poem all

---

[56] As cited in Joseph Frank, *Dostoevsky: The Miraculous Years, 1865-1871* (Princeton: Princeton University Press, 1995), 271.

the better (DJ, x). After the first few issues, *A Writer's Diary* repeatedly lurches between success and failure. Reading *The Idiot* and *War and Peace* we constantly encounter moments that seem to promise later developments that never come. When Prince Andrei refuses to move aside for a proud official leaving a council of the tsar's advisors, the official snarls and Andrei comments to Boris that he is "one of the most remarkable but to me most distateful of men, Prince Adam Czartoryski.... It is such men as he who decide the fate of nations" (W&P, 310). There could hardly be a stronger signal that the two proud men will confront each other again, but they do not. In Part One of *The Idiot*, Ganya three times calls Myshkin, ominously and eponymously, an "idiot," and the whole weight of the title seems to promise a climactic conflict between them. So does Ganya's prediction to Myshkin that "you and I shall either be great friends or great enemies" (I, 117). But by Part Two, Ganya descends from a major character to Myshkin's secretary, undergoes a personality change, and never seems able to regain major status.

The novel works by planting what might be called "plot nuggets": moments that have rich potential for future development if occasion warrants. We sense that "if." Early on, Myshkin remarks that his father died awaiting trial, "but I never have been able to find out what he was accused of" (I, 90). If we expect to learn the accusation, as we could confidently expect in a novel with structure, we will be disappointed. We are told that in addition to the Pavlishchev who raised Myshkin, there was "another Pavlishchev"—about whom we never hear again. Why mention the trial or the other Pavlishchev, only to forget these hints of the future?

In a novel based on structure, these and countless similar passages would be obvious flaws, but they fit *The Idiot*. In neither *The Idiot* nor *War and Peace* can one presume that the narration of an event guarantees its future significance. That could be true only if the future were already given, but these works genuinely develop in open time, as their themes demand. Some plot nuggets lead somewhere and some do not.

Such processual works provide a pleasure quite different from contemplating a well-made artifact. One feels like a spectator at an ungoing sports event or a game played by an expert but hardly infallible player. We become witnesses of the ineffable presentness when art is in the making.

### Serialization

To indicate sequential intentionality, processual works often take advantage of serial publication. In such cases, serialization is not just the way a work happens to appear but may be said to be intrinsic to the work. Each issue testifies to a separate act of creation. The reader recognizes that earlier issues appear without the author knowing what later ones will include or being able to adjust them to fit what appears later.

To be sure, serialization is often extrinsic, as it is with most nineteenth-century novels. Although it appeared in installments, *Bleak House* clearly reflects a comprehensive advance design. So carefully is it plotted that the most unexpected details and minor characters later turn out to have significance. We do not need Dickens's detailed chapter outlines for the novel to be convinced that a single intention governs the whole.

In short, serialization does not prove processuality, but processuality tends to make special use of serialization. It can, though it does not have to, allow the reader to experience the work's composition as an ongoing *event*.

In expandable works that grow from the middle, ever new editions take the place of new serialized installments. Burton's *Anatomy* went through five expanding editions between 1621 and the author's death in 1640, and could obviously have added more. Erasmus's *Adages* began modestly enough in 1500 with 818 sayings and acompanying notes occupying 152 pages, but after repeated expansions it grew to gargantuan proportions. The posthumous 1536 edition featured 4151 entries. Brief notes grew to lengthy essays, the most famous of which ("War is sweet to those who have not tried it") also appeared as a separate pamphlet. The brief note on the saying "the labor of Hercules" became a labor of its own as it grew to a long essay about Erasmus's own work compiling the Adages and enduring the "ingratitude and envy" of hostile readers.[57] Since Hercules' labors did have an end, it might have been better if Erasmus had made his self-referential comments about Sisyphus.

---

[57]     From the "Editor's Introduction," *The Adages of Erasmus* (Toronto: University of Toronto Press, 2001), xii.

### *Closure and Aperture*

Processual works are inherently incomplete, not accidentally incomplete in the way *The Mystery of Edwin Drood* remained when Dickens died. We may not know what structure *Edwin Drood* would have revealed, but we know there would have been one. None of the many attempts to finish this mystery turned it into a processual work lacking structure or closure.

By contrast, *War and Peace*, *A Writer's Diary*, *Tristram Shandy*, and *Don Juan* are not merely long books. They are books of indefinite length. *War and Peace* is literally interminable in the sense that, no matter how many parts Tolstoy added, he could have added more. He shocked people when he added another part to *Anna Karenina* after the heroine's death. No internal principle dictates that the stopping point reached by *Tristram* (or *Don Juan*) precludes continuation, and it is obvious that Dostoevsky's "monthly publication" could in principle continue as long as the calendar.

By definition, closure completes a pattern. It provides an ending in Aristotle's sense. It has, and can have, "nothing following it" because it completes a "whole" (AP, 52). As Barbara Herrnstein Smith remarks, "Closure, then, may be regarded as a modification of structure that makes stasis the most probable succeeding event.... That expectation of nothing, the sense of ultimate composure we apparently value in our experience of a work of art, is variously referred to as stability, resolution, equilibrium."[58] But there is no such point in a process work.

The most we get is the sort of partial closure that might round off a chapter or part, and ties up some of the loose ends of the work, as we do with *The Idiot*, *Tristram Shandy*, and *War and Peace*. So far as we can judge from reviews of the early portions of *War and Peace* as it appeared, readers did not suppose that the work would be anything close to the length it turned out to be, and were repeatedly surprised by its lengthening.

In fact, Tolstoy's 1450-page work acquired its present title only after it outgrew the confines of the one given to the first installments, *The Year 1805*. And it was not until Book III (which begins about page

---

[58]   Barbara Herrnstein Smith, *Poetic Closure: A Study of How Poems End* (Chicago: University of Chicago Press, 1968), 34.

700) that Tolstoy substantially altered his design to add the nonfictional essays that are now the work's most striking oddity. The book concludes with two essays that obviously could not complete a pattern including Books I and II. What is more, in subsequent editions Tolstoy moved the essays out of the text into an appendix, and back again, which suggests that their placing as the work's last words was hardly a structural inevitability.

In "Some Words," Tolstoy explicitly stresses that *War and Peace* cannot end. "I strove only so that each part of the work would have an independent interest." Tolstoy then wrote and struck out the following words, "which would consist not in the development of events but in development [itself]" (PSS, 13:55).

*Development itself*; development with contingency; partially unpredictable responses to partially unpredictable events—this is the spirit of Tolstoy's book as well as its main theme. Its most effective, if not always morally best, characters appreciate "development itself." When Rostov is faced with an impossible choice, he allows time to settle the problem in a way he cannot foresee. Kutuzov, of course, derides plans and recommends "patience and time." Perhaps most intriguing, the unattractive but effective Prince Vasily operates by a method resembling that of the book itself:

> Prince Vasily was not a man who deliberately thought out his plans.... Various plans and schemes ... which constituted his whole interest in life were continually forming in his mind, arising from the circumstances and the persons he met. He had not merely one or two such plans and schemes under way, but dozens, some of which were just beginning to take shape, some nearing achievement, still others dissolving. (W&P, 251)

If we substitute "plot lines" for "plans," we have a good description of the shape of *War and Peace*. The author plots like Prince Vasily, juggling many potentials and letting circumstances as they develop guide his choices when (and not before) they must be made. At any point in the novel, some plot lines are just beginning, others developing strongly, still others disappearing; which is why the work has so many loose ends and is incapable of achieving closure. Instead, it achieves the quite different effect of what I call *aperture*: principled openness.

### Presentness

In *War and Peace,* every moment is a present moment. There is no overall plan guiding the characters to a specific end; what they *do now* matters. That is why Kutuzov explains that the best preparation for a battle is not advance planning but "a good night's sleep": in a world of contingency, attentiveness and sensitivity to each moment's presentness makes all the difference. That is how the authorship of this book works as well, as Tolstoy makes the most of what develops under his pen. Processual works give us a sense of presentness as no structured work could.

In addition to serialization, *A Writer's Diary* makes the most of other reminders of processuality. The author argues with the other publications that criticize him. He whimsically presents as part of the work itself apparently mechanical information about subscriptions or the unexpected postponement of future issues. Dostoevsky invites readers into his laboratory as he writes.

So do *Don Juan* and *Eugene Onegin,* which imitate the way *Tristram Shandy* repeatedly catches its own composing in the act. "That observation is my own;--and was struck out by me this very rainy day, *March 26, 1759,* and betwixt the hours of nine and ten in the moning," Tristram informs us (TS, 64). Although this comment belongs to the fictional character Tristram, it seems to be the author's as well. In fact, the first volume of *Tristram,* from which this line is drawn, was published in December 1759 and announced on January 1, 1760, so Tristram's dating seems plausible as well as recent. We just missed being there with him.

Tristram offers his constant digressions as spontaneous, happening unexpectedly according to Locke's principle of the association of ideas. Spontaneity also leads to digressions from digressions, and to the author recalling, and telling the reader as he does so, that he hopes to get back to his main point if no further digressions intervene. So many ifs! Returning to his promised introduction of the midwife to the reader, Tristram promises—or rather predicts—"upon the best judgment I can form upon my own plan at present,—I am going to introduce to him for good and all: But as fresh matter may be started, and much unexpected business fall out betwixt the reader and myself, which may require immediate dispatch;—'twas right to take care that the poor woman should not be lost in the mean time;—because when she is wanted, we can in no way do without her" (TS, 35). His "plan" alters because "fresh matter" occurs "in the mean time." The "when" of "when she is wanted" refers to an anticipated but unspecifiable moment of writing.

In the next chapter, Tristram famously wonders at the oddity that, even though he has been writing his life as fast as he can for six weeks, he is not yet born. "These unforeseen stoppages, which I own I had no conception of when I first set out;—but which, I am convinced now, will rather increase than diminish as I advance,—have struck out a hint which I am resolved to follow; and that is,—not to be in a hurry;—but to go on leisurely, writing and publishing two volumes of my life every year;—which, if I am suffered to go on quietly, and can make a tolerable bargain with my bookseller, I shall continue to do as long as I live" (TS, 37). "If I am suffered to go on": contingencies, external and internal, intervene, and so the author has no idea what he will wind up writing or how long the book will turn out to be.

It is easy enough to find similar passages in Byron and Pushkin. Byron's eight-line stanzas are designed for spontaneity. He apparently writes two pairs of A-B lines and then relies on the moment's inspiration for a third pair and an appropriate final couplet. That last couplet seems to be contrived our of sheer inventive escape from the impossible situation in which the first six lines have placed him. This sense of close escape explains why bad rhymes often turn out to be good. Pushkin expands Byron's eight-line stanza to fourteen so as to allow still more digressiveness and more strange rhymes. Since any rhyme scheme imposes form, to set out with no idea what will be needed by stanza's end is to create risk and suspense for both author and reader.

In *The Idiot*, Dostoevsky incorporates recent news to create an effect of presentness. The sensational trial of Olga Umetskaia, on whom Nastasya Filippovna was obviously based, took place in September 1867, only months before the book began to appear. In November 1867, more information came out about the Danilov case, in which a cynical father told his son he might commit any crime to further his career, and Dostoevsky has Kolya tell Myshkin: "You have a father in Moscow teaching his son not to stick at anything to get money; we know it from the papers" (I, 125). *We know it from the papers*: these are the very papers the author and readers have recently read, and so it is as if the author was signalling the reader that the novel is open to ongoing events.

What is more, characters not only read the press but detect parallels with themselves! Nastasya Filippovna notices the resemblance Rogozhin bears to the famous murderer Mazurin, who, she notes, also came from a merchant family, lived with his mother, and inherited millions of rubles. She wonders if Rogozhin too has Zhadanov's fluid to conceal the smell of a corpse, as in fact he does.

The Mazurin case is not merely a "source" of *The Idiot*. Fictional characters are usually not aware of their sources, after all. Mazurin is not so much a source from outside the fictional world as a factor in it. When Rogozhin does kill Nastasya Filippovna, we do not have a case of foreshadowing, because in foreshadowing the sign is visible only to the reader, who detects the plan of the whole. But in this case the murder happens as it does largely because the characters are imitating Mazurin. The author is not engaging in foreshadowing; the characters are being copycats.

Nastasya Filippovna, and presumably Rogozhin, are reading the paper along with the author, *simultaneously*, or as close as possible to simultaneously. They wonder about their fates just as the author is meditating what will happen to them. And the readers are almost present at this very presentness.

### Between the Books

Serial publication offers another opportunity: to let events in the real world that take place between installments influence the work's development. When this happens, readers see that the whole work could not have been contained in any advance plan. With one section already published, an unforeseeable event outside the author's control prompts alterations. The work therefore must be the result of two or more acts of will.

Such a sequence offers the same threat to poetics that is offered to theology by God's reacting to surprising human choices. As God becomes historical, the author's creative process becomes part of the work. Both lose their outsideness.

So serious a threat does this possibility pose to traditional poetics that critics, like their theological counterparts, have strained credulity to deny it. The *a priori* tells us that God's changes of mind, disappointments, and tests must be mere figures of speech. In the same way, poetics insists that whatever appears to violate structure has itself been stuctured. If so, there can be no aperture, only anti-closure; no real digressions or process, only the illusion of them; no real spontaneity, only its scripted similacrum.

Since anti-closure, illusory digressions, and scripted sponta-neity do exist, advocates can always claim to have discovered yet another case. But why must all spontaneity be scripted just because some of it is?

In Part Two of *The Idiot*, characters discuss the celebrated Gorski case, in which the tutor for the Zhemarin family murdered the family members and their servants. Dostoevsky read the report in *The Voice* of March 10, 1868. That is, the news appeared after the novel was partly published and so could not have been part of any advance plan. Dostoevsky had hoped to send Part II, with its discussion of the case, in time for the March issue of *The Russian Messenger*, but was only able to send two chapters for the April issue. The news could not have been more current and readers could hardly have missed that the author was adjusting his novel as he went along. This and similar incidents make processual intentionality almost unmistakable. Only after a century, when we no longer know what stories are real and when they were current, do we miss such signs of processuality.

Part VIII of *Anna Karenina* is devoted to the Eastern War. Vronsky enlists while Levin argues with his guests about its morality. Contemporary readers could not have missed, as we do, that these events took place several years after Part One of the novel appeared. Their inclusion demonstrates beyond the possibility of doubt that the author responds to events outside his control.

Sometimes installments adjust based on the responses of readers to earlier installments. The success of an early part may have called for more, as happened with *Tristram*, *Don Juan*, and *Hudibras*, while the popularity of one or more characters may have led to their unexpected reappearance, as in *The Pickwick Papers*. *A Writer's Diary* includes correspondence with readers. Such responsiveness makes the reader a sort of "co-creator," as Dostoevsky explicitly states, and one cannot control a co-creator's actions. Intentionality becomes dialogic and evolves in surprising ways. Such methods dramatize the succession of wills.

### Reading and Rereading

When process governs, we can no longer make reading a form of anticipated rereading by guessing how ongoing events will fit into the overall structure.

Or we might put it this way: in a work with structure, ideal reading is re-reading, and even a first reading aspires to the condition of anticipated rereading. In a processual work, the reverse is the case.

First reading, rather than rereading, is closest to the work's spirit. That is why we might need to reconstruct the timing of the Eastern War amid installments of *Anna Karenina*. It is also why Dostoevsky kept the *Diary*'s division into monthly sections when he later published the work in book form.

In life, if we are to understand past events, we must think away the future that happened later. Otherwise, we will read the past anachronistically, with those future events somehow already present—as if no other futures were possible. In rereading a processual work, we must do something similar: recreate the *initial* experience of reading, with many continuations still possible.

Processual works create a sense of time without eternity. No author stands above, contemplating, like Milton's God, what must be, what in a sense already is. Rather, we sense that the story as it develops is one of many possible stories; that there are many points where something else might have happened. *Bleak House* is the one and only *Bleak House*, but there are many possible *Idiots* of which we have but one. We sense the shadows of the others.

In the world of Leibniz and of poetics, there is no "might-have-been," but in the processual work there is no "had-to-be." The literature of process takes us beyond providence, beyond structure, and beyond harmony to a world where things can either be or not be.

### Process and Contradiction

When I wrote my book on *War and Peace*, I tried to reconcile a number of Tolstoy's contradictory assertions (HIPV). In one place, Tolstoy professes that, contrary to familiar belief, the higher one stands on the social scale the less freedom one has; in another place he denies anyone has any freedom at all. Usually Tolstoy rejects any mathematicized approach to society, but in one place he does not. By and large, he knows what he opposes—the idea that great men and dramatic events make history—but not what alternative he endorses.

My book tries to come up with what might be called the "average" view: the position that conforms best to the whole work. But once one reads processually, a wiser approach presents itself.

If no single intention governs the whole, inconsistency is what one might expect. The author tries out formulations whenever his writing has led him to a new insight. The work represents not various ways of expressing one idea but a process of thinking things through.

By the same token, open theists need not be so disturbed that some, but not all, scriptural passages testify to a God in time. The Bible would be entirely consistent only if it existed atemporally. Why deny a perfect, immutable, atemporal God and accept a Bible of the same sort? To assume that scripture transcends the limitations of God is to engage in a kind of textual idolatry. Just as God evolves in time, so does the Bible.

Critics of *The Idiot* have differed on a fundamental point. Its ending has suggested to many, particularly those outside Slavistics, that it portrays the "curse of saintliness," the evil of Christian good.[59] These critics often cite Radomsky's comment about the destructiveness of Myshkin's pity, "What will compassion lead you to next?" Slavists, knowing Dostoevsky's Christianity, regard such an intention as impossible. They describe Radomsky as the sort of Westernizing rationalist who measures goodness by results and whom Dostoevsky despised. Both readings make sense.

The problem is that both presume that this work, like all others, proceeds from a single, unified intention, making the ending implicit from the beginning: whether the ending shows the evil of Christianity or the wrongheadedness of consequentialism, the work was composed with it in mind, and everything prepares for it. Both sets of critics see the work as product, but it asks to be read as process.

Once one reads processually, one can ascribe a different sort of intention to the author. Dostoevsky intended neither to endorse nor to refute the Christian message of goodness, but to perform an experiment to test it, a true experiment in which the outcome is not known in advance. The fact that the book's ending seems to demonstrate the harm of Christianity must have been unwelcome to Dostoevsky, but it indicates how honestly the experiment was conducted. Only if we recognize the work as process can we see an intention that governs the work but allows the ending to be whatever it would turn out to be.

\* \* \*

In the most famous passage in *The Idiot* a minor character surprises author and reader by somehow seizing control of the book. He voices

---

[59]    Murray Krieger, "Dostoevsky's *The Idiot*: The Curse of Saintliness" in René Wellek, ed., *Dostoevsky: A Collection of Critical Essays* (Englewood Cliffs, NJ: Prentice Hall, 1962), 39-52.

what turned out to be its central theme and the key sentiment inspiring most processual literature:

> Oh, you may be sure that Columbus was happy not when he had discovered America but while he was discovering it.... It's life that matters, nothing but life—the process of discovering, the everlasting and perpetual process, not the discovery at all (I 375).

Part Three

---

# WHAT IS MISANTHROPOLOGY?

## Chapter Four

### MISANTHROPOLOGY: VOYEURISM AND HUMAN NATURE

*By Alicia Chudo*

> It's a jolly thing that there always are and will be masters
> and slaves in the world, so there will always be a little maid-
> of-all-work and her master, and you know, that's all that's
> needed for happiness.
>
> — *Fyodor Pavlovich Karamazov*

I would like to introduce a new discipline, misanthropology, the study of the cussedness of human nature.

Anthropology as traditionally practiced claims moral neutrality but is in fact guided by a none-too-covert utopianism. There is nothing neutral about Margaret Mead's portrayal of sexual freedom in Samoa, which she represents as an island paradise free of bourgeois repression. The sort of cultural relativism espoused by Ruth Benedict served, and was meant to serve, as a tool for the reform of American moral standards.

Often enough, anthropologists and other social scientists commit what might be called the *disciplinary fallacy*. They begin by claiming to have an objective discipline and so they must avoid judging cultural practices. For an anthropologist, there is only behavior, not misbehavior. Linguists set out to study what people do say, not what they should say.

The problem arises when, at a later point, they conclude that their discipline has proven that there is no such thing as incorrect speech. Anything a native speaker says is by definition correct, just as anything a so-called primitive culture does is right by its own standards. For proof, just look at the work in the discipline in question: none of it faults bad grammar or primitive morals. True enough, but that is not because the discipline has *proven* relativism; it has *assumed* it.

The proof that such thinkers do not believe what they are saying is their selectiveness in condemning the passing of moral judgments. They do not argue that social science has proven there is nothing to condemn about patriarchy, sexual repression, or ethnic discrimination. Nor should they.

Misanthropology focuses on human evil, and so by its very nature rejects relativism. This discipline is not amoral. The misanthropologist contemplates the twentieth century — Auschwitz, the Gulag, the Khmer Rouge, Mao's cultural revolution, Rwandan genocide — and wonders, if these do not make a case against human nature, what would?

"But man is so fond of systems and abstract deductions," writes Dostoevsky's man from underground, "that he is ready to distort the truth intentionally, he is ready to deny what he can see and hear just to justify his logic" (NFU, 21). He will distort evidence not only to justify his systems but also to exalt humanity — that is, himself.

### Misanthropological Premises

Are people fundamentally social or individual? Are they at root good or evil? Should we rely on the insights of scientists, sages, and theorists to improve the world, and how much good can they do? Which vision is closer to the truth, utopianism or anti-utopianism, the vision of Edward Bellamy's socialist paradise *Looking Backward, 2000-1887* and William Morris's *News from Nowhere*, or that of Zamyatin's *We* and Orwell's *1984*? To these, and many similar questions, misanthropology offers answers. Not comfort, but answers.

Some disciplines begin with the individual and treat society as secondary. Mainstream micro-economics presumes that each person chooses to maximize his own "utility," while the economy as a whole sums up these individual choices. In Freud's view, people are fundamentally asocial egoists. Socialization must be forced upon us, at the cost of repression, which produces neurosis. I suspect that one reason Freudianism has had such impact in America is that it accords with core American beliefs.

By contrast, Lev Vygotsky and Mikhail Bakhtin viewed the social as primary. For Vygotsky, inner speech does not develop first and then, when externalized, give rise to social speech. Rather, speech with others is subsequently *internalized* to produce individual thought as inner speech. Bakhtin believed that a self develops gradually as a person gives his own accent to the innerly persuasive voices he has heard. "I" comes out of "We," much as individual speech patterns depend on mastery of a language held in common with others. No one resembles Adam, who broke the eternal silence with the first word; rather, each of us enters upon a pre-existing stream of communication.

Misanthropologists take the Russian view. Our shared humanity comes first, and we make ourselves individual—if we do—as a project that is never complete.

Adam Smith and the English eighteenth-century moralists adopted the social view, as do many social scientists, with the tacit conviction that it is more optimistic. People are not what Hobbes assumed, beasts who must surrender some primordial freedom so they do not destroy each other, but creatures who value most the "regard" of others. Surely, concern for others' good opinion indicates that we are fundamentally moral!

Alas, it does not. For one thing, people tend to win approval not so much by goodness as by strength. While they are alive, saints are mocked, but no one laughed at Genghis Khan. Real goodness strikes us as social infraction, a sort of *faux pas*. Plutarch tells the story of the man who voted to ostracize Aristides the Just simply because he was sick and tired of hearing him called "the Just." "Our evildoing arouses less hate and persecution than our good qualities," La Rochefoucauld notes sagely. What is more, "Men not only tend to forget benefits and injuries; they even hate those who have helped, and stop hating those who have harmed, them. The need to requite good and revenge evil becomes a slavery painful to endure" (L R, 35).

La Rochefoucauld chronicles how our fundamental sociality, our craving for others' regard, creates vanity, which in turn leads to self-deception and insincerity. So much do we rely on society for our sense of self worth that we fool ourselves into believing that we are what we make ourselves seem to be. "Hypocrisy is the tribute that vice pays to virtue" (LaR, 73).

Rousseau believed that people are fundamentally good but perverted by society. We must return to our natural state. Marx saw class conflict as the source of evil. Do away with classes, and evil will disappear. All utopians have imagined that if humanity could only abolish the social source of crime and cruelty—let us say, by eliminating private property—universal happiness would ensue.

Freud explicitly criticized the Bolsheviks for just this belief, and that is one reason he was banned in the Soviet Union. "The communists believe that they have found the path to deliverance from our evils," he writes mockingly in *Civilization and Its Discontents* (CAID, 66). "According to them, man is wholly good and is well-disposed to his neighbor," and if only private property could be abolished, "ill-will and hostility would disappear" (CAID, 66-67). Freud counters that "the psychological premises on which the system is based are an untenable illusion." Communism, or any appeal to universal benevolence, can unite some people in love "so long as there are other people left over to receive the manifestations of their aggressiveness" (CAID, 67-68). As if he foresaw the Great Purges to come a few years later, Freud concludes: "one only wonders, with concern, what the Soviets do after they have wiped out their bourgeois" (CAID, 69).

In all utopian views, evil must be seen as superficial, not fundamental, and human nature therefore malleable and perfectible. In the USSR, tragedy was held to be a false genre. Genetics was forbidden for the same reason as psychoanalysis, for suggesting some qualities are ineradicable. In America, Mead and Benedict reflected an anthropological tradition of distrusting Darwinism for its suggestion that our nature derives from our animal heritage and therefore lies much deeper than any particular social or economic arrangement. There are limits to what altered social arrangements can achieve.

The great skeptics—Qohelet (in Ecclesiastes), Gibbon, Swift, Voltaire, Dostoevsky—saw evil as fundamental. It does not always triumph, but should never surprise us. In religious terms, misanthropologists may be said to accept the doctrine of original sin. It is, as G. K. Chesterton once remarked, the only religious tenet that is provable empirically.[1] All history testifies to it, and to maintain the opposite involves thinking away all the evidence. When we are told that humanity can "escape from history," we should recognize this promise for what it is, an assertion that the totality of human experience tells us nothing about ourselves.

Pelagius imagined that people could save themselves by their own wills and efforts, while Augustine contended they could not because original sin corrupts the will itself. Self-deception flatters people, and, as la Rochefoucauld remarked, "self-love is cleverer than the cleverest man in the world" (LaR, 33). When we imagine we are behaving well, we may be glossing over bad motives. Augustine concluded that only divine grace could save us, which means, if one

---

[1]     As cited in Alan Jacobs, *Original Sin: A Cultural History* (New York: HarperCollins, 2008), x.

accepts his view of human nature but does not believe in the divine, that nothing can.

Anti-utopians know: there is no greater cause of evil than the attempt to eliminate it altogether. "I am perplexed by my own data and my conclusion is a direct contradiction of the original idea with which I started," declares the revolutionary theorist Shigalyov in *The Possessed*. "Starting from unlimited freedom, I arrive at unlimited despotism. I will add, however, that there can be no solution of the social problem but mine" (p. 409). Perhaps if one's goal were not "unlimited," some other, admittedly less than perfect, solutions would appear.

Once one makes perfection the goal, then surely no price is too much to pay. No matter how much carnage one causes, one can always argue that it is less than the sum total of all the evil presently in the world accumulating year by year forever. "They shout 'a hundred million heads,'" explains the revolutionary hero of *The Possessed*, Pyotr Stepanovich. "But why be afraid of it if, with the slow day-dreams on paper, despotism in the course of some hundred years will devour not a hundred but five hundred million heads?" (p. 415). You can't make an omelette without breaking eggs. Is it any wonder how in the name of humanity the Khmer Rouge could wipe out a third of the Cambodian population? In killing the Jews, the Nazis imagined they were doing what the Soviets did by killing capitalists. As Vasily Grossman observed, communism is racism by class. Utopianism brings all the blood of the Apocalypse, because it imagines a final struggle between good and evil: "Behold, I make all things new!"

When evil persists, revolutionaries imagine sabotage rather than rethink the supposed perfectibility of human nature. Correctly, they detect treason to the ideal everywhere. Robespierre himself dies on the guillotine, and the revolution eats its children. "*O Liberté, que de crimes on commet en ton nom*! (Oh Liberty, what crimes are committed in thy name!)," declared the Girondist Madame Roland at the guillotine. It is a line dear to misanthropologists everywhere.

## Misanthropology Versus Misanthropy

Misanthropology draws upon the tradition of misanthropy, but differs from it in a few important ways. For one thing, misanthropy is itself one of the human vices studied by misanthropology. For another, it views misanthropists as all too sure of their conclusions, which means they place excessive faith in their powers of discernment.

They are insufficiently skeptical of the mind's powers and often fail to recognize their own beliefs as perhaps overly broad theories. In fact, misanthropy represents the typical position of a disillusioned utopian, whose former faith has been reversed into unremitting contempt. "One day he gives us diamonds, next day stones." [2] Misanthropy is reverse sentimentality. As Apemantus tells Timon in Shakespeare's play: "The middle of humanity thou never knewest, but the extremity of both ends."

Critical debate about *Gulliver's Travels* has raged over whether the book is misanthropic or a satire on a misanthropy seen as a particularly noxious form of pride. Just how dark is the vision of Swift's book?

If we consider the Yahoos of Book 4, who are presented as humans reduced to their primordial state, we note that this state is highly social. These are not Hobbesian people before society but humans living in primal sociality, which turns out to be far worse. As Gulliver notices with disgust, the instincts of Yahoos involve rituals in which they tear, gnaw, and frequently defecate upon each other: "But how far this might be applicable to our courts and favorites ... my master [Houyhnhnm] said I could best determine" (GT, 489). Each Yahoo action reveals an uncanny resemblance to the more sophisticated behavior of Europeans. The real plot of Book 4 describes Gulliver's gradual realization that he is little more than a clothes-wearing Yahoo.

> When I thought of my family, my friends, my countrymen, or human race in general, I considered them as they really were, *Yahoos* in shape and disposition, perhaps a little more civilized, and qualified with the gift of speech, but making no other use of reason, than to improve and multiply those vices, whereof their brethren in this country had only the share that nature allotted them. (GT, 507)

Swift could easily have imagined our origins as pre-social, but he instead sees our past—and our future, if these Yahoos are indeed shipwrecked humans who reverted to their natural state—as social in the worst sense of the word. We are collectively loathsome, and civilized behavior reflects our essential, and social, wickedness.

---

[2]     This quotation and the following one are from William Shakespeare, *Timon of Athens*, ed. H. J. Oliver (London: Methuen, 1969), 83 and 108.

Give Yahoos reason, the Houyhnhnms observe, and they will use it to find new ways to torture each other or to indulge vices unimaginable to either an asocial or a rational being. As Dostoevsky's underground man remarks, "Civilization only produces a greater variety of sensations in man.... Have you noticed that the subtlest slaughterers have almost always been the most civilized gentlemen, to whom the various Atillas and Stenka Razins could never hold a candle?" (NFU, 21). Swift would not have been in the least surprised that the twentieth century has seen people develop ideologies leading to unprecedented murder, with or without advanced technology (the Khmer Rouge needed no computers).

Swift presents Gulliver as a disillusioned utopian lover of humanity who becomes misanthropic, a process to be expected of all utopian dreamers. "For as to these filthy *Yahoos*, although there were few greater lovers of mankind, at that time, than myself, yet I never saw any sensitive being so detestable on all accounts" (GT, 452). Earlier, Gulliver is rather disturbed by the King of Brobdingnag's response to his enthusiastic praise of England. Holding the diminutive lover of humanity and his homeland in his hands, the king "cannot but conclude the bulk of your natives to be the most pernicious race of little odious vermin that nature ever suffered to crawl upon the surface of the earth" (GT, 342).

Brobdingnag teaches Gulliver to appreciate the physical, as well as moral, deformity of human beings. While the king instructs Gulliver in cultural misanthropology, the country's beautiful women unwittingly teach him physical misanthropology. Because these women are so large, even the most perfect examples of the human body appear as they are, pitted, marred, filthy, and repulsive. "I was placed on their toilet directly before their naked bodies, which I am sure to me was very far from being a tempting sight, or from giving me any other emotions than those of horror and disgust" (GT, 325). And of course, people who are less than royal—beggars, for instance—are far worse, and probably more representative of the human. They offer Gulliver "the most horrible spectacle that an European eye ever beheld": their lice, for instance, "rooted like swine" (GT, 318). And parasites are evidently the rule, not the exception, for humans, whose bodies exude "nauseous" and noxious substances beyond enumeration. Our hospitality to parasites constitutes another way in which we are "social."

Gulliver draws the wrong lesson from cultural and physical misanthropology when he returns to England and can view humans only with extreme disgust. "And when I began to consider that by copulation with one of the *Yahoo* species I had become a parent of more, it struck me with the utmost shame, confusion, and horror" (GT, 521). We can see the close connection of misanthropy with utopianism when Gulliver manages to maintain both simultaneously. In his letter to his cousin Sympson, he complains that neither his book nor his social prescriptions have produced perfection. "For instead of seeing a full stop to all abuses and corruptions, at least in this little island, as I had reason to expect: behold, after six months warning, I cannot learn that my book hath produced one single effect according to my intentions.... And it must be owned that seven months were a sufficient time to correct every vice and folly to which *Yahoos* are subject" (GT, 205-6). Faulting European *Yahoos* above all for their pride, he sets himself above them and does not see that he is the proudest of all.

My own view is that *Gulliver's Travels* is both misanthropic *and* a satire on misanthropy: that is, Swift hates humanity for its ineradicable vices, and among these vices is misanthropy. A misanthropologist, while learning a good deal from Swift's catalogue of human ills, and agreeing with much of his indictment, would nevertheless draw a different conclusion.

Misanthropology is deeply anti-utopian, in part because of its disbelief in timeless, theoretically driven solutions, and in part because, like misanthropy, it has a keen sense of human perversity. It focuses on the almost necessary corruption of the best-intentioned schemes for reform (which are in any case rarely as well-intentioned as their backers imagine). The American Constitution may be seen as a rather misanthropological document. With its endless checks and balances, its division of power between three branches of government and two houses of a legislature, its prescription of staggered election years for senators, its division of power between federal and state governments, and its limiting of Congress to specific types of legislative powers and by a Bill of Rights, the Constitution expresses everywhere the belief that power is always likely to be abused. No utopian would construct such an invitation to paralysis. In the Soviet Constitution, the Communist Party, which was presumed infallible because it had the right theory, could do whatever it liked. Misanthropologists ask of any reform what effect it will have when (not if) it is abused, when initial enthusiasm wears off and interest group politics set in, and when unintended consequences govern what actually happens. Only if, even then, the reform would do more good than harm will they support it.

In that respect, misanthropologists would not accept Ambrose Bierce's definition of a conservative: "A statesman who is enamored of existing evils, as distinguished from the Liberal, who wishes to replace them with others" (DD, 35). Bierce's cynicism reflects the categorical mindset of a person who believes that either there is a right theory or there is nothing, and has then concluded that there is nothing. One cannot please a misanthrope because he regards all human behavior as necessarily awful, if not overtly than covertly; but a misanthropologist is so sensitive to human evil that he appreciates goodness all the more when he sees it. Because it is not to be expected, he honors it all the more.

As Swift was literature's greatest misanthrope, Dostoevsky was its greatest misanthropologist. He saw both the evil and the good in human nature as (1) irreducible to each other, (2) ineradicable, and (3) fundamentally social. And what are our fundamental, ineradicable social vices?

## Regard

In *Crime and Punishment*, Raskolnikov finds the drunkard Marmeladov run over in the street. He brings the crushed man home to his tubercular wife, prostitute daughter, and destitute children, who live in something resembling an indoor public square. In Dostoevsky's novels, suffering, shame, torture, and death usually take place before a crowd of spectators, who indulge in the quintessential social act of gaping. When Raskolnikov dreams of a horse beaten to death out of sheer sadistic delight, a woman enjoys the scene while eating nuts.

In Dostoevsky, the first sign of our essential sociality is that we are all voyeurs. In his scandalous scenes, spectators stare at a sufferer, who in turn watches how they watch him. In this case, Raskolnikov contemplates the whole exchange of voyeurisms.

The dying Marmeladov lies in a room "so full of people that you couldn't have dropped a pin. The policemen left, all except one, who remained for a time, trying to drive out the people who came in from the stairs" (C&P, 178). Katerina Ivanovna, Marmeladov's wife, flies into a rage at her neighbors' unseemly curiosity, but with her anger, tears, and horrifyingly fascinating gasps and coughs, only succeeds in making herself another object of interest. "'You might let him die in peace, at least,' she shouted at the crowd, 'is it a spectacle for you to gape at?'" It is, of course, and no one can resist watching. We all love the spectacle of each other's humiliation.

"You should respect the dead, at least!" Katerina Ivanovna shouts, and readers may imagine how Marmeladov, who is in fact not yet dead, overhears her words and becomes a sort of spectator at his own dying. In Dostoevsky, a scene is typically just that, performed as if on stage before an audience, whose interest is the greatest scandal of all. The act of reading the novel is itself another, vicarious act of voyeurism, and those who respond to the irresistible attraction of Dostoevsky's novels (as almost everyone does) become living examples of sociality in its primary, voyeuristic form.

At this point, the novel's narrator draws some characteristically Dostoevskian observations. In response to Katerina's reproaches, "the lodgers, one after another, squeezed back into the doorway with that strange inner feeling of satisfaction which may be observed in the presence of a sudden accident, even in those nearest and dearest to the victim, from which no living man is exempt in spite of the sincerest sympathy and compassion" (C&P, 178). People need each other, are incomplete without each other, because without others there is no voyeurism, no joy at witnessing horror. If torture is not the purest expression of our need for others, then voyeurism is.

"The sincerest sympathy and compassion" may be there, too, of course, but not by themselves. Opposite social feelings typically accompany each other. Perhaps humanity is so constituted that we always have in mind not only the perfectly just listener and judge—what Bakhtin calls our superaddressee—but also the *supervoyeur*, the constant and unseemly witness of all our inner thoughts and feelings. The devil who appears in *Karamazov* quite explicitly describes his principle role as witnessing spectacles. "You know how susceptible and aesthetically impressionable I am" (BK, 787), he tells Ivan, thus indicating that part of our taste for art derives from that "strange inner feeling of satisfaction ... from which no living man is exempt."

Dostoevsky would have had no difficulty in understanding what traffic reports call "gapers' delay," the slowdown of cars as drivers attempt to see how horrible an accident has been. Nor would he have had any trouble comprehending our interest in O. J. Simpson, Susan Smith, the Menendez brothers, and other trials. Dostoevsky himself followed and reported at length on the equivalent Russian trials of his day, and he was keenly aware that the reaction of the public was itself central to their import. In *Karamazov*, far less attention is paid to the jury than to the lady spectators at Dmitri's trial. Their titillated reaction to the murder is revealed in all its obscene interest, which, after all, the readers share. Lise Hohlakova reflects on such dynamics when she expresses a wish to witness a boy being slowly tortured to death while she eats "pineapple compote."

If it were to satisfy all our capacities, heaven would have tabloids. Inquiring spirits want to know! But it doesn't, according to Ivan's devil, which is why the other world is, while extremely edifying, insufferably tedious. The devil hopes to prevent earthly life from becoming just such "an endless church service" (BK, 781), and so he befriends the press. For without the devil and what he represents in human nature, there would be no newspapers, for "who would take them in?" (BK, 787-88).

One reason we want to read newspapers *when* they appear, and follow a trial *while* it is going on, is that closeness in time to horror makes us virtual witnesses of it. We need to feel that the crunch of bones, the flaying of skin, and the sort of humiliation "one experiences only in nightmares" are still taking place, or, at least, that their effects still linger. Presentness is liveliness.

In *The Possessed*, people gather at the fire consuming a large portion of the town:

> Some helped to put out the fire while others stood about, admiring it. A great fire at night always has a thrilling and exhilarating effect.... Then the horror and a certain sense of personal danger, together with the exhilarating effect of a fire at night, produce on the spectator ... a certain concussion of the brain and, as it were, a challenge to those destructive instincts which, alas, lie hidden in every heart, even that of the mildest and most domestic little clerk.... This sinister sensation is almost always fascinating. "I really don't know whether one can look at a fire without a certain pleasure." This is word for word what Stepan Trofimovich said to me one night on returning home after he had happened to witness a fire and was still under the influence of the spectacle. Of course, the very man who enjoys the spectacle will rush into the fire himself to save a child or an old woman; but that is altogether a different matter. (p. 523-524)

The logic of this passage evidently resembles the one from *Crime and Punishment*: our sociality, which every human being shares, consists of both the capacity for sympathy or self-sacrifice and the instinctive, irresistible feeling of satisfaction of viewing the suffering of others.

Neither one of these is a matter of individual self-interest, or the pursuit of advantage, for both are desired even at great disadvantage.

## Double Thoughts

An optimist might be inclined to see our evil social impulses as a perverted, eradicable form of the good ones, whereas a Freudian might be inclined to make the opposite reduction. Dostoevsky considered both reductions as naïve, one a case of sentimentality and the other of reverse sentimentality. The human soul is ever entertaining what Prince Myshkin in *The Idiot* calls "double thoughts."

In Part Two of the novel, the disreputable but goodhearted Keller comes to confess his evil deeds, and does so sincerely, as Myshkin appreciates. But Myshkin realizes that Keller also wants to borrow money, and anticipating the request offers it to him. Admitting to his ulterior motive, Keller explains that at first he prepared his confession, "bathed in tears," but then "a hellish thought occurred to me: 'Why not, when all's said and done, borrow money of him after my confession?' So that I prepared my confession, so to say, as though it were a sort of 'fricassee with tears for sauce,' to pave the way with those tears so that you might be softened and fork out one hundred and fifty rubles. Don't you think that was base?" (I, 293). Myshkin replies in a truly Dostoevskian way:

> "But most likely that's not true; it's simply that both things came at once; that often happens. It's constantly so with me. I think it's not a good thing, though.... I have sometimes fancied," Myshkin went on very earnestly, genuinely, and profoundly interested, "that all people are like that; so that I was even beginning to excuse myself because it is awfully difficult to struggle against these *double* thoughts; I've tried. God knows how they arise and come in the mind. But you call it simply baseness!" ...
>
> "Well, I don't understand why they call you an idiot after that!" cried Keller. (I, 293-94)

Precisely because both our best and worst impulses are social, they get confused. We decide retrospectively that one motive must have been the real one. We usually choose the worst, because we mistake cynicism for profundity. And so we oversimplify our intentions by reducing a complex process to a mere exfoliation of a single purpose.

This doubleness is "not a good thing." It is a strange fallacy, which Dostoevsky was at some pains to expose, that somehow the social nature of humanity necessarily offers grounds for hope or, still worse, constituted an argument for socialism. As if etymology were destiny, the words "social" and "socialist" almost seem to imply each other. This is this sort of fallacy that led so many to assume that because Bakhtin believed in essential sociality (which he did) he must have been a socialist or Marxist (he was not), an American confusion that provokes wonder in Russians.

How common it is to reason that if people are social they should have socialism! If only individualists recognized that even individualism is itself a social theory, the argument goes, they would join the other side. But if both socialism and individualism are equally social, then one must choose between them not by asking which is the social theory but on some other grounds, like which is more moral, or better spurs the growth of knowledge, or makes people happier.

In short, sociality offers no argument whatsoever for (or against) socialism. One might as well contend that because humans are animals they should all treat each other like beasts. Our social nature carries no nontrivial political conclusions. Still less does it offer grounds for optimism or encouragement to radical reform. Of course we are social, but for that very reason we might do well to curb some of our social impulses at the expense of others. After all, sadism, totalitarianism, snobbery, envy, and slander are by their very nature social, no less than are compassion and love.

### Human Diversity

*The Brothers Karamazov* might be seen as a debate between misanthropy and misanthropology, the former represented by Ivan and his Grand Inquisitor, the latter by Zossima and Alyosha. Ivan has all the best lines.

In the famous "Rebellion" chapter, Ivan describes man as a social animal for whom other people are necessary, either to torture them or (still more perversely) to be tortured by them. "People talk sometimes of bestial cruelty, but that's a great injustice and insult to the beasts," he tells Alyosha. "A beast can never be so cruel as a man, so artistically cruel. The tiger only tears and gnaws, that's all he can do" (BK, 283). Unlike the Turks in the Balkan wars, tigers do not slowly torture babies before their mothers' eyes—"doing it before the mother's eyes was what gave zest to the amusement" (BK, 283). Again the gaze, again the need for the "regard" of others, defines us as both social and evil.

Lest one think this example is directed against Turks or any other specific nationality, Ivan develops his own version of multiculturalism. Instead of saying, as our multicultural school curricula seem to do, that each group is wonderful in its own way, Ivan has put together a "collection of facts" showing that each people is nauseating in its own way. Nationalities may be distinguished by their preferred means of torture. The Swiss, for instance, engage in psychological abuse that a Russian or Turk would never dream of. Russians, on the other hand, prefer "the direct satisfaction of inflicting pain" not only on other people but also on animals. They love to lash a horse "'on its meek eyes'.... It's peculiarly Russian" (BK, 285).

Ivan's amazing catalogue of newspaper stories about child abuse involves exhibitionism, voyeurism, and turning others into unwilling witnesses. Each country, each nationality, and perhaps each historical period develops, with the full powers of human creativity, its variation on the timeless and intertwined dramas of torture and voyeurism. Think of all those paintings of Saint Sebastian or other tortured saints, of the flagellation and crucifixion: the holy purpose, though real, is inseparable from the horrible fascination with others' pain, itself a proof of our sinfulness and need for grace. These paintings are wiser than first appears. Paintings and stories of hell and the last judgment appeal in the same way, and Ivan narrates the "Journey of the Mother of God Among the Torments" much as he includes, in his Grand Inquisitor legend, an auto da fé. For all his horror at other people, Ivan also recognizes these voyeuristic impulses in himself, as we guess from the signature he uses for his own journalistic articles: "the observer."

Alyosha cannot doubt Ivan's misanthropic truths, but contends that people are also capable of love. Granted, we need others to torment them, but do we not also need others to care for them, as Christ did? Ivan answers that Christian love does not exist. "'I must make you one confession,' Ivan began. 'I could never understand how one can love one's neighbors. It's just one's neighbors, to my mind, that one can't love, though one might love those at a distance" (BK, 281). When Saint John the Merciful rescued a frozen beggar, held him close, and breathed into his mouth, putrid from some disease, he must have done so not from Christ-like love, which is impossible, but from some variety of pseudo-love: "from the self-laceration of falsity, for the sake of the charity imposed by duty, as a penance laid on him" (BK, 281).

Look how holy I am! The saint may have sought praise, taken pride in his own virtue, or enjoyed (in Dostoevskian fashion) his own self-humiliation.

Ivan argues that love for those "at a distance" is possible because such love is always false: from afar one loves not a person but some abstraction. That is why "beggars, especially genteel beggars, ought never to show themselves, but to ask for charity through the newspapers. One can love one's neighbors in the abstract, or even at a distance, but at close quarters it's almost impossible. If it were on stage, in the ballet, where if beggars come in, they wear silken rags and tattered lace and beg for alms dancing gracefully, then one might like looking at them. But even then we should not love them" (BK, 282).

Thus Ivan, an atheist and (former?) socialist, rejects the possibility of significant social improvement. Overcoming individualism and selfishness would not work because our evils are themselves social. "The question is," Ivan asks, "whether that's due to men's bad qualities or whether it's inherent in their nature" (BK, 281). That is, how deep does evil go: is it superficial, just bad qualities, or does it go the core, as part of our nature? Ivan chooses the more radical alternative.

Dostoevsky's spokesman, Father Zossima, differs from the novel's other monks because he accepts much of Ivan's argument. For Dostoevsky, a real saint is a realist. He knows human nature. Sunny, naïve idealism is itself a cause of evil, as his portrait of Stepan Trofimovich in *The Possessed* demonstrates. Like Tihon in *The Possessed*, Zossima in *Karamazov* is well versed in all the complexities and perversities of the human soul. He goes as far along Ivan's path as misanthropology will allow.

In particular, Zossima repudiates the false kinds of love Ivan describes, both the monkish and the socialist varieties. The former he regards as a species of mystic pride, and the latter as a misidentification of love's proper object, which must always be a specific person seen "at close quarters." He tells the story of a doctor, who observed trenchantly:

> I love humanity ... but I wonder at myself. The more I love humanity in general, the less I love man in particular. In my dreams ... I have often come to making enthusiastic schemes for the service of humanity, and perhaps I might actually have faced crucifixion if it had been suddenly necessary; and yet I am incapable of living in the same room with any one for two

days together.... I become hostile to people the moment they come close to me. But it has always happened that the more I detest men individually the more ardent becomes my love for humanity. (BK, 64)

Here is Dostoevsky's paradox: to love men socially one must love them individually, as particular people, not as representatives of groups. Loving "humanity" satisfies one's pride, attracts public regard, and so makes one feel superior to those who go about their petty concerns or practice small acts of kindness—"microscopic actions," as Dostoevsky liked to call them. "Love of humanity" reflects the *worst* of our social nature.

When Ivan maintains that it is impossible to love someone "close to me," Alyosha replies that Father Zossima has said almost the same thing: "he, too, said that the face of a man often hinders many people not practiced in love, from loving him" (BK, 281). But one can become "practiced" in loving particular faces. Voyeurism is a much stronger urge, but the impulse to love specific people, with all their flaws and deformities, is also part of our nature. Though weaker, it can be developed by constant effort. That is why Zossima teaches Alyosha not doctrine, of which he is suspicious, but techniques for loving. It is also why he insists repeatedly that no convincing arguments for God, dogma, or general theories of morality can ever be developed, but that faith nevertheless can grow "from the bottom up," by repeated acts of kindness. "There's no proving it," he tells Madame Hohlakova, "though you can be convinced of it.... by the experience of active love. Strive to love your neighbor actively and indefatigably. In as far as you advance in love you will grow surer of the reality of God and of the immortality of your soul" (BK, 63).

## Prosaic Love

> Jesus saith unto her, Woman, what has it to do with thee or me? Mine hour is not yet come.
>
> —*John 2:4*

Dostoevsky offers three key truths about active, prosaic love. The first is that its long-term effects are impossible to trace. In this respect, love is opposed to "enthusiastic schemes," whose good effects are supposed to be immediately visible. After performing an uncharacteristic act of kindness, Ippolit Terentyev (in *The Idiot*) observes that by his good deed, he dropped a "seed" in the soul of another, and, like a real seed, it may, after many generations, germinate into countless more good deeds, though we will never see how. "How can you tell ... what significance such an association of one personality with another may have.... You know, it's a matter of a whole lifetime, an infinite multitude of ramifications hidden from us. The most skillful chess-player ... can only look a few moves ahead.... How many moves there are in this, and how much that is unknown to us!" (I, 385). No theory can ever assess the unintended consequences of consequences of consequences, but they exist nonetheless, "hidden from us."

Second, "active love" operates when we view the world *processually*. Love is of the moment, *this* moment, and only such love has the right consequences. Although each good act will have "an infinite multitude of ramifications," it must be performed for the particular person before us now, as part of a particular way of living. The actions producing the best long-term results were not designed to do so; they were the right ones to take as part of the ongoing process of living rightly. In *War and Peace*, Tolstoy makes the same argument about historically effective actions, which are never made with some overarching plan in mind. One reason Dostoevsky and Tolstoy distrusted narratives with closure is that they encourage us to assess actions by specific results within a specific time frame. Closure, with its subordination of all actions to a pregiven plan, leads us to undervalue the presentness of the moment while overlooking the "infinite ramifications" beyond the frame.

Finally, our capacity for goodness and prosaic love involves a particular way of regarding others. Dostoevsky believed that in addition to the "master-slave" regard preached by that perverse Hegelian Fyodor Pavlovich Karamazov, and the voyeuristic gaze practiced by men in crowds or spies in corners, humanity is also defined by the gaze of a mother at her infant. There is more than one kind of gaze.

In Part Two of *The Idiot*, Myshkin tells the cruel and voyeuristic Rogozhin a series of stories about faith, which Myshkin understands anthropologically. He reports first a conversation with an atheist, who somehow seemed to miss the very point of belief. Myshkin contrasts this conversation with another, in which he saw a peasant woman crossing herself devoutly when her baby smiled at her for the first time.

"What are you doing, my dear?" (I was always asking questions in those days.) "God has just such gladness every time he sees from heaven that a sinner is praying to Him with all his heart, as a mother has when she sees the first smile on her baby's face." That was what the mother said to me ... this deep, subtle and truly religious thought—a thought in which all the essence of Christianity finds expression; that is the whole conception of God as our Father and of God's gladness in man, like a father's in his own child—the fundamental idea of Christ! (I, 208)

One is tempted to imagine that, in referring to "the essence of Christianity," Myshkin alludes and replies to Feuerbach's doctrine that "theology is anthropology" with the reverse assertion, that anthropology is theology. People are what they are because of divine love. God suffuses the world with love, which Zossima's brother Markel tries to teach others to feel as he does, palpably.

To Myshkin, Christianity is not a doctrine, or a pseudo-scientific account of the world's origin, but an attempt to express something primordially human: the mother's gaze. The child's first smile is the gaze returned. The exchange is anything but a trading of voyeurisms. Rather, it expresses the essence of faith, the Holy Spirit. "The essence of religious feeling," Myshkin concludes "does not come under any sort of reasoning or atheism.... There is something else here, and there always will be something else—something that the atheists will for ever slur over; they will always be talking about something else" (I, 208-9). That "something else" provides the indirect answer not only to the atheists, but also to the anti-theists and misanthropes like Ivan Karamazov. Though we resemble the devil in enjoying the sight of horror, we also, like the mother and God, can gaze with love beyond consequences.

These characteristics of active, Christian love are prosaic. The mother's gaze is commonplace and ordinary. It has far-reaching if undramatic effects and is to be valued without thought of any specific goal. "Cast a little bread upon the waters" (Ecclesiastes 11:1).

Active, prosaic love fits no master-narrative. It is complete in the moment. Philosophers of history go wrong when they try to construct an essential story of mankind, because such a story must always be either sentimental or misanthropic. Such histories draw their power and interest from the repulsive parts of our social nature, and Myshkin's anecdote has no place in them.

In *Karamazov*, Dostoevsky makes the exceedingly strange choice of portraying the Marriage at Cana as the supremely Christian moment of the New Testament. As the story is read to Alyosha over the corpse of his beloved Zosima, we are given both the Gospel text and Alyosha's silent responses. In this hidden dialogue we perceive Zossima's and Dostoevsky's idea of prosaic love. Jesus's miracle of turning water into wine, which he performs secretly at his mother's behest, has nothing to do with his mission. "Mine hour has not yet come." Alyosha asks himself: "Was it to make wine abundant at poor weddings He had come down to earth?" (BK, 434). In the most important sense, it was. The unnoticed, kind act, performed with no overall goal in mind, at a common event without historical significance: this is itself the great human miracle we all have in our power at every moment.

When Alyosha wakes from his trance, he feels his contact with others, but not "in the Karamazov way," as objects of lust, violence, and the gaze of voyeurs. Rather, he desires to pray for them and feels certain that others are praying for him as well. Prayer is itself a social act performed individually.

Nobody had a deeper sense of the social as an arena of gratuitous cruelty—of the world as a "house of the dead"—than Dostoevsky. Ivan Karamazov's "Rebellion" and "Legend of the Grand Inquisitor" form a misanthropist's bible. But in the chapter "Cana of Galilee," the story of Jesus's gratuitous gift and Alyosha's secret prayer, we discover a prosaic miracle: the overlooked icon of a misanthropologist's faith.

## Chapter Five

MISANTHROPOLOGY, CONTINUED:

DISGUST, VIOLENCE, AND MORE ON VOYEURISM

*By Alicia Chudo*

Human emotions, behaviors, and purposes often contain implicit philosophical content.

For example, as William James stressed, the sentiment of regret presupposes indeterminism, since to regret a choice is to imagine that something else might have been chosen. Likewise, guilt would make no sense without both indeterminism and moral norms. Insofar as envy derives from the sense that someone else has gotten what we deserve, it already contains the concept of just allotment. And greed presumes that the kingdom of God is not entirely within us.

In some cases, the philosophical content remains more elusive. I would like to consider here a cluster of human reactions to violence and to the pain of others that may be less straightforward than they seem. I focus on voyeurism, identification, and disgust; understanding disgust will require a brief digression about laughter.

## 1 / Another Look at Voyeurism

### The Violent Witness

When Dr. Johnson remarked that nothing so focuses the mind as the prospect of being hanged, he might have added the prospect of watching someone else being hanged. Or disemboweled. Or flayed alive. Or dissected.

I would like to focus not on violence, but on the act of watching it with interest, that is, on voyeurism. We usually think of acting as one thing and watching as quite another, but sometimes watching may be part of the total action. For that matter, it can be seen as an action in itself. The very term "voyeurism," which is always pejorative, already suggests that at least some looking is not morally neutral. We can be responsible for it, as we are for other actions.

When a person is publically put to shame—say, by being placed in the stockades, denounced from the pulpit, or forced to exhibit a scarlet letter—the knowledge that others are looking is an intrinsic, not incidental, part of the punishment. An act of physical punishment may be all the worse if it is done in public. Then the sufferer is an unwilling object not only of bodily torment but also of public exposure. He has become a spectacle and a source of voyeuristic pleasure.

Public commentators often ask whether fictional depictions of violence are corrupting? Should children be kept from watching gory television programs? Often enough, other commentators reply, isn't it extremely rare for someone to witness a film about a savage act and then go out and imitate it? Even children clearly know what is make-believe and do not just blindly imitate whatever they see.

These shallow answers reflect the naïveté of the initial question. To begin with, the question as it is usually phrased presumes that depicted violence is one thing and the act of watching it quite another, but a moment's consideration might suggest that watching may itself be morally compromising. Think of the Roman circus, which has become a virtual synonym for watching as morally corrupt action. There, watching is an intrinsic part of the spectacle, which would not exist without it. We might more properly ask not whether watching violence is corrupting but whether it is already corrupt.

The question as usually posed also ignores the role of habit. To be sure, very few people watch a single spectacle of titillating torture and then go out and make another person a victim. But even a single act of viewing may initiate awareness of a previously unsuspected kind of pleasure. If that pleasure is frequently indulged, it may become a need. Like all addictive desires, it may require ever greater doses and lead some people to crave the excitement that only a real victim can provide.

### As If

Finally, it is far from true that the awareness of fictionality (make-believe) precludes real voyeuristic pleasure. If that were so, pornography would not work. For that matter, whenever we identify with a novelistic character, suffer with her misfortunes, or exult in her success, we do so without ceasing to be aware that we are reading a novel. Such identification can lead to both moral improvement and moral corruption, as writers from Dante to Dickens have known.

When we identify with Anna Karenina, we accept her not as a real but as a *possible* person, and we experience what happens to her as possible events. The same is true with viewers of a horror film. Experiences possible in that sense may attract us to events possible in the other sense, that is, ones we might contemplate.

### I Feel Your Pain

From Homer to Hollywood, violence to others has proven intoxicating.

Torture practiced on ourselves rarely leads us to want the experience prolonged, but when others are the victims, too many people—people unlike ourselves, of course—enjoy watching or thinking about the experience. Sophisticated folk who laugh at tabloids cultivate a taste for what they call "transgressive" representations of horror.

As with all human weaknesses, those who think themselves above this taste are most likely to be ambushed by it. Intellectuals shocked by peasant violence idolize terrorists.[1]

People derive pleasure, often quite intense, from others' pain. Ivan Karamazov observes, "I know there are people who are worked up to sensuality, to literal sensuality, which increases progressively at every blow they inflict. They beat for a minute, for five minutes, for ten minutes, more often and more savagely" (BK, 286). The two pleasures of inflicting suffering and watching it go well together.

One enjoys watching another suffer, and so one becomes a torturer.

One can imagine Ivan's reaction to the fatuous argument that there is no reason for torture because it is a poor way of extracting information. Common sense ought to instruct that if torture were obviously pointless it would not be so common in all epochs. Apart from the fact that the argument is false—let the arguer imagine himself or herself withholding a secret under such circumstances—it presumes that the sole goal of torture is information. No one who has

---

[1]    On such taste in intellectuals see Michael André Bernstein, *Bitter Carnival: Ressentiment and the Abject Hero* (Princeton: Princeton University Press, 1992).

either received or deliberately inflicted deep humiliation could believe that. Nor is it much more profound to add the goal of controlling a population.

To be sure, the widespread knowledge of horrors beyond mere death can intimidate. Historians tell us that the Turks scared Venetians away from Mediterranean trade not just by seizing their ships and selling their crews into slavery, but also by flaying Venetian admirals alive. At this point, the traditional career for young Venetian noblemen began to seem considerably less attractive than the barely profitable cultivation of terra firma. Soviet show trials worked not just because some believed the absurd confessions, but because those who did not could imagine what treatment produced them. But even this dark view may not be dark enough.

Dostoevsky's *Notes from the House of the Dead* teaches that people love torture for no practical purpose at all, simply for its own sake. Corporal punishment exists not only to control others, but because the infliction of pain, including the fear of pain, provides a unique pleasure. Craving that pleasure is part of what makes us human. It is part of what Fyodor Pavlovich Karamazov calls "the Karamazov baseness."

The narrator of *The House of the Dead* speculates that there is a bit of the Marquis de Sade or the Marquise de Brinvilliers in each of us:

> I imagine that that there is something in this sensation [of inflicting pain] that sends a thrill at once sweet and painful.... Anyone who has experienced this power, this unlimited mastery of the body, blood and soul of a fellow man made of the same clay as himself, a brother in the law of Christ—anyone who has experienced the power and license to inflict the greatest humiliation upon another creature made in the image of God will unconsciously lose the mastery of his own sensations. Tyranny is a habit ... the mind and heart are tolerant of the most abnormal things, till at last they come to relish them (HoD, 240-241).

How mistaken we are to speak of torture as "dehumanization"! No, we must sense in the victim another *person*, one like ourselves, made of the same clay, in the image of God. Who wants to beat a corpse? Or a robot? It is time to stop using the word "humane" to mean kind and "humanity" as a synonym for benevolence, as if those qualities, and not their opposites, belonged to us as human beings. We in the university might also rethink what we mean by studying "the humanities."

This lesson about ourselves has been voiced often enough in misanthropological literature, from Swift to Orwell. In *1984*, O'Brien demands that Winston, under torture, explain the regime's reasons for its cruel practices. When Winston gives the Grand Inquisitor's answer—that control serves the good of the people because they cannot govern themselves—O'Brien delivers a jolt of agony and tells Winston that such an answer is positively stupid:

> Power is not a means; it is an end. One does not establish a dictatorship in order to safeguard a revolution; one makes the revolution in order to establish the dictatorship. The object of persecution is persecution. The object of power is power. (1984, 217)

### *Lacerations*

But are we really so bad? Isn't there a kind of reverse sentimentality in assuming only the worst of human nature? After all, misanthropology itself teaches that cynicism may involve self-deception by placing us above the illusions entertained by others. Dostoevsky's radicals often feel this superiority when they claim to have gone "beyond nihilism" since they have "rejected more." Cynicism can be a form of naïveté, much as doubting everything can be a form of credulity.

And so we may ask: is it not possible that, just as we take pleasure in another's pain, we are also genuinely pained by it? Do we not often sincerely reproach ourselves for the pleasure we do take? Yes, *schadenfreude*, properly understood, contains both reactions.

But it also contains a third. As witnesses of our own self-reproaches at enjoying the pain of others, we may enjoy our own pain! We take pleasure, are pained at our pleasure, and take pleasure in that pain, in an endless hideous cycle. This is a special kind of evil that relies on our good impulses to make us worse.

Dostoevsky called this phenomenon "lacerations" (*nadryvy*). We love tearing at our moral selves. We may humiliate ourselves out of pride. Such dynamics define the psychology of "the underground" that some have come to call ressentiment (with its sense of re-sentiment, sentiment repeated).

A taboo forbids what might otherwise be pleasurable; we take pleasure in breaking taboos, and so there is a taboo against enjoying taboo-breaking, which it is a special pleasure to break.

### Taste and Distaste

Moral education typically involves learning that there is something shameful in enjoying another's pain and something disgusting in enjoying our own. In Gilbert and Sullivan's *Mikado*, the hideous Katisha explains that she is "an acquired taste"; and as there are acquired tastes, there are acquired distastes. Moral education provides us with numerous acquired distastes. Once learned, they allow us to reject behaviors and resist pleasures almost instantaneously, as fast as we turn away from excrement, and much faster than could result from any process of moral reasoning. If you have to reason yourself out of enjoying torture, you are already morally hideous. Philosophers often seem to miss this point.

Acquired tastes often involve taking pleasure or finding beauty in what less sophisticated palates would find nauseating, such as consuming insects, rotting cheese, raw meat, or, one step further, the brains of still living animals. By the same token, acquired distastes leave us revolted by the pleasures of less educated people or of ourselves when we were still unformed. With ever finer gradations, taste and distaste mark status.

Unfortunately, one can teach people to overcome their distaste, as well as their taste, for immoral actions. No one wants to be called a "choir boy" or a "boy scout," and men who are too squeamish may be deemed effeminate. Others may enjoy the sight of that squeamishness. One can develop a taste for the sight of others' distaste for human suffering, which may constitute yet another reason to inflict it. One enjoys the pain initially inflicted and the pain of the squeamish audience: two enjoyments at once!

### The Scientist and the Voyeur

Undeniably, we are fascinated by torture, both physical and psychological, but what exactly is it that fascinates us?

We may distinguish two sources: we may be interested in what is revealed and we may be interested at our own (and others') reactions to the revelation. The first is the pleasure of the scientist, the second of the voyeur. Of course, the two can go together.

Consider celebrated paintings depicting surgery and dissection. Thomas Eakins's *The Agnew Clinic* shows surgery's most up-to-date practices. Unlike the surgeon in Eakins's earlier painting, *The Gross Clinic*, Dr. Agnew wears not street clothes but an up-to-date antiseptic white gown. He abides by the new practices that came in the wake of Lister's work on infection. One doctor is administering the anaesthetic, another taking the pulse, Agnew is holding a scalpel, and, most interesting of all, an audience of students, occupying half the painting, looks on. The painting was commissioned for a University of Pennsylvania medical school graduation (1889), at a time when the school boasted about its emphasis on dissection. It is still proudly shown on the Penn website, with each of the depicted people identified.

Ostensibly, we are watching a scientific demonstration and a clinical lesson; and we are watching an audience that looks on in the right scientific spirit. It is as if the painting were saying: any other attitude would be philistine.

*The Gross Clinic* depicts a similar scene, but with one notable difference. A woman—should we say a "mere" woman?—who is looking on covers her eyes in distress.[2] Are we supposed to regard her horror as a sign of what we should not feel and what medical students are too mature to feel?

Or is it possible that the painting acknowledges something wiser: that no matter how much the science may interest us, the sheer horror of dissection is always present and a covert source of enjoyment? If so, how are we to read the absence of any such signal in *The Agnew Clinic*? Could it be that, for all its "scientific realism," the painting achieves its power precisely by inviting us to ask "unscientific" questions that its audience apparently does not?

Like Conan Doyle's dog that did not bark, does this painting portray the questions no one asks? I would like to ask: could the painting be a commentary on the purely detached scientific attitude it supposedly recommends?

### Amputation and Us

In both Eakins paintings, the patient is anesthetized and barely visible. By contrast, the second floor of the International Museum of Surgical

---

2    She is conventionally identified as the patient's mother. Michael Fried describes the viewer's fascinated repulsion and interprets the "excessiveness" of the mother's gesture "as if covering her eyes required a convulsive effort" as "a commentary on the painting as a whole," including viewers' reactions. "Excessive" to whom? See Fried, *Realism, Writing, Disfiguration: On Thomas Eakins and Stephen Crane* (Chicago: University of Chicago Press, 1987), 65.

Science in Chicago displays an enormous painting of a conscious man undergoing amputation. The patient writhes while a surgeon approaches him with a saw.

Captions indicate that the painting has been exhibited to show us what surgery was like before anaesthesia. Some questions suggested by the museum will convey a sense of the painting: "Why would the surgeon amputate the patient's leg? Why are there four men holding the patient down? What do you think happened to the patient after his leg is amputated?" The museum's explanatory plaque informs us that the most common cause of death from such operations was shock caused by pain.

None of these questions or comments alludes to the sheer eroticism of a muscular, naked young man completely in the power of others, much less the voyeuristic fascination with another's torture. The museum instructs us what to see in the tone of "questions for deeper comprehension" at the end of a textbook chapter. More important, it implicitly tells us what not to see, lest we show ourselves to be philistines incapable of scientific detachment.

But however much we acknowledge the importance of scientific advances and the heroism of pioneering surgeons, is it possible to see a conscious person undergoing amputation without experiencing horror? If it is possible, is it desirable? Once one can amputate with (pardon me) "detachment," what else can one do?

In Eakins's paintings, the patient is unconscious, but that only puts the horror at one remove. Something prompts us to wonder whether we can indeed be so sure that the unconscious patient feels no pain rather than, let us say, feeling it without remembering it afterward? Some have thought that patients in comas do feel pain, and that we must not mistake the absence of the usual signs of suffering for the absence of suffering. Could that not be the case here?

Even if an anesthetized patient experiences no pain, he still resembles ourselves all too closely. He, too, was recently conscious as we are, and will soon be again. This resemblance makes it almost impossible not to imagine what the patient would feel if conscious. And we may easily imagine the patient himself, after the operation, wincing at the thought of what must have happened to him as if he could still feel it; and we can easily share the pain behind that wincing.

If the Eakins paintings are meant to raise these questions, they are profound. If not, they are disturbingly shallow. Such shallowness evokes its own kind of horror.

### Self-Exposure

Perhaps more than any other writer, Dostoevsky understood the peculiar mix of emotions we feel at watching another's torment. The very title of *The Insulted and the Humiliated* promises a look at psychological writhing, and almost all of Dostoevsky's works explore the inscape of insult. The insulted are usually aware not just of their humiliation, but also of the witnessing of their humiliation, an awareness that is itself witnessed, as they are also aware; and so on.

This infinite sequence also belongs to the psychology of the underground, as the underground man explains to us more than once. I say "to us" because the underground man treats his readers as if they were *present*, witnesses not exactly of the humiliating actions he describes but of the one he enacts in describing them. We are drawn into his drama, and even our disgust at his self-exposure and our resentment at being drafted into a scene of degradation turn out to initiate new humiliations, which we also view with disgust and resentment.

> You will say that it is vulgar and base to drag all this into public after all the tears and raptures I have myself admitted.... But why is it base?... And yet you are right—it really is vulgar and base. And what is most base of all is that I have now started to justify myself to you. And even more base than that is my making this remark now. But that's enough, or, after all, there will be no end to it; each step will be more base than the last. (NFU, 51)

In *The Insulted and Humiliated*, Prince Valkovsky describes a French exhibitionist who enjoys the cynical pleasure of "throwing off the mask" and, beyond that, of making the onlooker aware that she looks at the scene *willingly*, if not out of eroticism then out of fascination with self-degradation. The viewer does what she refuses to do, and does so in the very act of refusing. Fyodor Pavlovich perfects the same psychology, as we first see in the "scandalous scene" in the elder's cell.

Not just the witnessing but even the refusal to witness makes one part of the drama.

Perhaps Ivan Karamazov signs his articles "the observer" to indicate that he is the eternal nonparticipant, but the novel demonstrates that adopting such a stance is itself a morally questionable action. In this novel, it is also the source of overt crimes. Without it the novel would lack its plot. Ivan comes to feel guilty precisely for having been *only* an observer.

In Genesis 9, Noah curses Ham for having witnessed his nakedness, whereas his two brothers had covered their father without looking. There could hardly be a clearer appreciation of the fact that looking is an action, and I suspect the story of Ivan, his two brothers, and his father alludes to it.

In Dostoevsky, no scene of suffering is complete without its audience. Raskolnikov sees such immoral witnessing and refuses to take part in it. He rushes to save the mare beaten in his dream and does what he can for the Marmeladovs. Unlike Ivan Karamazov, he will not remain a mere witness, because such a stance is morally tainted. Unfortunately, so is action. One might almost infer that he becomes a criminal in order to stop being a witness.

## 2 / Identification

In life as in Dostoevsky, witnesses of horror experience a thrill, but what psychological reactions lead to that thrill? What does it express?

I think that for Dostoevsky voyeuristic pleasure at the suffering of others presupposes two distinct human reactions. Each fascinates by its sheer intensity and each raises important questions about life and the soul in a compelling way. Each thereby makes philosophy palpable. Ultimate questions play directly on the nerves.

The first reaction is *identification*, the second is *disgust*. Let us begin with identification.

When we identify with a sufferer, we draw near and imagine ourselves in his or her place. In order to understand the human condition, we may want to understand its extreme forms. We all know that we are mortal and that our flesh is subject to a thousand natural shocks. We cannot help wondering what dying and extreme pain are like.

And so we observe them in reality or in an evocative depiction, all the while imagining ourselves in the sufferer's position but drawing back just when the identification becomes too painful. We vicariously join the sufferer until we reach our limit of vicarious endurance. That is the dynamic of identification: tentatively place yourself in the sufferer's position, then draw back and reflect, and then, perhaps, repeat.

### Almost Too Close

Seeing how closely we can identify with the sufferer is a way of testing ourselves. We get to know something about ourselves not only as members of the human species but also as specific individuals. The nearer we draw to the limit of our endurance and to a surrender we can no longer stop, the more thrilling the test becomes.

Drawing almost too close: identification thrives on this kind of experience. In *Karamazov*, Lise explains the complex dynamics of approach and withdrawal when she describes a dream in which devils surround her. Just when they are about to seize her, she crosses herself. The devils retreat, but do not leave.

> And suddenly I have a frightful longing to revile God aloud, and so I begin, and then they come crowding back at me, delighted, and seize me again, and I cross myself again and they all draw back. It's awful fun, it takes one's breath away. (BK, 709)

Alyosha confesses that he has had the same dream. The two seem to share a fascination with terror and with testing themselves.[3]

### Striptease

La Rochefoucauld famously observed that "in the misfortune of our best friends, we always find something which is not displeasing to us" (YBQ, 443). Our sympathy for the friend can coexist with pleasure at one's superior lot. One's own good fortune always confirms the justice of the universe.

Dostoevsky liked to stress that we may be sincerely sympathetic with another's suffering, and yet also take pleasure in the thrill of witnessing disaster. Neither feeling precludes or is reducible to the other.

Even if we would risk our lives to save another, we cannot help being drawn to witness that person's most exquisite suffering. Why

---

[3]   Lise is struck by the fact that Alyosha and she have had the same terrifying dream. In *Anna Karenina*, serialized only a few years earlier, Anna and Vronsky have also have the same terrifying dream. Both novels take as a key theme the idea that looking is an action, and one with moral significance. When two people share a dream, they become joint witnesses in a way that is deeply mysterious, and that mystery makes the terror all the more powerful.

else would torture and execution once have been public events, and why are they now kept rigorously behind doors lest the spectacle corrupt onlookers? Both exposure and concealment testify to the same impulse.

In Myshkin's descriptions of execution in *The Idiot*, the condemned man's suffering includes enduring the gaze of others fixed upon him: "There were crowds of people, there was noise and shouting; ten thousand faces, ten thousand eyes—and all that he has had to bear, and worst of all the thought, 'They are ten thousand, but not one of them is being executed, and I am to be executed.'" (I, 59). Witnessing the execution, Myshkin himself experiences the same intense fascination, as he confesses to the Epanchins. Aglaia and Adelaida vicariously experience his vicarious experience, and are as fascinated as he:

> "I did not like it at all and I was rather ill afterwards, but I must confess I was riveted to the spot; I could not take my eyes off it."
> "I couldn't have taken my eyes off it either," said Aglaia.
> "They don't like women to look on at it; they even write about such women in the papers."
> "I suppose, if they consider that it's not fit for women, they mean to infer (and so justify it) that it is fit for men. I congratulate them on their logic. And you think so too, no doubt."
> "Tell us about the execution," Adelaida interrupted (I, 57)

The gaze of others emphasizes the intense loneliness of the prisoner's dying and thereby adds to his pain. "We all die alone," Pascal wrote, but we don't all find ourselves stared at as our life is ending. It appears that we are most alone not when we are entirely by ourselves but when our loneliness is made public.

Such loneliness derives in part from the palpable sense that the onlookers exist in a different sort of time, one in which, as Myshkin explains, the future is open, whereas for the condemned man the end is certain. The crowd wants to understand what such dying would be like. It wants to make its controlled identification with the prisoner the source of knowledge about ultimate mysteries of the soul, but for the prisoner it is his own soul that becomes an object of inquiry. He is not watching a dissection, he is being dissected and watching those watching the process.

The lonely prisoner is stripped beyond mere nakedness, for it is his very soul that is exposed. Each step towards execution involves more and more stripping, and the audience experiences a quasi-erotic arousal. Presumably, that is the hidden reason that women are not supposed to witness something so obscene, and why Dostoevsky has included the discussion of this question. In fact, he includes it twice, since Myshkin has already discussed it with the footman. Aglaia admits her intense curiosity, and Adelaida wants to end the discussion about women so as to hear more about the psychologically stripped man.

### Extreme Exposure

When the underground man suffers the most extreme agonies of humiliation, he feels as if he has been skinned so that the very air touches him to the quick. It is a metaphor of extreme exposure.

The more private something is, the less it should be witnessed by others and, therefore, the greater the voyeuristic delight at seeing it. Watching another's suffering, still more his dying, involves the most extreme violation of privacy. That is so because in both we lose all ability to conceal anything about what is most intimate. What could be more so?

The thrill of such voyeurism suggests that human selfhood involves something that we feel to be uniquely our own, which cannot be made public if we are to remain ourselves. Animals have sex in the open, which, as we are aware, constitutes a key difference—perhaps the key difference—between them and us. We have "private parts," they do not. Privacy virtually defines humanness, at least since the Fall. When Adam and Eve eat the apple, "the eyes of them both were opened, and they knew that they were naked; and they sewed fig leaves together, and made themselves aprons" (Genesis 3:7). They become recognizably human when they have something to hide.

To remain human, we must protect that difference from the animal at all costs. Humans who happen to witness dogs copulating in the street, horses in a field, or lions in a zoo are embarrassed before each other because the resemblance between what animals do and what we do calls attention to the very animality we must conceal. It suggests our fear at the possibility that anything nonanimal, anything that should be concealed, is an illusion. And we are embarrassed at our own embarrassment because it betrays the fear that, even more than our animality, we must conceal.[4]

---

[4]      The same applies to defecation and vomiting, when we cannot help

For each person, the private realm of self is unique, or there would be no reason to keep it private. *What we all share is the need to have something that we do not all share*, something that, for each person, belongs to him or her alone. Each of us is human because he is a unique person, a soul. Zombies fascinate us because they are people in all respects except that they have no soul. They raise the terrifying prospect that, as many materialists have contended, we are all zombies.

Human interest in watching others make love, suffer, or die testifies to the voyeuristic desire to witness what should not be witnessed, to trespass on the private realm that each person keeps sacred. In *The Republic*, Glaucon imagines that the value of the ring of Gyges, which confers invisibility, would lie in all the crimes and seductions one could commit without detection. But he overlooks the idea that the sheer act of eavesdropping on others' souls might be the greatest crime and offer the greatest thrill of all. The thrill of trespassing depends on our belief in a forbidden realm in others and therefore in ourselves. One way a person can affirm his or her own selfhood is to violate another's.

Voyeurism will everywhere and always violate the basic human taboo and yet, at the same time, affirm humanness.

### The House of the Dead

How to conceal the private and exactly what constitutes voyeurism may differ from culture to culture, but the concept of impermissible seeing distinguishes not one culture from another but humanness itself—or so Dostoevsky's anthropology suggests. Lack of privacy threatens human identity, which is why Dostoevsky singles out the fact that he was not alone once for four years as a particularly awful part of his imprisonment. That is one reason prison is "the house of the dead," that is, of former people whose human life has been annulled. The need for something not shared by others, something uniquely one's own, also explains Dostoevsky's deep hostility to socialism.

Neither prison camps nor phalansteries offer private quarters.

---

displaying the internal as it becomes external. Externalization does not involve shame when, as with crying, it derives from recognizably spiritual sources. Defecation, vomiting, and dismemberment provoke disgust, for reasons described below.

### Connoisseurs

Witnessing what is most private about another is morally prohibited because it violates selfhood. On the other hand, what violates selfhood affirms its existence, but in so doing it raises the possibility of selfhood's utter destruction. That possibility accounts for the fear, as well as the joy, of psychic espionage.

In his essay on teaching peasant children to write, Tolstoy describes the moment when Fedka discovers the joys of story-making:

> He was excited for a long time, and could not sleep; and I cannot represent the feeling of excitement, of pleasure, of pain, and almost of remorse which I experienced in the course of that evening. I felt that from this time a new world of joys and sorrows had been revealed to Fedka—the world of art; it seemed to me that I was witnessing what no one has the right to see....[5]

Witnessing another's first act of story-making or love-making occasions excitement, pleasure, and pain because it means spying on a turning point in the life of a soul: this is the sort of thing that "no one has the right to see" and which therefore occasions remorse. The craving to see it constitutes the voyeuristic impulse. One wonders whether Anne Sullivan experienced such feelings at the moment Helen Keller realized that a particular movement of the fingers meant "water."

If Tolstoy could eavesdrop directly on Fedka's thoughts, the violation might be all the more profound, as would the ability to sense directly another's bodily sensations whenever one wished.[6] Spying, overhearing, touching: it does not matter which sense we use to learn another's intimate secrets. Blind people can be voyeurs. Despite the etymology of the word, then, voyeurism is not really about seeing in the narrow sense of what we do with our eyes. It is about *knowing*.

To be human is to have secrets. Secret police exist so that there will be no secrets.

---

[5] Lyof N. Tolstoi, *"Who Should Learn Writing of Whom; Peasant Children of Us, or We of Peasant Children," "The Long Exile," and Other Stories* (New York: Scribner, 1929), 308.

[6] Perhaps the special thrill or horror entailed by brain imaging reflects the suspicion that we are seeing not just brain but mind, and the portion of ourselves we would keep most private.

Whether we read another's diary, eavesdrop on his or her romantic conversations, or "touch on" hidden sensitivities, we become voyeurs because of what we have come to know. Perhaps we should have referred not to voyeurs but to connoisseurs, if that term had not already been appropriated for a different meaning.

The priest who hears confession, the doctor who learns about intimate ailments, the psychiatrist who hears our most private fears and desires: these professionals enjoy a special status, and sometimes wear a special uniform, because to perform their function they must acquire knowledge that would otherwise make them voyeurs. We trust them not only to keep the information secret from all others, but also to resist their own voyeuristic impulses. Perhaps one reason some religions insist that priests and monks be celibate is that sinners do not want their confessors to be aroused when hearing of fleshly sins. Those whom we trust with intimate secrets must not be curious in the wrong way. And we, too, must regard our encounters with them as essentially different from other encounters, which is why it can be so unsettling to come across one's psychiatrist showering at the gym.

### Room 101

In *1984*, the telescreen ensures that no inch of space and no moment of time escape scrutiny. Even when Winston and Julia imagine they have found their own time and place—the real joy of their love lies in its privacy—that very impression is part of Big Brother's trap. The point of O'Brien's torture encounter with Winston is not to punish him but to violate self and soul so profoundly that Winston truly loves everything that has taken them away. Thus the novel ends with Winston's horrible appreciation of how he has finally lost his self:

> He gazed up at the enormous face [of Big Brother]. Forty years it had taken him to learn what kind of smile was hidden beneath the dark mustache. O cruel, needless misunderstanding! O stubborn, self-willed exile from the loving breast!... But it was all right, everything was all right, the struggle was finished. He had won the victory over himself. He loved Big Brother. (1984, 245)

The struggle was *self*-willed and he wins the victory over him*self*: it is selfhood that is lost.

In Zamyatin's *We*, the horror of the houses with glass walls is not that one can hide nothing, but that there is nothing to hide. But the horror of *1984* is still greater. Big Brother does not create a world without souls. On the contrary, he ensures that there will always be people with souls because the goal of the regime is not social engineering but precisely the violation of souls. The world we are creating, O'Brien explains, "is the exact opposite of the stupid hedonistic Utopias that the old reformers imagined." It will grow "not less but more merciless," and progress will be "progress toward more pain." The emotions it will foster are fear and "self-abasement"; and for there to be self-abasement there must be selves (1984, 220).

Winston has been lured into rebellion and self-cultivation so that his self can be violated all the more painfully. His very dreams have been spied upon. The ultimate torture of "Room 101"—which is "the worst thing in the world"—differs from person to person. It is whatever each person, in the depth of his soul, most dreads. It affirms individuality by violating it.

This violation takes place in the sight of a torturer who experiences "the thrill of victory, the sensation of trampling on an enemy who is helpless. If you want a picture of the future, imagine a boot stamping on a human face—forever" (1984, 220). Someone will always be present to inflict the self-destroying pain and to witness it. In the world of Big Brother, voyeurism and espionage are not means to an end, they are an end. That is the hidden meaning of the phrase Winston has always known: Big Brother is Watching You.

We too often overlook the fact that *1984* is about voyeurism.

## 3 / Laughter and Disgust

We have seen that as voyeurism involves identification, it implicitly affirms the existence of self. If we really thought of ourselves as entirely material, as no different from animals, and as having nothing resembling a "soul," voyeurism would lose its point.

We have also seen that in identification, one draws close to the other so as to witness and vicariously experience his or her selfhood, and then withdraws to a safe distance.

But voyeurism can take the opposite route if it involves our other reaction to the suffering of others: disgust. When disgusted, we first recoil, and then, fascinated by what we have seen and our own reaction to it, we may then draw close to examine these two sources of fascination. Disgust, too, contains implicit philosophical content.

### Atness

Theorists have often noticed that disgust is closely related to laughter. In his well-known study of disgust, Winfried Menninghaus even declares that "all theorists of disgust are, at the same time, theorists of laughter."[7]

The connection often noted is that laughter and disgust each distance one from an object. I like to say that they both partake of "atness": we feel disgust *at* something whereas hatred is hatred *of* something. One is more intimately involved with what provokes hatred than with what provokes laughter or disgust. On the positive side, wonder also displays atness.

Nevertheless, most things that are funny are not disgusting, and vice versa. Disgust seems to involve a sense of the threatening, whereas laughter, as Bakhtin famously observed, abolishes fear. To be sure, the same things may be both disgusting and funny, as in Rabelais, Swift, or the humor of twelve-year-old boys. But we have here the sort of phenomenon Hume discusses in relation to tragedy: two opposite emotions intensify each other precisely because they do not fuse but remain distinct.[8] That could not happen if they were somehow versions of the same thing.

Laughter and disgust share an important feature. Nothing in inanimate nature can be either funny or disgusting. The Grand Canyon

---

[7] Winfried Menninghaus, *Disgust: The Theory and History of a Strong Sensation,* trans. Howard Eiland and Joel Golb (Albany: SUNY Press, 2003), 10. See also Aurel Kolnai, *On Disgust,* ed. Barry Smith and Carolyn Korsmeyer (La Salle, IL: Open Court, 2004); William Ian Miller, *The Anatomy of Disgust* (Cambridge, MA: Harvard University Press, 1997); and Martha C. Nussbaum, *Hiding from Humanity: Disgust, Shame, and the Law* (Princeton: Princeton University Press, 2004).

[8] For Hume, in tragedy the beauty of the oratory and the genius of representing horror create a situation in which "the uneasiness of the melancholy passions is not only overpowered and effaced by something stronger of an opposite kind, but the whole impulse of those passions is converted into pleasure, and swells with the delight which the eloquence raises in us." David Hume, "Of Tragedy," in *English Prose and Poetry, 1660-1800: A Selection,* ed. Frank Brady and Martin Price (New York: Holt Rinehart, 1961), 243.

may be sublime and an erupting volcano threatening, but neither is funny or disgusting. One may make them funny or disgusting only by seeing them as metaphors, let us say, for parts of the human body, but then it is the human that proves essential. In between the human and inanimate lies the world of animals, where disgust but not humor easily arises. The rotting body of a dog may nauseate, but animals can only be funny if we choose to see them in human terms.

The ridiculous and what Menninghaus amusingly calls the vomitive both involve physiological responses: we smile or laugh, become nauseated or vomit. Fear by its nature also seems to involve physiological responses, as hatred does not. In all three cases, fear, laughter, and disgust, the physiological response is involuntary or, rather, faster than voluntary control. Good speakers may get a hostile audience to laugh at something that, given their beliefs, they should not find funny. The undeniable physiological fact of their laughter indicates that they acknowledge contrary evidence they would rather abjure.

### Laughter

According to Henri Bergson, we laugh when we recognize that the immaterial soul has ceded control to the purely material or to the body acting on its own. The failure of attentiveness, flexibility, and vitality reveals the mechanical, automatic, and purely physical. "The soul imparts a portion of its winged lightness to the body it animates; the immateriality which thus passes into matter is what is called gracefulness. Matter, however, is obstinate and resists. It draws to itself the ever-alert activity of this higher principle, would fain convert it to its own inertia and cause it to revert to mere automatism."[9] Such reversion constitutes the humorous.

We intuitively try to imagine that we are minds in control of our selves, but the body often operates by its own inertia: "The attitudes, gestures, and movements of the human body are laughable in exact proportion as that body reminds us of a mere machine" (Bergson, 79). Moreover, the mind itself sometimes displays an unthinking

---

[9]     Henri Bergson, "Laughter," in *Comedy: "An Essay on Comedy" [by] George Meredith, "Laughter" [by] Henri Bergson,* ed. Wylie Sypher (Garden City, NY: Doubleday, 1956), 78.

momentum and is even funnier than the body when it, too, acts like a machine operating outside our will. That is one reason that Freudian slips can be funny: a mechanism independent of our conscious wills eludes its control and reveals what we would rather conceal.

As we intellectuals ought to know, absentmindedness is inherently funny. As we intellectuals ought to know, absentmindedness is inherently funny. Or consider Orwell's example of a mixed metaphor in a Communist pamphlet: "the fascist octopus has sung its swan song."[10] The two metaphors seem to be strung together by rules acting mechanically on their own, since no one really paying attention could have produced the absurdity of an octopus singing.

The history of comedy might almost be described as the history of representing the seven deadly sins plus the one that attempts to conceal the others, hypocrisy, each of which seem to operate on its own. Bergson's theory explains why it is much easier to make a comedy out of the more bodily sins—gluttony, greed, and lust—than of the more spiritual ones: wrath, envy, and pride. The greatest comedies deal with highly self-conscious vices, such as pride and hypocrisy, because it is harder to show self-consciousness escaping conscious control. For similar reasons, comedies about slothfulness are rare: how does one show non-action operating on its own? That is why *Oblomov* is such an achievement.

Bergson likes to cite Pascal, who is anything but a comic writer, and I think the reason is that both have a keen dualistic sense of the mind entombed in a body. They also sense consciousness entombed in a mental world that often acts like a body because it operates by habit. For Pascal, full consciousness is the rarest and most wonderful thing in the world—wonderful in the root sense of exciting wonder that somehow it could exist at all and that it could then be tethered to physical and mental flesh.

> Man is but a reed, the most feeble thing in nature, but he is
> a thinking reed. The entire universe need not arm itself to

---

10      George Orwell, "Politics and the English Language," in *Collected Essays and Letters of George Orwell, Vol. 4: In Front of Your Nose, 1945-1950*, ed. Sonia Orwell and Ian Angus (New York: Harcourt Brace, 1968), 134. Orwell observes: when images clash like this "it can be taken as certain that the writer is not seeing a mental image of the objects he is naming; in other words, he is not really thinking."

destroy him. A vapor, a drop of water, suffices to kill him. But if the universe were to destroy him, man would still be more noble than that which kills him, because he knows that he dies.... The universe knows nothing of this.[11]

Overlook the wonder of consciousness imprisoned and become ridiculous. Appreciate it and discover the essence of the comic in life.

Tolstoy captured the very essence of comedy when he described Pierre's reaction to having been imprisoned in a hut. All of a sudden Pierre bursts into laughter:

> "Ha, ha, ha!" laughed Pierre. And he said aloud to himself: "The soldier did not let me pass. They took me and shut me up. They held me captive. Who is 'me'?... Me? Me—is my immortal soul! Ha, ha, ha! Ha, ha, ha!..." and he laughed till the tears came to his eyes.
>
> ... High overhead in the luminous sky hung the full moon.... And farther still, beyond these fields and forests, was the bright shimmering horizon luring one on to infinity. Pierre contemplated the heavens, and the remote, receding glimmering stars.
>
> "And all that is mine, all that is within me, and is me!" he thought. "And they caught all that and put it in a shed and barricaded it with planks!" (W&P, 1217)

### Disgust

My idea is this: Comedy is by its nature Platonic and dualistic, but when we experience disgust we implicitly endorse an Aristotelian philosophy.

Aristotle's doctrine of forms and the soul is not dualistic. For Aristotle, form is inseparable from matter, because it inheres in matter and gives it shape. Form does not exist on its own, any more than there can be color or shape without a thing that is colored or shaped. Believing in the independence of forms, as Plato did, is like supposing that because we can mentally abstract the properties of color, somewhere, in absolute purity, color must exist by itself.

---

[11]    Blaise Pascal, *Pensées,* trans. A. J. Kailsheimer (Baltimore: Penguin, 1966), 95. Translation amended.

For Aristotle, soul shapes the matter of living things. Psyche is Aristotle's term for the form of a living object, and psychology is the study of the formal factor that makes a living object what it is.[12] Psyche is therefore not separable from body. More accurately, form (or soul) is a shaping power, an entelechy, that is in the process of shaping matter. Thus, in nutrition (performed by the "digestive" soul), food becomes assimilated into flesh. Living involves not just form but also forming.

We can arrive at a good first approximation of the nature of disgust if we say that it constitutes our reaction to *the failure of soul* in the Aristotelian sense. We experience disgust when living matter escapes the shaping power of form, when soul weakens and so leaves relatively unformed organic being. Bodies disintegrate and rot, disease deforms, parasites invade, processes normally kept private or internal are exposed to view: all these disgusting events testify to the failure of Aristotelian soul.

That is one reason Rembrandt's famous dissection painting, *The Anatomy Lesson of Dr. Joan,* is especially nauseating. It shows the corpse of a man just dead whose viscera have been removed and whose brain is being carefully taken apart (the outer membrane has just been removed). The face stares blankly at us, as if to remind us that ever so recently it bore witness to a soul governing itself and the rest of the body. Form still lingers, or else there would be no point in the dissection. Form taken apart before it falls apart; that is what this painting portrays.

I therefore believe Martha Nussbaum is incorrect when she says that we experience disgust at our own animality and materiality, a conclusion that seems driven by her political and social agenda. It is not human materiality but the failure of form to govern materiality that disgusts. After all, the very materiality of beautiful, erotic bodies attracts us. Marilyn Monroe's flesh was not perceived as disgusting. Each period's ideal of beauty expresses a different conception of how form should govern matter.

Nussbaum wants to reject disgust as the basis for any social policy because disgust, in her view, reflects a Platonic dualism that rejects body. Such dualism, she believes, is false, and leads to what she calls "shady social practice, in which the discomfort people feel over the

---

12       I paraphrase the paraphrase of W. T. Jones, *A History of Western Philosophy,* vol. 1 (New York: Harcourt Brace, 1952), 196.

fact of having an animal body is projected outwards onto vulnerable people and groups" (Nussbaum, *Hiding,* 74). But disgust is not Platonic but Aristotelian. What disgusts is not body *per se,* but body that escapes from shape, form, and soul.

### Rot and Skin

While laughter betrays the mind's unsure relation to the body and the body-like qualities of the mind itself, disgust is about the mind-like qualities of body. It is about the shaping power inherent in an organic being that makes it what it is and allows its processes to go on as they should.

If so, we should expect that what we find most disgusting is what is most like us and yet has lost shaping power: the rotting human corpse. In the literature of disgust, the rotting corpse does play the role of exemplar. By contrast, "the body beautiful"displays form perfectly shaping matter with nothing left over, or with perhaps one small exception, like a tiny mole, that all the more forcefully reminds us of the forming power operative elsewhere.

Ovid tells the story of Apollo, who himself symbolizes perfect form, stripping the skin of Marsyas, who had challenged him to a flute contest and lost.

> And as he cried the skin cracked from his body
> In one wound, blood streaming over muscles,
> Veins stripped naked, pulse beating; entrails could be
> Counted as they moved, even the heart shone red
> Within the breast (cited in Menninghaus, 79).

Stripped skin turns the body into a mass of biological processes no longer held together by any guiding force: skin, which holds together physically, stands in for soul, which holds together processually. To lose one's skin is to lose one's soul, and Marsyas screams, "Why are you tearing me from myself?" (Menninghaus, 79).

### Table Manners

In Brobdingnag, Gulliver has trouble eating the most delectable food because he can see flies, as large as larks, "alight upon my victuals, and leave their loathsome excrement or spawn behind, which to me was very visible, though not to the natives of that country" (GT, 314-5).

Gulliver is also disgusted at how the gracious queen eats, "which was for some time a very nauseous sight. She would craunch the wing of a lark, bones and all, between her teeth, although it were nine times as large as that of a full-grown turkey" (GT, 311).

Norbert Elias famously argues that the history of table manners shows a gradual attempt to distance one's self from the sheer animality of eating: over time, people develop codes that forbid the diner to touch his anus, blow his nose, or put dirty hands into communally shared dishes.[13] People gradually learned to prepare food so that it becomes symbolically transformed, not mere animal flesh but veal marsala, or as English allows us to say, not pig but pork. We move from hands to a knife to elaborate silverware, or in the Far East to chopsticks, which dictate that food be cut into very small pieces as unbestial as possible.

In Aristotle's terms, it is as if the cooking and serving of food already began the process of the soul's assimilation of matter into form, which is why in some cultures (and for some people) food is supposed to remind the consumer of the animal as little as possible. Many find internal organs, from the brain to the kidney, disgusting, and some extend this disgust to meat on the bone or with the skin. Vegetarianism may arise not only from humaneness but also from disgust. A roast pig with the head visible or the dish the French call *tête de veau* is either disgusting or a delicacy, for "delicacy" often means that the diner has the high culture to see the work of artistic preparation where others cannot. Only a barbarian or a connoisseur (in the usual sense) would eat brains.

### Mind Has Fled

In Bruges I saw Gerard David's two-paneled painting entitled "The Judgment of Cambyses," which was based on a story in Herodotus and commissioned for the Bruges town hall. The first panel shows in the background an official taking a bribe, and in the foreground his arrest. In the second panel's gruesome foreground, we see the punishment: he is, like Marsyas, having his skin slowly stripped from his body. In the background, his son has inherited his father's post but as a reminder against corruption must always display his father's skin.

---

13    See Norbert Elias, *The Civilizing Process* (Oxford: Blackwell, 2000), 45–182.

What is truly awful about this painting is not so much the stripping of the skin but the expression of the man's face, which does *not* show pain, suffering, or despair. Those horrors have evidently already been endured, and so we see what succeeds them: a complete mental absence. The still-living man's mind has departed along with his Aristotelian soul, which has died while the man's organs still function by sheer inertia. This is truly a living corpse (*zhivoi trup*) with a dead soul (*mertvaya dusha*).

Something quite similar appears in Titian's painting of the flaying of Marsyas, which is much more horrible than the story as Ovid tells it. Apollo is delicately stripping skin from Marsyas's body, which is hanging upside down, while a little lapdog incongruously licks up blood from the ground. The dog's meal hints at the digestive soul, which presumably Marsyas still has.

What is worst of all is that Marsyas no longer appears to be suffering. He is beyond suffering because he is now a still living body from which the mind—the higher sort of soul that for Aristotle differentiates us as human—is now absent. Various figures of different species, humanoid and animal, look on in voyeuristic curiosity, evidently fascinated by the repulsive scene.

Here again we have before us the ultimate mystery of soul. The Aristotelian understanding of soul, dramatized by stripping, can also generate fascinating disgust. What does the complete absence of mind show about our humanness?

### Dostoevsky and Holbein's "Christ in the Tomb"

Horribly enough, David's and Titian's paintings convey the sense that soul cannot transcend body. The paintings embody a conception the very opposite of one Dostoevsky admired, which was of saints who could laugh with contempt at the torturers burning them alive.

Now consider the Holbein painting of "Christ in the Tomb" that, in *The Idiot*, so fascinates Myshkin, Rogozhin, and Ippolit. All three agree that it is a painting that could make one lose one's faith. Why? The answer cannot be simply that it shows Christ's suffering, because, as Ippolit notes, it has been Church doctrine since the earliest ages that "Christ's suffering was not symbolical but actual, and that his body was therefore completely subject to the laws of nature" (I, 388). Portraying Christ's suffering should endorse, not shake, faith.

The problem, I think, lies not with the suffering itself, but with what has happened as a result of the suffering. Jesus's face has the same horrifying blankness as the official in David's painting. Ippolit notes that artists typically paint Christ with extraordinary beauty of face in spite of the agonies he suffers. But in this face "there is no trace of beauty. It is in every detail the corpse of a man who has been wounded, tortured, beaten by the guards and the people … and after that has undergone the agony of crucifixion, lasting for six hours at least." In that face one sees that "the great wide-open whites of the eyes glitter with a deathly glassy light" (I, 388). *No one is there.*

The horror of the painting is that the soul, or rather the part of it that makes one human, has evidently disintegrated before death. Only the lowest part of the animal soul—sensitivity—remains, while the higher soul that makes one human has departed. If this is how it was with the Savior, then we cannot credit a dualistic model in which Christ gives up the ghost, saying, "it is finished": by then, his soul was already dead. Therefore it cannot have left his body at death, harrowed hell for three days, and then returned to his body to rise again.

This painting is not Platonic, but Aristotelian: the soul subsides in the body, in the form of the body; and as the body loses form, it loses soul. Soul cannot exist outside the body and can be destroyed piecemeal even before the body. That is why it is hard to accept that anyone seeing the dead Jesus like that could believe that He would rise again. Ippolit asks: "If the Teacher could have seen Himself on the eve of the crucifixion, would He have gone up to the cross and died as He did?" (I, 389).

When the shaping form, the human image, is lost, so is the soul. Faith can survive agony much more easily than it can survive disgust. I think that is why, immediately after his description of the painting, Ippolit formulates his question in terms of image and imagelessness: "Is it possible to perceive as an image that which has no image?" Can the one who has lost his soul still have a soul to rise?

* * *

We watch dramas, see paintings, and read literary works that raise ultimate questions about the soul with voyeuristic curiosity. Sometimes they invite us to identify, and then we can easily be horrified that the soul can be so violated. At other times, they provoke disgust, which suggests that the soul might no longer be there at all. Which is more horrifying, or more fascinating, it is hard to say.

## Chapter Six

## MISANTHROPOLOGY IN VERSE: AN ONEGIN OF OUR TIMES

*By Alicia Chudo*

### I

As Walter brooded "weak and weary"
On Poe and onomatopoeia
He wished he could return to Theory,
Forget trochaic diarrhea,
Abandon texts you force to fit,
Leave literature for "comp lit."
In one short term he'd have his wish
And read no Fielding, only Fish,
No poems, just *texts* and *parataxis*.
*Desire* takes the place of joy,
*Thematization* of Tolstoy,
As theory transmutes work to *praxis*.
So long as schism yields to schism
He'll never read without an *-ism*.

### II

So thought a would-be critical theorist
Who found poetic fire chilling,
An anti-bourgeois pro-careerist,
Our heir to Richards, Brooks, and Trilling.
Admirers of Pushkin and *Onegin*
(Whose devotees now go a-beggin'),
My hero, with no more ado,
I proudly introduce to you:
Young Walter Samuel Alladish
Attended Duke and Santa Cruz
Where you, dear reader, loved t'amuse
Yourselves with theories dark and faddish
Until you found the one to suit
All texts you'd care to hermeneut.

## III

His mother's antics always bored him.
A Bolshie heir to factories,
She financed marches and ignored him.
(His dad still wore phylacteries.
He muttered, shrugged, and shook his head
And gave his boychik up for dead,
Especially when "in the know"
The youth embraced the PLO,
Confiding that there was no way
A comp lit major could demur
From opposition *de rigeur*,
Since *victim studies* now held sway.
He mentioned Heraclitus' river.
With eyes rolled up, his dad sat *shiva*.)

## IV

The young Alladish loved to play;
He aped his teachers and forgot
That he was he and they were they
And whether role was self or not.
His shrinks detected abnormality
And called the deviance *performality*,
Which leads at last to *mimicism*.
(His dad just called it cynicism.
But no one listened to the father
Who thought in terms of "right" and "wrong"
And not in terms from Freud or Jung.)
Alladish never thought to bother
If absent selfhood is pathology
Or present self, ontotheology.

## V

His dissertation now completed,
Alladish as assistant prof
Old class notes every day repeated
Until his students had enough.

He played each theorist's perfect clone,
And answered the department phone:
"W. S. Alladish is the name,
Comp Lit and Theory is the game."
What power wished was his desire.
Avoiding junior prof neurotics,
He shared the chairman's semiotics
(He knew who was the Signifier)
And fenced (not first) with those she fenced with.
(The first, he knew, would be dispensed with.)


### VI

With time he was the perfect miser;
No pedagogy ever bound him.
He served as undergrad advisor
Though students never yet have found him.
Except for two: the first knew beer,
The second had the chairman's ear.
What more was needed? Friends assured
He won the Pedagogue Award.
His junior colleagues all averred
The students loved him just as they did;
Which means, in private, they all hated
The man they praised but jointly feared.
They stressed the splendid role he'd played.
(That's how a reputation's made.)


### VII

His graduate students he'd advise
They never had to read a "classic"
And certainly not read it twice
Unless you held beliefs Jurassic
That "authors wisdom should impart"
And "texts are integral as art."
Such views he deemed, above all, sorry.
One makes one's meanings *a priori*.
"To guarantee interpretation
You have to know the text is empty,

Means what you please, said Humpty Dumpty.
No difference with evaluation.
We make each painting in the gallery.
And that is how we earn our salary."[1]

## VIII

"All English profs who love to read,
Historians who value facts,
You're relics we've long ceased to need,
That 'same old cast of cataracts.'
For facts, agreed both Marx and Kant
Are made to order as you want.
The only thing that makes them 'true'
Depends on what you need to do.
All other theories are erroneous,
All science equally as specious
As atomism in Lucretius
Or Platonism in Petronius."
He never fails to earn a kudo
By calling one more science pseudo.

## IX

He taught TV, games, comics, porno
While always *privileging* the new.
Improving Habermas, Adorno,
He synthesized them with Bourdieu.
The canon was his constant enemy;
It serves the interests of *hegemony*.
So-called aesthetic valuation
Preserves the forms of *domination*.
A course in classics always fails
In gender, class, and social history.
We must demystify the mystery
Of Dead White European Males
And show it's either us or them.

---

[1]     Written in Durham.

(You'll never learn that from a DWEM.)


X

By "us" he meant the combination
Of sufferers and academics.
His ever-growing reputation
Was based on deftly turned polemics:
Some die from bourgeois exploitation,
We teach with but three months vacation.
Some starve, and some have wounds that fester;
We teach two courses per semester!
We have to publish, others wonder
What happenstance will feed them next.
To help, we deconstruct the text
And tear its signifier asunder.
To battle the reactionary
We show all signs are arbitrary.


XI

He hated every "pious message"
And so his students called him "Pilate."
"You needn't read; for any passage
Just choose your theory and apply it.
You have to write on *Adam Bede*?
One random page is all you need.
Good theories come with guarantees,
So work on any text you please."
Thus Walter sought an invitation
To talk at a prestigious meeting;
Without a thought he might be cheating,
Prepared to give an explanation
Of Pushkin's curious allure,
All phrased in terms of *écriture*.


XII

*Onegin*'s a novel told in verse,
And poetry he found a bore.

All narratives he hated worse;
This poem he managed to ignore.
The new advanced lit education
Let Walter pass examination
In *areas* the student chooses
And other forward-looking ruses.
And now he had to give a lecture
About a work he didn't know;
But Walter had his *method*, so
He wrote on Pushkin's *empty texture*.
His theme and theory worked in tandem,
And Walter picked a page at random.

### XIII

Here's Walter at his writing table.
With implements he dully fingers,
He reads as long as he is able.
He picks his text and briefly lingers
Ten minutes on the chosen lines
And then their meaning undermines.
And here, alas, an explanation:
Not knowing Russian, he resorted
For evidence to be aborted
To Nesposobny's verse translation—
Enough to make another falter,
It didn't matter squat to Walter.

[Fragment from *Eugene Onegin: A Novel in Verse*]

### XIV

"My uncle, principled old ass,
Fell ill so well it was no joke,
Compelled respect with great finesse
(A case that others well might note)
And could have wished for nothing more.
But what a God-forsaken bore
To serve a sick man night and day

And not to stir a step away;
What lethal hypocratic cunning
To entertain one half alive
Adjust his pillow, heave a sigh,
And sadly for his pills go running.
And mutter through a practiced moan,
'When *will* the devil claim his own?'"


### XV

So thought our hero in his chaise
While speeding past the posting stations,
By Zeus's will and Russia's laws
The heir to all his dear relations.
Friends of Lyudmila and Ruslan!
Who want to know this novel's plan:
*In medias res,* without ado,
My hero I present to you.
Eugene Onegin, long my friend
Was born upon the Neva's banks
Where maybe you, like all us cranks,
Were born, now shine, will meet your end.
There I, too, used to have a spree,
But now the north is bad for me.[2]


### XVI

An honest servant of the state,
His father earned less than he'd spend.
Gave countless balls, filled each guest's plate,
And then went bankrupt in the end.
Eugene was rescued by kind Fate:
On him *Madame* at first would wait.
*Monsieur* replaced her one fine year.
"The boy's precocious, but a dear."
A wretched Frog, *Monsieur l'Abbé,*
In order not to vex the lad

---

[2]     Written in Bessarabia.

Would never teach him good from bad,
Instructed in a jesting way,
Ignored his "pranks," or maybe talk
Of taking kiddie for a walk.


## XVII

And when he reached the stormy years,
"That time of hope and sweetest doubt,
Of youthful dreams and pleasant tears,"
*Monsieur l'Abbé* he had kicked out.
I give you reader, young Eugene
Who captivates the social scene.
A London *dandy* came to view
And made his Petersburg *debut*.
His French was flawless, all allowed,
He knew when, how, and what to say,
His speech a dance, his dance display,
He moved with ease, with grace he bowed,
And what else is there? It was clear
He was a charming cavalier.


## XVIII

Some time or other, some old way,
We all have learned some proper lies,
So we can voice the right cliché
To get someone to think us wise.
Onegin, though, had still more learning,
So judges stern and men discerning
Pronounced him, with a sigh, a pedant.
They claimed he even had the talent
To speak with charm, with polish state
The latest in imported truths.
Important topics in the news
He passed in silence, or would wait
Till ladies yawned, and then he chose
A pointed epigram to close.

### XIX

Among us Latin's now *passé*:
But then Onegin knew enough
To charm ennui or spleen away
By citing some wise epigraph.
He'd prove that Juvenal lashed folly;
When writing notes, he'd close them *vale*.
At feast, he'd say "Trimalchio dines";
From Virgil he could botch two lines.
And though he had no inclination
To sift through chronologic dust
He could an anecdote adjust
To fit the present situation.
Some pithy tale he could recite
To grace whatever might seem trite.

[end of Alladish's reading]

### XX

"Ennui, hypocrisy, and spleen
Reflect the Signified's senescence;
This carnival (he cites Bakhtin)
Recalls the hero's fear of *presence*.
All value is eliminated,
The poem's de-axiologated.
Its autotelic hygienics
Bequeaths *Onegin* to 'Eugenics.'"
Alladish took most joy in dooming
All human interest in the text.
Of course, you guess what he did next:
The work, he proved, is *self-consuming*.
It has no meaning through and through.
(For him, at least, it's largely true.)

### XXI

With gender theory's rage exceeding
He blamed Descartes for anorexia

And dreamed up a new way of reading,
Which he called *carnival dyslexia.*
This theory made his reputation.
It authorized new obfuscation,
The old ones now a known arrangement.
Alladish found the new *bestrangement.*
Interpreting began anew.
The terms he coined were all displayed
In hermeneutic games now played
So critics had enough to do.
To undermine the *status quo*
They copied Walter's *style nouveau.*

## XXII

*"Dyslexic textualities*
Command inversion of the signs.
Disrupting staid realities
The critic *dislocates* the lines.
He moves an ending to the center
And so allows new sense to enter.
Replace or change a primal word
Whose opposite can be inferred.
So meaning might be sublimated,
Use criticism's archest cunning
(When all else fails, resort to punning).
Relations must be *dis-related.*
Erase or cover all the traces
Of stable texts and social places."

## XXIII

With Walter's powerful connections
Dyslexic readings won the day.
Success in turn ensured election
As president of MLA.
No Ayatollah could be wiser
Rewarding every sympathizer.
Alladish complimented most
Those adding *post-* to last year's *post-.*

With all his rapid revolutions
And with the certainty of rhyme
He won awards from Guggenheim.
New panels passed his resolutions.
He soon became the new *Times* sage
With columns on the op-ed page.

### XXIV

But my muse, with her wizened ears
And long passé humanity
The sounds of older ages hears
Until I doubt my sanity.
In all new academic roles
I see the shadows of dead souls,
In MLA's new Ayatollah
The figure of Savonarola.
I call the shade of Lev Tolstoy
To banish this new catechism
By writing *What Is Criticism?*
And scatter theorists who annoy
This humble bard, Alicia Chudo
(Of course, the name's, like theory, pseudo).

**Alicia Chudo** teaches Russian and Comparative Literature at Midwestern University. Her first book, *Sadistic Victims: Self-Abasement in the Novel and Self-Righteousness in Criticism,* won the Jonathan Swift prize from the American League of Misanthropes. Her notorious study *And Quiet Flows the Vodka: or When Pushkin Comes to Shove: The Curmudgeon's Guide to Russian Literature and Culture* (Northwestern University Press, 2000) earned the contempt of Russians and Russianists the world over. Her most recent article is "Susan Sontag as Metaphor."

Part Four

# What Is Literary Education?

## Chapter Seven

# NOVELISTIC EMPATHY, AND HOW TO TEACH IT

> I have to answer with my own life for what I have experienced
> and understood in art, so that everything I have experienced
> and understood would not remain ineffectual in my life....
> Art and Life are not one, but they must become one, united
> in the unity of my responsibility.
>
> — *Mikhail Bakhtin*[1]

## A Crisis of Massive Proportions

Go to the English department, gather round the coffee pot, and listen
to the Great Kvetch. Someone is sure to cite some recent lament about
an underestimated crisis threatening the world.

"We are in the midst of a crisis of massive proportions and grave
global significance," Martha Nussbaum begins her recent book, *Not
for Profit: Why Democracy Needs the Humanities* (NFP). And what is this
crisis of massive proportions? No, not imminent economic collapse,
nor looming environmental disaster, nor the spread of nuclear
weapons. At least we discern such threats, but the worst of all "goes
largely unnoticed, like a cancer; a crisis that is likely to be, in the long
run, far more damaging to the future of democratic self-government"
(NFP, 7-8). When a writer invokes the insidious progress of a cancer,
you know she hopes to forestall the objection that little visible evidence
supports her argument.

This cancer threatening democracy and the world is: *declining
enrollments in literature courses*. And declined they have. In a much-
cited article in *The American Scholar*, William M. Chace (a professor
of English and former president of Wesleyan University and Emory
University) reports that from 1970/71 — the peak year for enrollments —
to 2003/4, the number of English majors declined from 7.6% to 3.9%,
and majors in foreign literatures from 2.5% to 1.3%.[2] The Modern

---

[1]  I have modified the translation in M. M. Bakhtin, "Art and Answerability,"
AA, 1-2.

[2]  William M. Chace, "The Decline of the English Department: How it

Language Association's Teagle Report of 2009 reports a decline (in absolute numbers) of 18% for English majors between the high-water mark of 1971 and 2004, and 27% for foreign literature majors since its high-water mark in 1969. As a percentage of total degrees awarded, the decline is much steeper.[3] But why is this crisis so important to anyone except humanities professors?

Somewhere, I suppose, there is a shoemaker envisioning the collapse of civilization due to the rising price of leather.

Unless we solve this crisis, Nussbaum warns, democracy, decency, and "critical thinking" will all disappear. But to solve a crisis one must identify its cause. So why is it that students are choosing to study economics or chemistry rather than literature?

Nussbaum widely avoids one Luddite answer increasingly given: because of technology, students now have short attention spans and so cannot be expected to read Dickens or Tolstoy. Are chemistry and economics better suited for the attentionally challenged? Does anyone really doubt that it is easier to pass an English class with little work than the pre-med curriculum? But Nussbaum still wants to blame the students and the culture that has shaped them.

When I was growing up in the Bronx, the owner of the local Jewish deli, whose meats smelled vaguely rancid and whose bagels seemed to start out already a day old, attributed his failing business to the vulgarization of taste. In every age the unappreciated consider themselves geniuses born in the wrong time. Since I started teaching literature some thirty-five years ago, humanities professors have been attributing declining enrollments to their students' materialism, careerism, and philistine desire for profit. As the title of her book indicates, Nussbaum arrives at the same self-serving answer.

The book's conclusion cites Harvard president Drew Faust, who regrets "a deep decline the percentage of students majoring in the liberal arts and sciences, and an accompanying increase in preprofessional undergraduate degrees." Faust asks whether universities "have

---

Happened and What Could Be Done to Reverse It," *The American Scholar* (Autumn 2009), http://theamericanscholar.org/the-decline-of-the-english-department/. For discussion of this article in *The Chronicle of Higher Education*, see http://chronicle.com/forums/index.php?topic=63571.0.

3      Modern Language Association, "Report to the Teagle Foundation on the Undergraduate Major in Language and Literature," http://www.mla.org/pdf/2008_mla_whitepaper.pdf, 15.

become too captive to the immediate and worldly purposes they serve? Has the market model become the fundamental and defining identity of higher education?" (NFP, 124). No one ever lost the allegiance of the faculty by blaming "the market."

Can it really be that students are more materialistic now than in those proverbial eras of backwardness, the 1950s and 1980s? Professor Chace notes that despite reduced materialist incentives since the recession, and "the debacle on Wall Street," students "are still wagering that business jobs will be there when the economy recovers." Chace, as it happens, is one of the few who asks whether literature professors might themselves be selling the academic equivalent of bad-tasting bagels. "Unable to change history or rewrite economic reality," he comments, English professors "might at least have kept their own house in order. But this they have not done." He suggests that the decline might have something to do with "the failure of departments of English across the country to champion, with passion, the books they teach and to make a strong case to undergraduates that the knowledge of those books and the tradition in which they exist is a human good in and of itself…. They have distanced themselves from the young people interested in good books." If so, then perhaps students avoid literature classes not because they are wagering on business degrees but because they reason that if English professors do not seem to believe in literature, why should they?

For decades, literature professors have been teaching that the canon is a mere construct; that social power relations alone determine what is considered great literature; and that there are no intrinsic or objective standards of greatness. To think otherwise is to endorse the greatest philosophical enemy of social justice, "essentialism," that is, the belief that people or artifacts have inherent qualities. Literature is just another social document, and the turn to "cultural studies," where the works once considered intrinsically great enjoy no "privilege" over other documents, has followed.

But if Shakespeare is not intrinsically great, and if great works teach us nothing one cannot learn more easily elsewhere, why bother reading them? It does not seem to occur to most English professors that if what predominant theories assert is correct, students would be fools to study literature. Could the decline in enrollments reflect not so much materialism or preprofessionalism as good sense?

One reason I wonder at these debates is that my experience has been so different from the trend. As it happens, I teach Northwestern

University's best-enrolled humanities course, with 600 students, and the academic year before last, two of the courses with the highest enrollment (the third featured live sex demonstrations).

These are classes in Russian literature. In one, students read Dostoevsky's *Brothers Karamazov* and Tolstoy's *Anna Karenina*, and in the other, they read *War and Peace*.

In most universities, enrollments in "Tolstoyevsky" courses hover at around twenty, since students who search for literature courses under "English" do not know to look as well under "Slavic Languages and Literatures." I am even more gratified that a large number of students report on official evaluation forms that, though they had been skeptical of "all the hype," this course really did make them understand why literature is worth serious study.

No student has ever told me that he or she does not take more literature courses because, in these difficult economic times, one needs to devote every moment to maximizing future income, which, after all, is what really matters. On the contrary, students respond by describing some literature course they have taken, which left them thinking that, apart from "appearing educated" or getting an easy A, they had nothing to gain from taking any more. When I heard their descriptions of these classes, I saw their point. No hint of that experience appears in MLA reports.

If students take English, we are told, they will learn "critical thinking." Apart from the fact that every discipline claims to teach some form of critical thinking—is it absent from philosophy and cognitive science?—perhaps the problem is that the students are already adept enough at thinking critically to take literature professors who do not believe in literature at their word.

### Teaching as Subtraction

What can students learn from literature they cannot learn elsewhere? Why should they bother?

Literature professors rarely ask these questions. For understandable reasons, they assume the importance of their subject matter. But students are right to ask them. Any course is expensive: in money, in time, and in what economists call opportunity costs. To study seventeenth-century English lyric, one foregoes another course not just in something practical, but also in something that is also intellectually challenging.

Will Rogers once remarked, "We are all ignorant, only on different subjects." To teach anything well, you have to place yourself in the position of the learner who does not already know the basics and has to be persuaded that the subject is worth studying. One has to *subtract* knowledge and assumptions one has long since forgotten having learned. It's like reminding yourself you once did not know how to walk. Without such empathy and subtraction, teaching is unlikely to succeed.

All too often, undergraduate courses tacitly presume that students will become literature professors. And that is natural enough, since those are the sort of students literature professors most easily imagine. But if one wants to persuade future chemists, businessmen, and physicians to read novels, this approach will likely prove counterproductive.

For anyone but future English professors, does it make sense to teach theory in undergraduate courses? Would students not be wise to reason: either literature is less interesting than these theorists, or one first has to know very difficult and obscure methods before one even starts to read great works? If one has neither the taste nor time for such preliminaries, then literature will remain forever out of reach.

The first task is to get the student to *want* to read literature. Students see the point of wisdom, guidance in how to think about their values and decisions. We tend to laugh at such a conception as somehow philistine. An English class isn't church, nor is romantic poetry the Book of Common Prayer! When students want to know "the meaning of life," we smile—the sort of smile we assume students can't detect. However, people's ability to perceive condescension is usually sharper than we imagine.

Clara Claiborne Park—best known for her book about raising an autistic child, *The Siege*[4]—devoted an essay to the experience of teaching literature in a community college. At the end of the semester, one farmboy asked her: "Mrs. Park. We've read what Homer says about the afterlife, and what Plato says, and now we're reading what Dante says and they're all different. Mrs. Park. *Which one of them is true?*" She recalls her reaction: "I smile, of course. I suppress, just in time, the condescending laugh, the easy play to the class's few sophisticates,

---

[4]  Clara Claiborne Park, *The Siege: The First Eight Years of an Autistic Child, with an Epilogue, Fifteen Years Later* (Boston: Little, Brown, 1982).

who are already laughing surreptitiously.... But the open seriousness on the boy's face encourages reflection. Who, in this class, is reading as Plato and Dante would have expected to be read? And who is asking the right questions, I and my sophisticates, or this D-level student whom I have just time to realize I shall put down at my peril?"[5] As Tolstoy would ask, who should learn reading from whom? Don't teach simple students to be "sophisticated," teach the sophisticates to ask simple questions in a more profound way.

Ask yourself: why do you think Tolstoy, Dickens, and George Eliot wrote their novels? Surely it was not to provide obscure puzzles for scholars to solve! So much professional training leads us to forget what undergraduates know, that literature needs to mean something or it is not worth studying.

Park chose the title of her essay—"Rejoicing to Concur with the Common Reader"—to challenge the professional establishment. She was alluding to Dr. Johnson's famous comment about Thomas Gray's "Elegy in a Country Churchyard": "I rejoice to concur with the common reader; for by the common sense of readers, uncorrupted with literary prejudices, after all the refinements of subtilty and the dogmatism of learning, must finally be decided all claims to poetic honors." By citing these lines, she utters them anew. They remind us that the dogmatism of learning and laboriously acquired refinements can obscure the obvious. This is never a message professionals like to hear.

## Philology Substitutes

What Johnson's passage does not say, but Park's essay does, is that professionals have a stake in not concurring with the common reader whenever possible. Professionals have to justify their status above laymen. Since many people love Jane Austen and Dickens, literature professors must do something that requires training and differs from what a nonprofessional could do. There must be something requiring initiation and certification.

---

5     Clara Claiborne Park, "Rejoicing to Concur with the Common Reader," *Rejoining the Common Reader: Essays, 1962-1990* (Evanston, IL: Northwestern University Press, 1991), 1-2. The epigraph for this volume contains the same sentences from Bakhtin as does the present essay.

Serious university instruction in English began by imitating the study of classical languages and requiring a lot of philology. As Slavists my age or older will recall, that used to be true of our discipline as well. I have a recently retired colleague who passed examinations demanding he translate on sight thirteenth century Bulgarian into fifteenth-century Polish. Even in my watered-down Yale program, I had to trace every word in a passage from Old Church Slavonic back to Proto-Indo-European, forward to modern Russian, and across to other Indo-European languages. When I entered Oxford as a graduate student in 1969, the requirements for an undergraduate degree in English included pages of topics in Old Norse and Old English, eventually proceeding to Middle English and the Renaissance. And then, on the last page of requirements, one line read: "English literature 1660 to the present." When I inquired what was meant by "the present," I was told that it had just been moved up from 1880 to 1914.

Such accomplishment required professional training. Without it, no reasonably literate person could read *Beowulf* or the *Volsungsaga* in the original. If one thinks of the sociology of the professions, it becomes pretty clear why the "new criticism" was bound to disappear. Like all critical schools, it had been applied so widely and its methods had become so familiar that something different was needed if professors were to publish or even retain their interest. The new criticism, however, posed the added problem that it could be done without much expert knowledge. It made, and was designed to make, literature available to nonspecialists. In so doing, it tacitly raised the question of why literature professors are needed in the first place.

So the profession developed *philology substitutes*, which do, without philology, what philology used to do. How much time do graduate students spend learning a critical vocabulary so as to say what might be said much more simply! We take pride in reading the Emperor's New Prose.

When Denis Dutton was alive, his journal, *Philosophy and Literature*, used to award an annual, unwanted prize to a prominent theorist guilty of especially bad writing. Winning samples exhibited the worst characteristics of contemporary theory—jargon, obscurity, pretension, vatic tone—in a dose so high as to reach what Dutton called "intellectual kitsch."[6] Homi Bhabba and Judith Butler shared, unasked,

---

[6]    For more on Dutton's contest, and similar competitions in badness, see the

the 1998 award, so one can see that Dutton did not choose obscure people as exemplars of obscure writing. These are not mute inglorious Miltons. Butler's prize-winning passage reads:

> The move from a structuralist account in which capital is understood to structure social relations in relatively homologous ways to a view of hegemony in which power relations are subject to repetition, convergence, and rearticulation brought the question of temporality into the thinking of structure, and marked a shift from a form of Althusserian theory that takes structural totalities as theoretical objects to one in which the insights into the contingent possibility of structure inaugurate a renewed conception of hegemony as bound up with the contingent sites and strategies of the rearticulation of power.[7]

I do understand this passage, but I wonder if that is a good thing. How many graduate students imagine that by mastering arcane language, and even learning to compose in it, they have actually accomplished something! And how many undergraduates, asked to read material like this, have decided to take a discipline whose complex terminology actually has precise meaning, like organic chemistry.

The Book of Proverbs tells us that wisdom "crieth without; she uttereth her voice in the streets" (Proverbs 1:20)—in the streets perhaps, but not in Crowe Hall!

To acquire wisdom, students ask—naïvely, we say—"what the author is saying." Perhaps professionalism explains why for almost a century we have developed one theory after another denying that the author's intentions, or authors themselves, matter. And yet, I know no one who reads without presuming the opposite. As with any communication, one has to assume it is constructed to effect a purpose, which implies human design.

Even if we know there is no single designer, as with epic poems that are the product of a long tradition, we posit a fictive author who sums up the tradition. We pretend there was such a person as "Homer." Otherwise, the work would not be a work at all, only a series

---

chapter on "witlessisms" in L&S, 96-111.

[7]     Cited by Dutton from Butler's "Further Reflections on the Conversations of Our Time," from *Diacritics* (1997), http://denisdutton.com/bad_writing. htm.

of pointless inscriptions. We have no choice but to posit authorship because, as with any communication, that is the only way to make it mean something. The author can be the unconscious, use disguises, and produce something resembling dreams as Freud describes them, but we must still personify this unconscious as an author with a purpose, as Freud does. Otherwise the dream would be precisely what he says it is not, a series of random physiological responses with no overall logical connection. He calls his book *The Interpretation of Dreams* to indicate that dreams are meaningful artifacts that, unlike mere neurological discharges, warrant interpretation.

### The *Cliffs Notes* Test

No author, no point. But if there is a point, why not simply state it? If what *Bleak House* says can be summed up in a paragraph, why not just read the summary? In fact, students often do make their way through required literature courses by reading a plot-and-message summary. If one cannot give a coherent reason why that won't do, then why should the student assume anything important is left out? The professor has to pass what might be called the *Cliff's Notes* test.

Just as assigning theory in beginning courses conveys a message about the dispensability of literature, so syllabi can suggest that, whatever might be affirmed publically, *Cliff's Notes* is good enough. Many years ago, when student course evaluations were published in printed form, I remember coming across responses to a course on Dickens. One comment at first amused me: "Don't take this course unless you want to read a lot of Dickens!" It seemed like an inane thing to say until I grasped what the student meant. The class assigned a Dickens novel a week to be discussed in two lectures. The first was devoted to Dickens's life and the other to the social conditions of the time. So much reading, with so little understanding of the work! It obviously made no difference whether one read *Bleak House* or *Cliff's Notes* (or nothing at all).

Even courses that do discuss the text defeat themselves when they assign a long novel a week. It is impossible for anyone but a highly accomplished reader with an empty schedule to read *Anna Karenina, Our Mutual Friend,* or *Middlemarch* attentively in a week. When professors ask students to do the impossible, they are in effect winking at shortcuts. And if one is not going to pay attention to each sentence, why *not* read the summary?

### Three Ways to Kill a Novel

#### 1. Execution by Technique

My informal survey suggests that very few students have taken high school or college literature classes that inspire further reading. Instruction kills interest in three main ways.

The most common approach might be called *technical*. It involves mastering a set of terms and methods to apply to any text. It is a sort of pre-theory.

Who is the protagonist, and who is the antagonist? Does the story have a narrator? Where is the denouement? Is there foreshadowing? Above all, this approach directs students to look for symbols and allegories. It is easy enough to discover Christ symbols. How many crosses or crossroads appear in *Crime and Punishment*! Water symbolism can almost always be found, since someone sooner or later will wash, drink, or see a lake or river. In *Huckleberry Finn* the Mississippi symbolizes freedom, while the Widow Douglas's house symbolizes civilization. In *Anna Karenina,* trains symbolize fate. Or modernization. Or the "transports" of love. Frou-Frou symbolizes Anna.

This approach can take a more sophisticated form. The teacher then is sure to speak not of "the work" but of "the text," that is, the words on the page and how they are woven together. It is as if "work" were what laymen said, while we professionals speak of "text." But in fact there is a crucial distinction between the two, the same one that Bakhtin drew between sentences and utterances.[8] Someone has to *say* an utterance to some real or potential listener for some reason. In an utterance, someone is trying to *do* something. If one imagines what Tolstoy and Austen were up to, one realizes immediately that they aimed to create not sentences, but an utterance using sentences, and, by the same token, not a text but a work.

If so, then the critic or student must first experience the *work* as a sensitive reader. Only then can he or she begin to analyze that experience and how it is created. The *text* is a tool for creating the experience, but unless one has the experience in the first place, one cannot analyze

---

8      Caryl Emerson and I discuss Bakhtin's theory of language, and the significance of this distinction, in chapter four of *Mikhail Bakhtin: Creation of a Prosaics* (Stanford: Stanford University Press, 1990).

it. One might as well confuse a building with its blueprint, and imagine that living in the blueprint will keep out the rain.

Students need to have such experiences, and not just be told of their results. It is crucial for them to see how one arrives at the interpretation and to live through that process. Otherwise, why not just memorize some critic's interpretation?

Some two decades ago I gave a series of lectures in Norway, where a theoretically sophisticated version of the textual approach reigned. One prominent scholar replied to my *Anna Karenina* paper by observing: "All my career I have been telling students not to do what you have done, that is, treat characters as real people with real problems and real human psychology. Characters in a novel are so many formal features, nothing more than words on a page. It is primitive to treat fictional people as real, as primitive as the spectator who rushed on stage to stay the hand of Judas." Well, if that is what she was teaching students, she was teaching them wrong. Characters in a novel are neither words on a page nor real people: they are *possible* people. When we think of their ethical dilemmas, we do not need to imagine that such people exist, only that such people and such dilemmas *could* exist.

But if we did not blind ourselves with professional notions, wouldn't it be obvious that we react to novelistic heroines as possible people? The "Judas" comment, which I first heard in so many words from a Jakobsonian instructor in graduate school, is a red herring. It is designed, like the Norwegian scholar's question, to allow only two alternatives, real people or textual features, and not the one we all intuitively know, people that are not real but could be. Readers who mistake theatre for reality are vanishingly rare, but almost everyone is moved by characters they know to be fictional. We never imagine searching archives for records confirming events in the lives of Anna Karenina or Dorothea Brooke, but we do wonder what we would do in their circumstances. Would we wonder about being in the circumstances of words on a page?

When students place themselves in a character's position, or recall they have been in a similar one, the last thing one wants to do is to tell them not to be so unsophisticated. It is obvious that George Eliot and Tolstoy did not have to work so hard to reproduce the way real people think, unless readers were meant to imagine people who really could exist. Students who imagine being such people are accepting the invitation the author and work extend. That is where the process of caring about works might well begin.

## 2. Death by Judgment

Somewhat less common is the approach that demands moral and social judgment. One faults or excuses author, character, or the society depicted according to the moral and social standards prevalent today, by which I mean those standards shared by professional interpreters of literature.

"If only divorce laws had been more enlightened, Anna Karenina would not have had such a hard time!" And if she had shared our views about (whatever the current consensus is discussing), she would have been so much wiser. Somewhere in a Solzhenitsyn novel there is a character who wonders why she has to read Tolstoy, Turgenev and the other Russian classics when they make ideological errors that today any twelve-year-old can identify. I asked one of my students who said she had never enjoyed reading literature what books she had been assigned, and she mentioned *Huckleberry Finn*. Pondering how to kill a book as much fun as that, I asked how it had been taught. She explained: "We learned it shows that slavery is wrong."

In this approach, the works of the past illuminate how far people have come or, perhaps, how much ahead of their time some writers were. The more they shared our beliefs, the better they were. Of course, numerous critical schools that judge or exonerate literary works are more sophisticated than that class on *Huck Finn*, but they all make the same mistake of presuming the correctness of one's own views and then measuring others against them. By its very nature, that stance makes it impossible to do anything but verify what one already believes. Students recognize very quickly that such reading is an elaborate form of self-compliment.

In *War and Peace*, Tolstoy writes of historians who judge figures of the past:

> In describing the part played by these historical personages who, in their opinion, caused what they call *the reaction*, the historians severely condemn them. All the famous people of that period, from Aleksandr and Napoleon to Madame de Staël, Photius, Schelling, Chateaubriand, Fichte, and the rest, pass before their stern tribunal and are acquitted or condemned according to whether they promoted *progress* or *reaction*.... In what does the substance of these strictures consist? It consists in the fact that a historic character like Aleksandr ... did not have the same conception of the welfare of humanity fifty years ago as a present-day professor who from his youth has been occupied

with learning, that is, with reading books, listening to lectures, and making notes (W&P, 1351-1353).

Just as one's own actions are "prudent" while the same actions performed by one's enemy are "cowardly," so "reactionary" is what our opponents are and "progress" is what we are trying to achieve. But unless one holds the highly dubious belief that History (with a capital H) has an inevitable direction, the word "progress" means nothing more than "what we believe." Who does not desire "progress"? Who wants things to get worse?

La Rochefoucauld remarked that "everyone complains of his memory but no one complains of his judgment" (LaR, 49). We may forget some fact, but we know our beliefs are right. Wisdom, however, entails imagining how the argument looks from the other side, that is, without presuming that the other person is venal, ignorant, malicious, or stupid, at least any more than one is oneself. For much the same reasons, it is puerile to summon Shakespeare, Milton, Austen, and Tolstoy before the stern tribunal of comp lit professors. Why not imagine what valid criticisms these authors would advance if they could see us?

*Us.* When I say "us," I do not mean all those *other* people of our society who do not share the views of Those Who Analyze Texts. When Intellectuals condemn what is wrong with "us," they usually mean Americans without postgraduate degrees. It's a strange use of the first person plural that excludes the first person singular and perhaps a few others. We need a new grammatical category—let's call it "the self-excluding we." By the way, the "self-excluding we" exists elsewhere, for example, when parents talk to young children: "We're having a little diarrhea today, aren't we?"[9]

Ambrose Bierce defined "egotist" as "a person of low taste and bad morals, who thinks more of himself than he does of me."[10] He might have added that when we say others are "in denial," we usually mean that they obstinately refuse to believe what we do.

One has to allow other perspectives to show the limitations of our own. Otherwise, one cannot learn anything and literature easily

---

[9]    And in the present essay.

[10]   So I remember the line that in my edition of Bierce reads: "a person of low taste, more interested in himself than in me." DD, 52.

becomes pointless. But if one engages in a real dialogue, new insights can emerge.

### 3. *Murder by Document*

One can kill a work a third way: treat the literary work as a *document* of its time. "The author didn't write in a vacuum, you know!" Dostoevsky shows us what urban life was like in nineteenth-century Russia. Dickens depicts the deplorable conditions of workers of his time. True enough, but a factory inspector's report might do even better.

The problem with this approach is that it puts the cart before the horse. One does not read Dostoevsky to learn about nineteenth-century Russia, one becomes interested in Russian history from reading its classics. After all, every culture has many periods, and one can't be interested in every period of every culture, so the argument about nineteenth-century Russia is bound to fail except with people already interested in Russian history.

What makes a work literary is that it is interesting (or meant to be interesting) to people who do not care about its original context. Of course, with any work one *could* reconstruct the exchange between author and original audience, and it might even be helpful to do so, but what makes the work literature worth reading is what goes beyond that. Dostoevsky illuminates psychological and moral problems that are still pertinent, even outside Russia!

In each of these approaches—the technical, judgmental, and documentary—true things are said. Works do indeed use symbols, they can show us slavery is wrong, and they illuminate their times. The problem is what these approaches do *not* achieve: they fail to give a reason for reading literature.

## Application

Is there something one can learn from literature one cannot learn as well or better elsewhere? Actually, there are numerous things, as numerous and various as the genres of literature and the geniuses who have written in them. Since many of the greatest minds around the world have written literature, the very fact that such a question needs to be asked suggests that we have strayed far off track.

I remember as a graduate student hearing that critics no longer believe that Proust is sugar-coated Bergson. I was surprised to learn they ever had. Why would we ever have needed Proust at all in such a case, since we already had Bergson, who is, after all, a lot easier to read? To my surprise, the explanation for the change in critical opinion had nothing to do with the source of my surprise. It was simply that no one cared about Bergson any more.

Then, as now, a great deal of Dostoevsky criticism discovered in his novels an exemplification of Russian Orthodox theology. These readings have always seemed forced to me—Dostoevsky was too shaky in his faith and heterodox in his views—but a more important problem with such criticism presents itself. If this were true, who would need Dostoevsky? Most readings of Tolstoy's fiction also disappointed me because, if they were correct, he simply wove a nice story about some ideas more clearly enunciated in Copleston's history of philosophy.

In all such approaches, the critic apparently knows everything the author had to say and more. If an author's work conveys Kantian or Hegelian ideas, the critic detects them and thereby determines its meaning. Beyond the sources, the critic has also mastered, as the author could not have, what more recent thinkers have said about the same issues. The critic can read Heidegger and his expositors. Tolstoy's narrative may have made these issues more easily graspable, but so would *Heidegger for Dummies*. If that is all Tolstoy has to offer, who needs him?

When critics approach literature with a theoretical method, they can usually explicate meanings beyond the author's awareness. Since such critics evidently know more than the authors they discuss, the question again arises: why read Trollope when one can read critical theory applied to him? Take this as a rule of thumb: whenever a critic speaks of "applying" a theory, something has gone badly wrong. All those introductions to graduate studies that apply a theory a week to a given "text" go a long way toward making their subject matter dispensable.

The work subject to "application" becomes merely an illustration of how the theory works, sort of like a patient with a toothache brought in to show the dentist's skill. Students are smart enough to know that in this model, one patient is as good as another. There will always be someone to cure, and what is important is the technique of curing. One studies dentistry, not patientry.

Perhaps this model owes a debt to the view variously espoused in Plato, the romantics, and several more recent schools, that poets do not understand their own works but serve as mere transmitters of truths beyond their ken. It is obvious that this tradition can picture the writer as a mere "scriptor," rather than author, through whose pen social forces reveal themselves. So does the classic Marxist idea of the "superstructure" and "the base," with a writer unwittingly expressing the economic interests of a social class.

From theory to theory many things change, but the structural place reserved for the critic remains. He sees more deeply while unmasking disguises to show what is really going on. Is it any wonder that critics find such a role agreeable? You might as well be startled that priests embrace their indispensable role in saving souls.

## Novelistic Discoveries

But is it possible, as naïve readers suppose, that a great work contains wisdom exceeding any theory? Could it be the case that writers are wiser and deeper than critics? What if it would be more sensible to regard Bergson as watered-down Proust, rather than the reverse?

And perhaps unprofessional readers and other authors are correct when they judge Tolstoy an especially keen observer of other people and of his own mind? What if the strikingly realistic sense of his works, on which readers constantly remark, reflects his strikingly fine perception leading to discoveries about how people think? Then it would no longer be difficult to understand why one should study Tolstoy. The philosophers he read would not already contain his ideas but would have served as catalysts of his discoveries.

Bakhtin insisted that such discoveries indeed belong to great authors, major works, and important genres. For this reason, I have been arguing for decades that, if one defines "theory" by what has prevailed in America in recent decades, then Bakhtin is the great anti-theorist. I first became attracted to his thought when I read him in preparation for writing my dissertation about Dostoevsky. I was immediately struck that he had not so much interpreted Dostoevsky according to a theory but had derived various theories from attentive reading of Dostoevsky. His book seemed less a critical interpretation than a work of philosophy inspired by Dostoevsky.

I admire Bakhtin for resisting the temptation to place himself above the writers he discusses. He imagines his work as a stab at paraphrasing, so far as that is possible, the profundity of Dostoevsky's and Rabelais's "artistic thinking." By "artistic thinking" Bakhtin means not thinking about art but thinking in the form of art.

Bakhtin supposes that Dostoevsky's ideas are so elusive, and yet so valuable, that a good explication, however unequal to the masterpieces explicated, can tell the reader something important and otherwise unavailable. That is the approach I take in my classes.

And so, when I see Bakhtin himself made into a method to "apply," I grow disheartened. As there are schools of feminism and post-colonialism, so there is now "dialogism." Literary works are evaluated—no surprise—by how well they live up to the school's "dialogic" standards.

In his unfinished book on the novel of education, Bakhtin contends that when we presume writers fictionalize philosophers we forget that sometimes philosophers "tractify" fiction. The novelists often make the discoveries that the discursive thinkers "transcribe." To cite Bakhtin's example, a commonplace of intellectual history holds that eighteenth-century thought lacked a historical sense, which is largely true if one is thinking of philosophers. But eighteenth-century novels began the process of representing people not by fixed qualities but by processes of change. They pioneered an "image of man" as always *becoming*: people alter over time in complex interactions with each other and with society, which, in turn, also "becomes." Having come to see people this way, novels arrived at new insights about psychology, morality, and values. Nineteenth-century novels took these insights still further to develop what Bakhtin considered the richest sense of people ever conceived.

To be sure, nineteenth-century philosophers and essayists also wrote important treatises devoted to these themes. But it would often be more accurate to say that they were teasing out the implications of novelistic discoveries than that novelists were sugar-coating the ideas of philosophers. In many cases the novelists were far ahead and, indeed, remain unequaled.

## A Proof

There is an obvious proof that the great novelists knew more about human psychology than any social scientist who ever lived. If psychologists, sociologists, or economists understood people as well as George Eliot or Tolstoy, they could create portraits of people as believable as Dorothea Brooke or Anna Karenina. But no social scientist has ever come close.

To be sure, the new behavioral economics, with which students are often familiar, has claimed to have overcome the shallowness of traditional rational choice economics. One would think they could hardly miss, but they do. Read behavioral economists or popular syntheses, like that of Dan Ariely, and you will encounter portraits of decision-making so breathtakingly shallow that one can only sigh.[11] Ariely has started giving advice on love relationships grounded in behavioral economics.[12]

At least rational choice economists, at their best, do not claim that real people of flesh and blood actually think according to their model. They often cite Milton Friedman's classic article from the early 1950s, "The Methodology of Positive Economics," which argues that the test of a good model is not whether it is psychologically realistic.[13] The test, rather, is whether the model, positing that people acting "as if" certain simplifying assumptions were true, yields reliable predictions of collective economic behavior (Friedman, 40). If that is what they claim, one can fault them only on their predictive accuracy. Those who make no claims about psychology cannot be wrong about it. Unfortunately, many traditional economists forget this "as if," while

---

[11]    See PI. Another good survey is Hugh Schwartz, *A Guide to Behavioral Economics* (Alexandria, Virginia: Higher Education Publications, 2008).

[12]    A reader writes to Ariely that his six-year love relationship is not as thrilling as it used to be but just "comfortable." In that case, Ariely replies, "I suspect that what has emerged is not sufficiently beneficial for you—and given this, I would say get out. As the economist Tibor Scitovsky argued in 'The Joyless Economy,' there are two kinds of experiences, pleasures and comforts, and we have a tendency to take the comfortable, safe and predictable path way too often. This is particularly sad, Scitovsky argues, because real progress comes from pleasures. It comes from taking risks and trying very different things. So, perhaps this is a good opportunity to give up your comfort and give pleasure a chance." I quote extensively so the reader will not suspect a paraphrase is exaggerated. See Dan Ariely, "The Don't-Let-It-in-the-House Diet: A Behavioral Economist Tackles Readers' Dilemmas," in the Life and Style section of *The Wall Street Journal*, August 3, 2012, http://online.wsj.com/article/SB10000872396390443687504577563133964708876.html?mod=googlenews_wsj.

[13]    Milton Friedman, "The Method of Positive Economics," in *Essays in Positive Economics* (Chicago: University of Chicago Press, 1953), 3-43.

behavioral economics is based on such claims. Their models bear as much resemblance to real people as a point bears to a three-dimensional object.

## Novels as Thought Experiments

> We have got on to slippery ice where there is no friction and so in a certain sense the conditions are ideal, but just because of that, we are unable to walk. We want to walk: so we need *friction*. Back to the rough ground!
>
> —*Wittgenstein*

While behavioral economists rely on simplified "laboratory experiments," philosophers sometimes construct thought experiments.[14] Thought experiments boast an impressive history. They have played significant roles in the sciences (Galileo's on falling objects, Einstein's elevator, Schrodinger's cat) and the philosophy of mind (a recent example is Searle's Chinese room).

These experiments persuade by simplification: they abstract essential features from a situation so we can perceive their implications more clearly. Contradictions may become visible, logical consequences apparent, or concealed assumptions bared. But clearly, they can persuade only insofar as they do not omit what is essential to the question under consideration.

Galileo made his remarkable discoveries by abstraction: if irrelevant "noise," such as friction, could be thought away, how would bodies fall? He presumed, and turned out to be right, that in physics

---

[14]    On thought experiments, see the article "Thought Experiments," 2011 version, in *The Stanford Encyclopedia of Philosophy*, http://plato.stanford. edu/entries/thought-experiment/; Roy Sorenson, *Thought Experiments* (New York: Oxford University press, 1992); Thomas S. Kuhn, "A Function for Thought Experiments," in *The Essential Tension* (Chicago: University of Chicago Press, 1977), 240–265; and James Robert Brown, *The Laboratory of the Mind: Thought Experiments in the Natural Sciences* (London: Routledge, 1993). For an excellent critique of philosophers' use of thought experiments, see Kathleen V. Wilkes, *Real People: Personal Identity without Thought Experiments* (Oxford: Clarendon Press, 1993).

the complexity of the world conceals simple laws underneath. But does that mean this assumption applies everywhere?

Contrast Galileo's simplifying assumption about physics with Carl von Clausewitz's classic account of war. Clausewitz describes the supposedly scientific, "Galilean" theories of war that have been formulated by abstraction. Generals who believe these theories lose. The reason is that such accounts abstract out the *essence* of war, what must be recognized if one is to understand it. That essence includes everything that from a Galilean perspective constitutes mere noise. Clausewitz explains:

> If one has never personally experienced war, one cannot understand in what the difficulties really consist, nor why a commander should need brilliance and exceptional ability. Everything looks simple; the knowledge required does not look remarkable, the strategic options are so obvious that by comparison the simplest problem of higher mathematics has an impressive scientific dignity. Once war has actually been seen, the difficulties become clear; but it is still extremely hard to describe the unseen, all-pervading element that brings about this change of perspective.[15]

Tolstoy was to call this unseen element "the elemental force," and the crucial point about it is that it is not a single thing but a way to refer to countless small forces that are constantly present and render all simple theories ludicrous. The generals in *War and Peace* follow just the sort of theories Clausewitz discredits—Clausewitz briefly appears in Tolstoy's book—in the belief that they have a "science of war." When they lose, they dismiss the interfering factors as mere chance, of no interest to a scientific theory. By contrast, Tolstoy's wisest generals, Kutuzov and Bagration, know that such "chance" is what war is all about.

Prince Andrei begins by believing in a science of war and eventually learns that there can be none, because battle is a matter of "a hundred million diverse chances." Good generals, he realizes, have not the right abstraction but the practiced ability, based on experience, to react appropriately to situations no theory could anticipate.

---

15      Carl von Clausewitz, *On War*, ed. and trans. Michael Howard and Peter Paret (Princeton: Princeton University Press, 1984), 119.

Or, as Clausewitz explains, "Everything in war is very simple, but the simplest thing is difficult. The difficulties accumulate and end by producing a kind of *friction* that is inconceivable unless one has experienced war" (Clausewitz, 117). For Galileo, friction is what must be thought away, while for Clausewitz it names what must be retained. Thought experiments relying on abstracting out the friction will therefore be of little use in understanding war or any other aspect of human life where friction is essential.

Clausewitz describes in general terms the many sorts of factors that produce friction, including weather, terrain, organizational snafus, accidents of countless sorts, and, crucially, *moral* factors. Under this term he includes the unforeseeable complexities of individual psychology, the effect of danger and terror, and many other emotions for which the soldier's earlier life has offered little preparation. Tolstoy's generals realize the important of morale, which cannot be formalized. Social factors of the most varied sort also make a difference.

The more friction matters, the more abstraction—on which thought experiments depend—will falsify. Such abstraction proves a useful tool in ethics only if one imagines ethical decisions as made, or as properly made, in abstract logical space. Thought experiments could then apply as well to Martians as to humans, to Muslims as to Presbyterians, to thirteenth-century French noblemen as to contemporary factory workers in Mississippi. The subtle psychological differences of individual people also should not matter.

Tolstoy was familiar with this sort of thought experiment. In *Anna Karenina*, Sergei Ivanovich tries to prove an ethical point by asking what Levin would do in a hypothetical situation. He thus tries to prove a moral point by a deftly constructed thought experiment. Levin properly replies that he would have to decide what to do when *in* that situation. This is the correct answer, for only then he could take into account all those factors the thought experiment abstracts out. This is another reason that, in ethics, *presentness* matters.

All such ethical thought experiments tacitly presume that the complexities of people as social and psychological beings can be bracketed to get at the essence of the matter. To the extent that ethics demands an understanding of what cannot be modeled in logical space—to the extent that it inescapably involves friction—thought experiments will mislead. Friction is not mere friction.

Ethics is a matter of prosaics. But what if the thought experiment included the prosaic details? Could one not construct a thought experiment showing people in their psychic complexity, their history, the climate of their minds, their values both recognized and unrecognized, their habitual way of perceiving others and the immediate considerations occupying their attention when a decision is being made? What if it also showed each person's relations, and potential relations, with the others, the course of their thoughts, the questions they mentally pose to themselves and imagine posing to others? It might also place people in their society with its many conflicts, complexities, and oddities, as they change at different rates. And could it not show the shifting ethical norms of changing groups, and anything else that might be pertinent?

In fact, we have such thought experiments. They are called realist novels.

When students learn to read novels this way, their relevance is apparent. Everyone makes ethical decisions in situations that call for a deep, rich, and prosaic understanding.

## Self-Deception in Philosophy and the Novel

When I was writing my book on *Anna Karenina*, I became fascinated with the complex dynamics of self-deception dramatized by Tolstoy. Anyone who knows the realist novel will recognize self-deception as a recurring theme. For novelists, we are not just what we think and remember, but also what we avoid thinking and remembering; and not just what we happen to misperceive, but also what we choose to misperceive. "Pride and prejudice" lead us to see one thing rather than another, to draw a less than plausible conclusion, and to justify to ourselves what we know we ought to condemn. All Jane Austen's novels deal with this theme, and it rapidly became a trademark concern of the genre.

Discovering that philosophers have recently taken an interest in self-deception, I turned to their work. The problem troubled them because it raised some obvious "paradoxes," as they like to say. How can one lie to oneself, when, after all, the self lied to is the same self that does the lying and knows the truth? Isn't self-deception a bit like concealing something in one's pocket so another person cannot find it and then imagining that the same ruse can work on oneself?

But what if (some philosophers suggest) self-deception refers to the holding of two contradictory beliefs whose contradiction the believer has not noticed? Or is that not really what we mean by self-deception? "Let us begin by supposing," writes Herbert Fingarette, "that the circumstances, evidence, or argument favouring a certain belief are presented to Jones, who holds a contrary belief."[16] But the argument is so complex that Jones does not recognize the contradiction, or he is too dull to do so. It would then be wrong, contends Fingarette, to speak of self-deception.

Fingarette is right about that. We hold countless beliefs and the sheer limitations of time and attention prevent us from assessing each in relation to all the others, so there may well be conflicts, but that is not what we mean by self-deception. In some way, self-deception must involve agency, a willingness not to see a contradiction or to recognize what one would rather not recognize. It requires some sort of effort.

Perhaps Fingarette and the philosophers he examines go astray with the reference to figures like "Jones." Jones, as the name suggests, is no one in particular. Jones has no biography or social connections. He is an entirely different *sort* of being from Ivan Karamazov or Anna Karenina. Jones does not develop over time. As with behavioral economists' examples, this one works by considering an abstract agent at a moment; in this case, a moment in which self-deception does or does not occur. But people do not live in a moment. They live processually. That is why novels are long.

Perhaps Jones does not hold a contrary belief; perhaps he is simply afraid of a threat to something he believes. Often enough, contrary evidence does not register because, as the possible contradiction is being approached, alarm bells go off and deflect one's attention. Those alarm bells result from years of handling disturbing information about quite other topics, mental habits that operate without any choice at the moment in question but which are still the result of choices in the past. The choice to self-deceive is not located at a single moment. No example about a person without a biography could grasp such an example.

Suppose Jones wants to avoid having his beliefs disconfirmed and so makes sure he associates only with people who tell him what he wants to hear and gradually loses "the capacity to see through this. Even in such a case," Fingarette contends, "I do not think we would say that such a person deceived himself. He has knowingly put himself in a position where he can be deceived, but he is not deceiving himself"

---

16    Herbert Fingarette, *Self-Deception* (Berkeley: University of California Press, 2000), 22. The book makes a number of interesting distinctions.

(Fingarette, 31). But placing ourselves, time and again, in situations in which the conclusion one wants to reach can be effortlessly drawn is precisely *how* we often deceive ourselves.

Anna Karenina wants to have an affair, which she believes to be morally wrong, because it is bound to hurt her husband and cause injury to her son. If she could arrange to believe that she is not hurting her husband— say, because he does not care about anything but social proprieties or because he is incapable of feeling anything at all—then she need not blame herself for hurting him. If she could only start to find him so repulsive that she simply cannot live with him, then she has no choice and is again not to blame. I shorten the list of beliefs she would like to arrive at. They are consistent neither with what she knows nor with each other.

The problem is, she knows that her husband can suffer, does love her, and would be tortured by jealousy. She cannot *will* herself to believe the opposite just because it would be convenient to do so. If she tried, the falsehood would be apparent to her. She therefore does what most of us do.

At any given moment, we can perceive a situation in a range of ways, shaded one way or another, but none palpably untrue. One can focus on one end of this range without a sense of lying. Self-deception often begins with such a choice of focus. Looking is an action we can perform in many ways. Since we have occasion to look at every moment of our lives, we have the choice to be generous or cruel, broad- or narrow-minded, at every prosaic moment.

Readers watch Anna choosing to focus on what presents her husband as less feeling and less vulnerable. Over time, the perception that lies at one extreme of plausibility moves to the center, and her attention switches to a new extreme and still less charitable view. Eventually, over many months and countless moments of looking, she succeeds in seeing him as she wishes, although there are moments when contrary evidence can get through.[17]

I have presented what Tolstoy describes over hundreds of pages much too schematically. Because novels allow us to get inside a character's mind, hear how she speaks to herself in inner speech, and detect the objecting voices she implicitly answers, we become familiar with Anna's mental actions. We witness the complex dynamics of self-

---

[17]     I discuss self-deception in *Anna Karenina* in SMW.

deception as it develops, overcomes obstacles, avoids evidence, and addresses the possible objections of other people she knows. We see her precarious developing beliefs unsettled by unwelcome memories from the remote past. Sometimes when her husband behaves uncharacteristically, he can unwittingly take her by surprise, and contrary to her desires she feels for him. Then she has to expend extra effort to talk herself out of what she sees, and each expenditure of effort tacitly reminds her of her falsity. Tolstoy both traces this process in detail and explicitly comments on it as it is happening.

Anna's self-deception includes choices extended over many moments but not wholly present at any single one. It involves a variety of mental actions pertaining to memory, perception, the course of thoughts when they wander, and many other prosaic inner gestures happening at countless moments every day. All these combine into a rich picture showing how people arrange to believe what they know to be untrue.

Indeed, what it means "to believe" also shifts. There are evidently shades of belief that hold unbelief of different kinds in check. Even the distinction between conscious and unconscious actions comes to seem far too simple. These are the sort of things one cannot show in a brief example about "Jones."

For some reason, philosophers do not turn to these novels. I find it strange: here we have what by common consent are the most convincing portraits of people ever written. These portraits offer plausible descriptions of the internal mental processes we never see in others and have trouble noticing in ourselves. They focus on the very problem under discussion. And yet, philosophers do not turn to them. It is as if they examined poverty by careful analysis of the word "poor" while a great slum lay outside their window.

Once students learn to trace Anna'a thoughts, and watch for similar mental activities of their own, they recognize the value of novelistic accounts of self-deception. And the same happens with many other habits, choices, and issues that confront them daily.

## Identification and Empathy

Philosophers can teach us that we ought to empathize with others. Anthropologists and sociologists recommend understanding the perspectives of distant cultures, while historians do the same for past centuries. But these disciplines do not involve actual practice in empathy. Great literature does, and in that respect its study remains unique among university-taught subjects.

When one reads a novel, one *identifies* with characters. In so doing, one experiences from within what it is like to be a member of the opposite sex, belong to another social class, work in an unfamiliar profession, live in a different society, or take other assumptions and values for granted. One experiences feelings and perspectives that one either knew about only by hearsay or never even suspected.

And one does not do so a single time. One does not have to have finished reading *Anna Karenina* to see the world from the perspective of an upper-class nineteenth-century Russian woman. Rather, in the course of reading page after page one finds oneself feeling what she feels in reaction to new circumstances, other people, unexpected memories, and earlier feelings.

One does the same with the other major characters. Upon reflection, the best definition of "major character in a novel" might be a character whom readers are allowed to experience from within. *Anna Karenina* gives us an astonishing number of major characters. And so we have constant practice in seeing the world from new perspectives and grasping what it is to be a different person.

Readers *practice* empathy. And what one practices, one find easier to do and, eventually, does by habit. It becomes second nature.

Time and again, the author lets us overhear, as we never could in life, the character's thoughts, often in the very words and voice the character uses when silently addressing herself. No wonder readers speak of characters as if they were old friends and of completing a novel as a farewell. Readers know, of course, that characters are only fictional, but at the same time, they get to know them intimately, in some ways more intimately than flesh-and-blood friends. We eavesdrop on their consciousness and co-feel their private feelings.

To enable this eavesdropping, the realist novel developed its greatest formal innovation: the extended use of what some have called "free indirect discourse" or what Bakhtin named "double-voiced discourse." Narration of a passage remains in the third person, but the perspective, choice of words, and sequence of thoughts reflect the character's inner speech. And so the passage carries all the emotional charge the character experiences. As the character's emotion alters in the course of thinking, readers can trace its evolution. They are present, feeling along with the character, in a way not possible in any other discipline or cultural artifact.

What literature generally and novels in particular are good for is an education in the skills of empathy.

## Living Into and Simultaneous Regret

I recall several years ago reading Edith Wharton's novel *The House of Mirth* and finding in the upper-class, social-climbing, beautiful, antisemitic heroine values I dislike and personal qualities that in life repel me. And yet, as she descended gradually into suicide, I felt intense psychic pain. That is one way I know Wharton is a splendid novelist. I experienced what it was like to be someone like Lily Bart and to undergo her feelings vicariously. I cared about them even when I was disapproving of her behavior and her way of thinking.

The old saw, "to understand is to forgive," is often taken to mean that if one really understood all the factors behind another person's decision one would recognize his behavior as inevitable. One sees that if everything were identical, one would behave the same way, and so one would forgive what could not be otherwise and what one would do oneself.

That is *not* the sense of novelistic empathy. Tolstoy enables me to sense what it is like to be Anna Karenina, to experience in part what her despair feels like. My own pain traces the extent of my identification. But I can empathize without justifying or forgiving. Sensing another consciousness from within allows me to see why I *might*, not necessarily *would*, behave the same way.

To really sense another person from within is to sense that person's choices. Inevitability is a category that can only be applied from without. From within, the most important thing about any person is that he senses more than one possible future, depending on what he chooses. He retains the capacity to surprise others and himself. He remains, as Bakhtin would say, unfinalizable.

One's own time is always open. And so empathy, far from leading to a sense of inevitability, creates an enhanced sense of the palpability of choice. When a character behaves badly, the reader who identifies with her experiences the pain of simultaneous regret.

Regret can be simultaneous, rather than happen after the fact, because empathy is not merging. It entails both identification and the maintenance of an outside position. It is, as Bakhtin explains, a "living into" (*vzhivanie*) another while still being oneself. One feels the other "from inside its own essence" and senses "life in its actual aliveness" while simultaneously remaining outside. Such "living into" is something I do, and am aware of doing as I do it. When I empathize, I retain "my own unique place…. It is *I* who empathize actively … empathizing is *my* act," an event in my life and an act for which I am responsible. One can therefore regret a choice while empathizing with the person who makes it and experiencing it as it is being made.[18]

## Experiencing Suicide

From within Anna's consciousness, the readers feel the intense pain leading her to suicide. They sense the way her spiteful and self-destructive thoughts feed on themselves, hear the voices suggesting she is overlooking something important, and feel her turning her attention away from the warning. At every moment the reader experiences Anna choosing to continue thinking as she does, and hopes she changes her mind. Even when reading the book for the tenth time, I feel myself telling her not to do it.

After Anna jumps, and is lying on the train tracks an instant before being run over, she realizes she has not been thinking right and regrets her decision. Readers following her thoughts and feelings share the sense of utter agony, share it insofar as they are living into her and acting as co-participants in her act. For Anna, the agony of that brief moment exceeds all the despair leading to her jump. Perhaps she experiences more pain in that instant than in all the rest of her life combined.

Outside a novel, this moment, the most intense of her life, would have to remain invisible and unshared. No one could even tell us about it, much less make us sense it. But our sharing it, through our relationship with Anna that is partly of our own choosing, becomes an event in our own lives. Reading a novel is not just reading *about*, it is living with.

Guiding the students through this experience constitutes the most effective caution I know against excessive indulgence in suicidal thoughts.

---

[18]     M. M. Bakhtin, *Toward a Philosophy of the Act*, trans. Vadim Liapunov, ed. Vadim Liapunov and Michael Holquist (Austin: University of Texas Press, 1993), 14-15.

## Subjectivities

From without, everyone else's actions constitute behavior. Behavior demands explanations in terms of external causes, such as social forces, psychological laws, or, as students today like to add, neurobiological mechanisms. But no one can view himself or herself that way. That, I take it, is the point of the joke about two behaviorists in bed, as one says to the other: "That was great for you, how was it for me?"

The subjectivity of other people's experiences is not normally accessible to us. We know directly, even if we profess otherwise, that an objective description of the world cannot include everything, because there are subjectivities. At the very least, there is mine. As the philosopher Thomas Nagel puts it, "objectivity is essentially incomplete" because "some things can only be understood from the inside, and access to them will depend on how far our subjective imagination can travel."[19] That imagination can actually travel quite far, if guided by a master like Tolstoy.

We already have some experience in knowing other subjectivities. When we remember our own past experiences—say, what it felt like to be much younger—we both inhabit and stand outside that experience. We feel what it was like, and feel what it is now like to feel what it was like. Great novels help us do the same with other people as we do with our earlier selves. We sense what it is like to be Anna Karenina while also sensing what it is like to identify with Anna Karenina.

And we watch her doing what we do: recalling, sometimes unwillingly, what it used to feel like to be her. Anna looks back, remembers, regrets, apologizes. When she believes she is dying in childbirth, she brings to mind what it was like to love and respect her husband. She recognizes how she has deliberately forgotten those feelings while telling herself they did not exist, and so she appreciates directly her process of self-deception for what it was. She describes it in terms similar to the ones I used above.

This moment is a complex one, and hard to describe. She feels the earlier feeling, while at the same time re-experiencing the somewhat later feelings of blocking it out. The two moments coexist as separate past moments in her present experience. And we, recalling our different moments of identifications with her in the process of reading,

---

19    Thomas Nagel, *The View From Nowhere* (New York: Oxford University Press, 1986), 18.

have a similar sense of feeling layered upon feeling. This is the sort of temporal layering I have never encountered in a philosopher's thought experiment, but it is what great novels do all the time.

As we vicariously experience the character's act of remembering many moments, we also re-experience our own feelings at each of those moments of identification with her. We remember our own feelings in experiencing hers. They become part of who we are. We become a person who has lived through Anna's experience. This grafting of biographies is also something missing from other disciplines.

### Novelistic Morality

As a genre, realist novels suggest that morality begins with empathy. "Compassion is the chief and perhaps only law of human existence," Prince Myshkin thinks in *The Idiot*, and he thinks here for the genre (I, 218).

The guiding thought is: "There but for the grace of God go I." Identifying with characters makes a reader feel: I could easily have been like her, faced what she faces, and suffered what she suffers. Things are only fortuitously otherwise.

As the story goes, this classic saying about empathy belong to John Bradford. Languishing in the Tower of London, he witnessed prisoners led to execution and remarked: "There but for the grace of God goes John Bradford." And, in fact, he was himself soon martyred. And so the saying, amended to apply to anyone who voices it, carries the sense not only of a near escape but also of future danger. It suggests how close one is to being someone else. And so it teaches us to view others as subjects like ourselves.

Some philosophers insist, as Kant did, that morality has nothing to do with empathy. It entails doing what is right because it is right. The imperative is universal and categorical, and would apply to Martians as well as to human beings if Martians were capable of understanding it. The implicit philosophy of the realist novel maintains the contrary.

In novels, any reliance on abstract rules in place of human feeling is seen as at best naïve and at worst cruel. Decency is a better guide than rationality. The basic plot of the political and philosophical novel—by Turgenev, Eliot, Conrad, Dostoevsky, Tolstoy, and others—tells the story of a person who believes in an abstraction only to learn both its ludicrous simplicity and its unwitting harm. Morality begins not with the right philosophical tenet but with the willingness and ability to place oneself in another's position.

In Part One of *Anna Karenina*, Kitty, who has decided to marry Vronsky, must turn down a proposal her old family friend Levin is about to make. Expecting that Vronsky will also offer to marry her, Kitty experiences a thrilling sense of her own beauty and power. She feels "intense excitement," a sensation "akin to that of a young man before a battle" (AK, 51). But as she enters the room where Levin awaits her, she switches her point of view and places herself in his position. "And then for the first time the whole thing presented itself in a new, different aspect; only then did she realize that the question did not affect her only—with whom she would be happy, and whom she loved—but that she would have to wound someone whom she liked. And to wound him cruelly" (AK, 52). She feels the hurt she must cause him. This is how we know that Kitty is fundamentally a good person.

I have never heard someone say, "Yes, you only see things from my point of view, why don't you think of yourself for a change?"

"We are all born in moral stupidity, taking the world as an udder to feed our supreme selves," writes the narrator of *Middlemarch*.

> Dorothea had early begun to emerge from that stupidity, but yet it had been easier to her to imagine to herself how she would devote herself to Mr. Casaubon, and become wise and strong in his strength and wisdom, than to conceive with that distinctness which is no longer reflection but feeling—an idea wrought back to the directness of sense, like the solidity of objects—that he had an equivalent center of self, whence the lights and shadows must always fall with a certain difference (M, 205).

The feelings and viewpoint of another self *wrought back to the directness of sense, like the solidity of objects*: that is where novelistic ethics begins and what novels are uniquely good at teaching. The other person has "an equivalent center of self," much like our own. We must decenter ourselves to place ourselves in that equivalent center, and in reading novels we practice doing so.

## Impersonation

How does one convey to students this aspect of novels? One cannot just direct attention to the text, because empathy is not a feature of the text, but of readers' interaction with it. It is part of the *work*.

Students need not just to learn about empathy but also to engage in it, and recognize themselves engaging in it, as they read. To encourage them, one could ask the sort of question that has long been regarded as unprofessional: do you *like* this character, and why? Students might write down their impressions as they finish parts of the book. They could then compare later impressions with earlier ones, which tend to be forgotten. Any long novel should be assigned in parts so that students can live with it over time and have the characters' lives intertwine with their own.

As the term proceeds, one can ask students how their sense of characters has changed. Do they like the character more or less, and why? Do their earlier impressions strike them as naïve? What can they learn about the process of revising their impressions? The real stories of *Emma* and *Pride and Prejudice* include the reader, who, after many misjudgments, learns from his or her own misperceptions, much as the heroines do. If one assigns such a novel for a single class, or does not direct students' attention to their own reactions as they read, one is in effect omitting part of the story. It is like assigning a seriously abridged edition. That is true with realist novels generally.

When lecturing about a novel, I have found it useful to impersonate the author. At the beginning of the course, I announce that the lectures will be given not from my perspective, but from the perspective of the author as I understand him. Should I comment on some recent event or issue, students will be hearing what Dostoevsky or Tolstoy, not I, would say about it.[20]

Such impersonation demands absorbing the author's perspective so thoroughly that one can think from within it, and then (as Bakhtin would say) "draw dotted lines" from his concerns to ours. Students hear the author's voice and sense the rhythms of his thought, and then, when they go back to the book, read it from that perspective. Instead of seeing puzzling words, they hear a voice.

It is therefore crucial to read passages aloud, with the students silently reading along. They learn to hear plays of irony, subtle shifts in

---

[20]   Mark Edmundson describes the objective of interpretation as "to bring the past into the present and to do so in a way that will make the writer's ghost nod in something like approval. This means operating within the author's terms, thinking, insofar as it is possible, the writer's thoughts ... inspired ventriloquism," or what I call "impersonation." See Mark Edmundson, *Why Read?* (New York: Bloomsbury, 2004), 53.

tone, and the double-voicing of inner speech. I describe what is going on, then read the passage so they hear the play of voices. One can also ask students to imagine what a character not addressed in a sample of inner speech would say if she could overhear it. How would Dolly respond if she could hear Stiva attributing his infidelity to the fact that she is no longer attractive nor interesting, "merely a good mother"? One can imagine the inner tonalities in inner speech that the work does not record but invites us to imagine. Whose answers are tacitly presumed as the character thinks?

One could use such passages as an excuse to teach "theory," but that would be a mistake. Rather, students should sense they are learning how to bring a novel to life. If the work becomes an occasion to teach the theory, then the course implies that the theory is what is really interesting. If you teach as I have described, students will in a sense be learning theory—should they ever read about double-voicing or free indirect discourse they will recognize the argument—but their experience will be a thrilling sense of bringing novels alive. "So this is why people get so much out of Tolstoy!"

At that point, students will not have to take the author's greatness on faith. They will sense that greatness and sense themselves as capable of doing so. Neither will they have to accept the teacher's interpretation without seeing how it was arrived at or what other interpretation might be possible. No one will have to persuade them why *Cliff's Notes* won't do.

Students will acquire the skill to inhabit the author's world. Her perspective becomes one with which they are intimate, and which, when their own way of thinking leads them to a dead end, they can temporarily adopt to see if it might help. Novelistic empathy gives them a diversity of ways of thinking and feeling. They can escape from the prison house of self.

## Impersonating Characters

One can also impersonate the novel's characters. They too offer a diversity of voices and points of view on the world. What makes a novelist great is, perhaps above all, the ability to bring to life people and perspectives at odds with her own. Everyone in Disraeli sounds like Disraeli, but George Eliot gives us a world of different people.

When students can hear characters' voices and imagine what they might think when confronted with new situations, those characters become inhabitants of their world. Their voices and perspectives on life come to live within them.

In one famous scene in *Karamazov*, Fyodor Pavlovich remembers that he was once asked: why do you hate so-and-so so much?, "and he had answered, with his shameless impudence, 'I'll tell you. He's never done me any harm, but I once played a nasty trick on him and I've never forgiven him for it.'"[21]

First, you have to read this extraordinary comment aloud in a voice filled with appropriate nastiness, self-display shading into self-humiliation, irony, and wit. If you do it right, students will laugh. Then you have to gloss the line, describe the whole dynamics of guilt that provokes a person to dislike those whom he has harmed. Help them imagine moments when they have witnessed something similar.

Next, point out that although everyone sometimes feels this way, very few admit they do. Most people do not have the "shameless impudence" to say so, even to themselves. Rather, they devise spurious reasons for hating the person they have harmed, and invent injuries that person has done to them. But old Karamazov is in one sense more honest than that. If hypocrisy is "the tribute vice pays to virtue," then he is not being hypocritical because, as a person with no morals at all, he has no need to pay that tribute. Such "honesty" makes him all the worse. While we all have the nasty reaction he describes, Fyodor Pavlovich makes a *principle* of it.

You can invent scenarios in which one might hate one's victim. Make these scenarios prosaic ones which the students can easily imagine, and sometimes they will supply one or two. I remember one student suddenly turning pale and saying aloud, "Oh, my God!"

Ask the students whether, in such a situation, you might dislike the other person less if you found out he had *really* wronged you. Such questions can make the dynamics of guilt, and of Dostoevskian perverse psychology, into something they know from within, something they have in fact felt and are now aware of: feelings that, after reading Dostoevsky, they can recognize should they feel them again and counteract if they wish.

Finally—and this is a very important step—you tell them: now, *this* is a line that only Dostoevsky could have written. If you had seen

---

21    So I intone it, though it actually ends: "and ever since I have hated him" (BK, 99).

it out of context, and been asked who wrote it, you would know that either Dostoevsky or someone imitating him must be the author. Why is it important to do that?

Because when you can do that with an author, when you can recognize the qualities that make him who he is—the author's "quiddities"—then he lives within you. When you have a model sentence of the author in mind, you can use it as a catalyst for producing more of them, and the insights that go with them.

The structuralists used to say that English is not every sentence ever spoken in English but every sentence that *could* be spoken. To know a language is to know its potential, to be able to work with it, to do new things. And that is true of knowing an author or character. The first step to being able to do that, to making another voice live within you, is to recognize it precisely when you see it. First comes recognition, then free imitation.

After a term of Dostoevsky read this way, students can often hear the "Dostoevskian" voice everywhere and recognize it in themselves. They can extend it, juxtapose it with other voices or perspectives, argue with it. They sense their ears and eyes opening. This is what novelistic wisdom feels like.

### Afterword: What Empathy Isn't

In his classic essay "On Liberty," John Stuart Mill famously argued the case for placing oneself in an opponent's position. "He who knows only his own side of the case knows little of that," Mill advises.[22] Mill finds it odd that people would claim their beliefs are rational when they have not heard objections to them. How does one call people on the other side closed-minded without even knowing what they say?

Mill explains that one does not know the other side's position by virtue of knowing one's own side's characterization of it. One might as well have a trial in which the jury hears only the prosecutor, who presents the defendant's case as he sees it.

A rational person must bring opposing arguments "into real contact with his own mind" (Mill, 44). To do so, he must make the effort "to hear them from persons who actually believe them; who defend them in earnest, and do their very utmost for them" (Mill, 44). And

---

[22]    John Stuart Mill, *On Liberty* (New York: Prometheus, 1986), 43.

one must listen to the most intelligent and well-intentioned persons on the other side, rather than (as the committed typically do) present the most venal and stupid people as all the other side has to offer. Unless the best people on the other side can recognize your paraphrase of their position as accurate, you do not really know it. And if you do not know it, you are the one who thinks irrationally and closes his mind.

Unfortunately, Mill adds, with almost no exceptions the intelligent people he knows "have never thrown themselves into the mental position of those who think differently from them, and considered what such persons may have to say: and consequently they do not, in any proper sense of the word, know the doctrine which they themselves profess" (Mill, 44). *The mental position of those who think differently*: Mill is talking about intellectual *empathy*. One needs to be able not just to recite opposing opinions but also to feel from within why a person who is intelligent and well-intentioned—no less so than oneself—would believe them.

Novels extend Mill's point from political and intellectual arguments to emotional and personal ones. They deal with other people in all the complex ways we encounter them. They enable us to put ourselves in the emotional, as well as intellectual, position of other people. Readers sense what it feels like to think differently not just about abstract ideas, but also about the most prosaic realities.

In fact, novels assess ideas, too, in terms of what it *feels like* to believe them. They examine how the ideas fit into a whole personality, way of living, or experience of social life. Experience, not dialectics, teaches Bazarov, Lydgate, and Ivan Karamazov the limitations of their beliefs. And readers learn (as one character in Dostoevsky puts it) to "feel ideas."

By inviting readers to inhabit the perspectives of other people, novels show how differences of every sort appear to both (or where appropriate all) sides. I sometimes ask students to look forward. Someday you may quarrel with your spouse and find yourself wondering how he or she could think such a thing. But wouldn't it be worthwhile to place yourself in your spouse's position and grasp the perspective that makes him or her ask the same question about you? If you could each comprehend the other's incomprehension, you would have made progress. Students appreciate that when novels teach us to do this, they are teaching us lessons of importance to their lives.

Just as it is disheartening to hear people unable to paraphrase opponents' arguments dismissing them as closed-minded, so it is disappointing to read people condemning stick-figure versions of others for their lack of empathy. It is all too easy to hate others for being hateful or to dehumanize them as incapable of empathy automatically.

A joke from the days of Brezhnev told of an American boasting to a Soviet citizen that in America he was perfectly free to run down the street shouting "President Johnson is a criminal!" So what, came the reply. In Russia I too can run down the street shouting "President Johnson is a criminal!"

Just as one does not prove one's devotion to free speech by tolerating views with which one is in accord, so one cannot prove one's empathy by assuming the position of those who think and feel like oneself.

In the book I discussed at the beginning of this essay, Martha Nussbaum correctly observes that the humanities can teach empathy. They allow us to understand other intellectual positions from within, "imagine sympathetically the predicament of another person" (NFP, 7), and engage in what she calls "critical thinking" about our own beliefs. With these and many similar statements I wholeheartedly agree.

The problem is that Nussbaum does not seem to mean what she says. Page after page, her book stresses the importance of empathizing with the beliefs of humanities professors resembling herself. But the book never invites us to empathize with opposing beliefs and the people who hold them. One "thinks critically" only about the other side. Their motives are always bad ones. They lack empathy! Far from exhibiting empathy, this book exemplifies how to use the term empathy to preclude empathy itself.

People rarely need coaching to appreciate the rectitude of their own opinions. What requires instruction and effort is discovering how a person with whom one is quarreling, or a member of another political party, sees things. Throughout this volume, Nussbaum mentions numerous current social issues, but time after time, and without exception, she presents the predictable position as the only possible one for a decent person.

When I began to teach at Northwestern, I passed by a professor's office decorated with a large sticker, common at the time, shouting "QUESTION AUTHORITY!" From within, I heard the professor berating a student with words I shall never forget: "How can you think that?! Hasn't my course taught you anything??"

As Nussbaum tells the story, those dedicated to economic growth, rather than the humanities, insist that care be taken "lest the historical and economic narrative lead to any serious critical thinking about class, about race and gender, about whether foreign investment really is good for the rural poor" (NFP, 20). "Educators for economic growth" want to be sure that people turn out morally obtuse because "moral obtuseness is necessary to carry out programs of economic development that ignore inequality" (NFP, 23).

Set aside the fact that social science, as well as humanities, courses are often devoted to making such points. These are hardly empathetic portraits of all those proponents of economic growth. Outside of Spiderman comics, no one sits around rubbing his hands with glee about doing evil. People with whom one disagrees do not conspire to promote moral obtuseness or create needless suffering. From their perspective, they are promoting justice.

Perhaps this point is obvious to me because I grew up among Communists who justified Stalin's purges and liquidations, the killing of millions of "class enemies," while sincerely believing that what they, not their critics, advocated was justice. I did not doubt their sincerity. But in Martha Nussbaum's universe, entrepreneurs, conservatives from many lands, Hindu nationalists, and others with whom she disagrees actively and knowingly promote evil.

Unless they have a proper humanist education, "males learn that success means being above the body and its frailties, so they learn to characterize some underclass (women, African Americans) as hyperbodily, thus in need of being dominated" (NFP, 35). Moreover, "white people who feel great compassion for other white people can treat people of color like animals or objects, refusing to see the world from their perspective. Men often treat women this way...." (NFP, 38). So they do. But isn't it also worth asking whether nonwhite peoples ever look on white people or other nonwhite people as animals or objects? It wasn't Europeans who committed the Rwandan genocide, nor did white people run the Khmer Rouge. Do women never refuse to feel compassion for men or other women?

In countless passages of this sort, the direction of criticism goes relentlessly in one direction. I understand thinking this way. I know it can be part of a desire for justice. But I find it remarkable to offer such thinking in recommending empathy.

* * *

Great art enables one to see the world from unfamiliar points of view and to experience life as others do. It can allow us to empathize even with those who do not value empathy, like Casaubon in *Middlemarch* or Tolstoy's Karenin, who regards his own considerable capacity for empathy as a weakness.

After Nussbaum has appealed to the right sentiments, it turns out she wants to open only the minds of others. The minds of those with whom she agrees are apparently already empathetic enough.

True empathy begins when we bracket our own perspective in order to experience that of another person. Perhaps it is easier to do so with people on the other side of the globe than with those of a different social class, political party, or religion living in one's own town. With people far away, nothing personal as at stake. That is why Dostoevsky's Father Zossima remarks that it is so much easier to love humanity or people "at a distance" than to love one's neighbor.

But just as we recognize Kitty's goodness when she imagines her actions from Levin's point of view, so we need to do the difficult thing and empathize not only with distant people but also with those nearby.

We need to sense in each other person "an equivalent center of self." And there is no better way to practice such sensing than by reading great novels. If one can help students do that, they will want to read more. And that is the real test of a humanist education.

Part Five

## WHAT IS WIT?

## Chapter Eight

## CONTINGENCY, GAMES, AND WIT

### Mess

The first principle of prosaics is: the fundamental state of the world is mess. Thus, to satisfy our need to feel in control we must overcome the very nature of things.[1] We must impose order on contingency, minimize the unforeseeable, and ensure the triumph of mind over raw experience. That, perhaps, is the fundamental purpose of culture.[2]

### Order and Entropy

Broadly speaking, we have three ways to achieve order and predictability. First, we may construct a science that explains away contingencies and hope that the order identified in one domain can somehow prove the model for all others. Second, we can advance a putative science that claims to do for the social world what hard science did for astronomy. Finally, we can build an avowedly artificial order designed to banish contingency, as we do in many man-made environments, in art, and in games.

Newton's amazing discovery of the laws of motion and gravitation explained a vast number of diverse phenomena in the same simple

---

[1]     I first used the concept of "fundamental mess" beginning with "Prosaics: An Approach to the Humanities," *The American Scholar* 57, no. 4 (Autumn 1988): 515-28. For the idea of "mess" I am indebted to Gregory Bateson, "Why Do Things Get in a Muddle?," in SEM, 3-8.

[2]     I use the term "contingency" in Aristotle's sense to mean an event that "can either be or not be."

terms. It led many to assume that everything else, however apparently complex, must before long reduce to a similar simplicity. Whatever has not yet been "Newtonized" soon will be: the world consists of what has been explained and what will be explained, and that is all. Such thinking rules out the very possibility of counter-evidence. But to rule out counter-evidence is to engage in a discourse not of science but of faith. Newton formulated no fourth law stating that whatever his first three had not explained some future one would, and if he had, that untestable "law" would by its very nature be based not on evidence but on sheer analogy.

When we do not actually have a science, we may, as our second strategy, persuade ourselves that we do. Ever since Newton's *Principia* (1689), "moral Newtonians," as Elie Halévy famously called them, have sought to explain social events as Newton explained planetary motion (GPR, 6). They have repeatedly "discovered" social laws that allegedly make, or soon will make, human events as predictable as Mercury's orbit. Auguste Comte, who coined the word "sociology," first called this proposed science "social physics," and thinkers as diverse as Locke, Laplace, Bentham, Marx, Spencer, and Freud have all fabricated a putative social science in the hard sense.

These two methods—assuming that the hard sciences we have offer sure models for sciences of everything and constructing putative social sciences that claim to be hard sciences—depend on the faith that disorder and unpredictability must be merely apparent. Thinkers imagine that if the vast diversity of social phenomena were traced back cause by antecedent cause, they would gradually converge on a few simple laws. It seems indubitable that order, not mess, defines the fundamental nature of things.

But why make such an assumption? Could the world, or at least the social world, not be governed by a principle analogous to entropy, the maximization of *dis*order? Experience teaches us that left to themselves, things tend to become a "muddle," as Gregory Bateson observed (SEM, 3). If one takes no special effort, neat things get messy, but messy things never get neat. That is why order requires work.

By the same token, what if causes traced to antecedent causes do not simplify but ramify? Why is it impossible that, even if everything should be law-governed, the laws should outnumber the phenomena they explain? In that case, the world, even if governed by deterministic laws, would behave exactly as if it were not.

Tolstoy's *War and Peace* argues both points: things tend to disorder, and the chain of causes ramifies. The dream of a social science is therefore absurd, as ludicrous as the supposed "science of warfare" accepted by the novel's German generals. Prince Andrei learns the Tolstoyan truths that battle is irreducible chaos beyond the reach of any conceivable social science. "What science can there be," asks Prince Andrei, "in a matter in which, as in every practical matter, nothing can be determined and everything depends on innumerable conditions, the significance of which becomes manifest at a particular moment, and no one can tell when that moment will come?" (W&P, 775). "As in every practical matter": Andrei's point about contingency applies not just to battle but also to all social life. "At a particular moment": *presentness* matters in the sense that at least some moments are not simply the automatic derivative of earlier moments. They possess what Bakhtin called "eventness" and "surprisingness." They contain an ineliminable element of contingency.

## Art

If we cannot control the weather, we can move indoors. As our third strategy to reduce contingency and unpredictability, we construct our own environments. We live in "living rooms." What makes such environments artificial is that they are governed, or are supposed to be governed, by an order we have made and therefore understand. In the real world, we possess no guarantee that whatever order might obtain in nature fits the predispositions of our minds—only think how strange quantum physics is! But interior decorating is our own creation.

Of course, despite all effort, we never achieve total order. We recognize the neat environments in home brochures as fake because we know what our rooms really look like. If unpredictability could be banished, why would we still need insurance?

Art constitutes another kind of environment designed to banish contingency. It works better than housing construction. Not only do novels not require new roofs every twenty-five years, they are often made supremely well from the outset. After all, the artist can go over his work to eliminate whatever does not fit. Contingency then disappears, at least in principle. Of course, the text of a poem may eventually undergo unpredictable changes. The very existence of textual editing as a discipline tacitly indicates that even poets cannot eliminate all contingency. Textual editing teaches the same lesson as insurance: we cannot control everything, even our own creations.

## Games: Time and Space

> Play ... creates order, is order. Into an imperfect world and into the confusion of life it brings a temporary, a limited perfection. Play demands order absolute and supreme.[3]

> Play ... is thus an attempt to substitute perfect situations for the normal confusion of contemporary life.[4]

We do have one way to do away with unwanted contingency: games. Every significant play theorist has noticed this special feature of games. Although not all resemble chess in eliminating contingency, others at least control it, and controlled contingency may not really be contingency at all.

Nothing forbidden by the rules can ever happen in a game. So radically do games differ from life in this respect that Huizinga and his successors have located games in a wholly different *kind* of milieu. Games exhibit "a stepping out of 'real' life into a temporary sphere of activity with a disposition all of its own" (Huizinga, 8). They unfold in a special time and place. We can immediately appreciate the difference between games and life by reflecting that games allow for a "time out" and life does not. One cannot take time out of time. In life, suspending one activity entails engaging in another, even if only "doing nothing." The very notion of sloth presumes that time flows even when we rest, or else it could not be wasted. The time we waste wastes us. Chekhov characters imagine their actions as a mere rehearsal for the real time to come—but of course they are not rehearsing for life but living life as if it were rehearsal.

The same distinction applies to space. One can leave a playground or walk away from a chessboard, but one cannot step out of real space. One is always somewhere; in fact, one is always right here, right now.

---

[3] Johan Huizinga, *Homo Ludens: A Study of the Play Element in Culture* (Boston: Beacon, 1950), 10.

[4] Roger Caillois, *Man, Play, and Games*, trans. Meyer Barash (Urbana: University of Illinois Press, 2001), 19.

## How Game Rules Differ from Physical Laws and Social Laws

Games exhibit rules that allow or prevent certain actions, but not in the way social laws do. If one breaks the law, one still belongs to the social world. One becomes a "criminal," which is itself a social role. But an athlete who brings a gun to a tennis court is no longer playing tennis, and someone who moves a rook diagonally is not a criminal chess player but is no longer playing chess. Society includes outlaws, but games do not include "outrules." Caillois distinguishes a cheat, who still works within the game, from a spoilsport or "nihilist," who breaks the game itself (Caillois, 7). A cheat is like a lawbreaker, but there is no social analogue to the spoilsport, because one cannot leave the social world. There is no spoillife.

Contingent events not allowed for by the game's rules cannot happen, because if they did they would not be *in* the game. One appeal of games is that they, unlike the rest of life, can prevent unwanted events simply by *ruling* them out of existence. Games can of course be interrupted, but that is because gameplaying, like every action, is itself an event in life. But an interruption *of* a game is not an interruption *in* a game.

A law of physics cannot be broken, because if it were it would be refuted and thus no longer a law at all. Game rules cannot be broken for a quite different reason, because they *define* this possibility away. No such option exists with social laws, which can forbid but not preclude actions. In fact, only things that do happen are ever forbidden.

To be sure, utopian thinkers have imagined a world that could be totally controlled and would in that sense be analogous to a game. That is what Trotsky meant by a leap from the kingdom of necessity to the kingdom of freedom, freedom here meaning not individual choice but the ability of humanity to order anything. "Man in socialist society," he wrote in one famous passage, "will command nature in its entirety, with its grouse and sturgeons."[5]

Nevertheless, utopian laws cannot be perfect because they still rely on *preventing* events, and one can try to prevent only what is

---

[5]   Leon Trotsky, *Literature and Revolution* (Ann Arbor: University of Michigan, 1971), 252. Scholars sometimes refer simply to "the grouse and sturgeon passage."

possible. Neither the laws of physics nor the rules of Monopoly require show trials. Games need not resort to terror, because definition works far better. Without force, and by the sheer power of definition, the "magic circle" of extratemporal time and extraspatial space achieves perfect order.[6]

### Playability and Representation

Games model reality. More accurately, they model reality as if it were ordered. Rules prescribe what can and cannot happen, so that events in the game in some sense represent events in life.[7]

At one end of a continuum lie games that, like chess, model some part of the world quite abstractly. There is no particular reason a bishop should move only diagonally, or a castle should move at all. Pawns do not undergo basic training, no one secures supply lines, and the technology of chess battle never alters. By contrast, the military tries to make its games as realistic as possible. The closer they are to the realistic side of the continuum, the better they can teach strategy useful in real warfare. Nevertheless, war games, no matter how realistic, differ from real wars because rules still define possible moves. In real war, anything goes, and there is no umpire.

A game's proximity to reality cannot be determined from within the game. From within, one can measure coherence, complexity, and playability. One can learn strategy games while forgetting what they supposedly represent. Who knows what a "rook" is, and what chess player has ever been helped by knowing? Monopoly originally modeled Atlantic City, but sets using street names from elsewhere remain the same game.

### Games with Contingency

In principle, it should be possible to model any aspect of life in a game. We may therefore pose a question: can the game continuum include an

---

[6]     The phrase "magic circle," common in writing about play, belongs to Huizinga, 10.

[7]     Caillois insists that rules govern most games, but not "make-believe." I am not so sure. Clearly, implicit rules specify unacceptable actions in playing "house." And while make-believe is play, whether it is a "game" depends on one's definition. See Caillois, 8.

extreme point where a game is so realistic that it includes contingency itself and models how people deal with it? Can rules defining possible events allow radically unexpected ones?

After all, in war, and in many other activities, what matters most is how one reacts to what has not occurred before and could not be anticipated. That is why the best general in *War and Peace*, Kutuzov, reminds other generals that the best preparation for a battle is "a good night's sleep." To the extent that contingency defines a situation, the presence of mind that depends on rest matters more than another strategic plan developed late at night. Can a game capture *that* aspect of war?

In games, one overcomes obstacles and meets challenges, as allowed and defined by the rules. What about obstacles *not* defined by the rules? Could a game involve challenges to the very logic of (rule-based) games? Could suspense derive from the player's attempt to turn unanticipated kinds of events into a part of the game?

I say unanticipated *kinds* of events to stress why games of chance like roulette do not model contingency in this sense. Roulette involves chances, of course, but only certain chances, as defined by the rules and, in this case, by statistical laws. The kinds of things that can happen can be exhaustively determined. The ball may stop at an even or odd integer, but never at a fractional or irrational number; the game allows for red and black, but never blue; and one cannot bet on triple zero even if one stupidly wished to.

To be sure, the outcome of any player's or any day's betting cannot be known in advance. But statistical probabilities can. If thirty-eight numbers can come up at roulette—1 through 36, zero, and double zero—and the odds paid for a correct guess are 36-1, then the more games played, the more likely the house will make money.

Despite probabilities, gamblers do sometimes beat the house, or no one would play and the house would make nothing. Paradoxically, the possibility that the house can lose is what makes it profitable. Relatively predictable profitability over the long run therefore entails short-run unpredictability. Roulette and similar games are about "beating the odds," which is possible but by definition unlikely; that is why the game can be so interesting. Everything about the game, in short, depends on the existence of chance, but in a tightly controlled, mathematically specifiable framework.

Other games do not allow odds to be calculated. Something closer to genuine contingency exists. No one can predict a baseball's "bad hop." The fielder must possess the presence of mind to respond to a weird bounce or sudden wind. Suspense in sports derives in part from the possibility of such unforeseeables. The game tests the player's skill, surprising perhaps even to himself, at meeting situations that may never have happened that way before. Good play depends not only on ability and practice but also on a good night's sleep. Unforeseeable possibilities distinguish real baseball from computerized models. Real baseball cannot be played entirely "by the numbers."

In baseball, unlike roulette, something new can always happen. But not just anything. The kinds of events that can figure in the game must be recognizably of the right sort. Sudden changes in weather can create new possibilities, at least until the umpire calls a time out. But bullets fired at an outfielder cannot. On the border lie events—the sound of a gunshot resembling a thunderclap?—that may qualify either as legitimate contingencies within the game or as outside interference. The umpire must decide. Indeed, it is because cases unspecifiable in advance exist that umpires enjoy discretion.

Novel situations arise in baseball, but baseball is not *about* such situations. If it were, major league parks would not have been domed to keep out weather and Astroturfed to make the field uniform. Of course, the fact that only some parks strive for such regularity, while others preserve a more natural outdoors, creates an element of the arbitrary that is itself contingent. But if baseball were about contingency, one would see more and more parks that, far from reducing it, would make it more likely.

### Games of Improvisation

Unlike baseball, some games are *about* contingency. Modeling encounters with the unpredictable, they test the player's ability to handle an unexpected challenge.

In such games, players must improvise, and the game is dull unless they have a chance to do so. Improvisation is not just something that might happen, but something that constitutes the game itself. A World Series game does not require bad hops to be interesting, but games of improvisation require the analogue to bad hops.

In Pushkin's unfinished novella "Egyptian Nights," an Italian *improvisatore* volunteers to compose a poem on the spot about any topic the audience might suggest. Poems so made impress in a way that identical verses printed in an anthology would not. Not just *what* is composed but *how* it is composed, not just the text but the process of its coming to be, is essential to its interest as an improvisation. The poet of a printed work chooses the topic, how much time to spend, and how much to revise, none of which the reader knows or needs to know. By contrast, the *improvisatore*'s audience knows that the topic was selected by another and witnesses immediate and unrevised composition.

Improvisations derive suspense from the possibility of failure. Otherwise there is no game, just as roulette demands that the house can lose. With printed poems, by contrast, failures are neither seen nor designed to be seen, because unless the poet or publisher deems them successful, the poems do not appear at all. The same logic pertains to musical and dramatic improvisations. They can, and sometimes must, fail.

Unlike roulette, improvisational performances demand skill. Chance alone does not determine the winner. Rather, mind encounters the unforeseen. Improvisations come closer than most games to modeling that encounter.

### Repeatability and Unrepeatability

What we might call *games of repeatability* allow the same situation to be repeated every time one plays. Single-player video games often involve the same initial scenario. By repetition, one learns to play more skillfully. Many games with more than one player, like chess and Monopoly, also start with the same initial position.

Improvisations, by contrast, depend on each situation's novelty. In such games of *un*repeatability, the discovery that the player, having met the same situation before, has practiced a strategy would destroy the game. An *improvisatore* cannot return the next day with verses prepared overnight, since that would no longer be an improvisation.

In games of unrepeatability, what matters is how one reacts *now*, when the challenge arises. To be sure, one can still improve by practice, but one practices reacting with presence of mind to the unexpected. In other words, *presentness* matters.

### Spectator Improvisations

Both baseball and improvisational games involve presentness, but some improvisations include a source of contingency baseball does not. They make the spectators into players.

In baseball, any attempt by fans to affect play constitutes interference, but in *spectator improvisations,* as we might call this type of game, the spectators are supposed to intervene. No "interference," no game. They present problems for the improviser to solve. This double role of spectators introduces a new source of the unexpected.

With such improvisations, spectators must devise a challenge. It would not do for the improviser to name his own theme. In that case, he could just name an easy one or even have memorized the poem beforehand. Themes must come from the spectators, and so they, too, face a test. The question "how good a challenge can the spectator devise?" is as much a part of the game as "how well does the improviser handle the challenge?"

"Love" would be too easy a theme. A manifestly unpoetic one might prove more interesting. How about the nondeductability of mortgage on a second house? Or one can make the topic difficult in a more surprising way. In Pushkin's story, the *improvisatore*'s first spectator is himself a poet, Charsky, who cleverly suggests a topic apparently precluded by the very nature of the game: "Here is a theme for you ... the poet chooses the subject of his songs himself: the crowd has no right to command his inspiration."[8] How does one make up a poem illustrating the suggested theme that poems cannot be based on suggested themes? Charsky means to place the *improvisatore* in an inescapable trap. If the *improvisatore* cannot devise the suggested poem, he fails; but if he can, then the crowd does have the right to command his inspiration and so the poem has not fit the suggestion after all. It simply fails in a different way.

Unfazed, the *improvisatore* composes a poem that expresses the proffered theme without self-contradiction, as Charsky himself concedes. "'Astonishing,' answered the poet. 'How can it be that someone else's idea, which had only just reached your ear, immediately became your own property, as if you had carried, fostered, and nurtured it for a long time?" (Pushkin, 255). The *improvisatore* succeeds because, as Charsky demanded, his lyric does use a theme suggested by another. His theme is the mystery of inspiration, which would place it beyond anyone's command. But he has also so deeply assimilated the theme that he has transformed it into his "own property," and so

---

8       Alexander Pushkin, *Complete Prose Fiction,* trans. and ed. Paul Debreczeny (Stanford: Stanford University Press, 1983), 254.

in making the poem he has "chosen the subject of his song himself." What began as external has become internal, and only then led to a poem. Charsky has suggested the theme, but the *improvisatore* has not been commanded by another but inspired by what has become his own idea. The two ideas just happen to coincide.

But how is such an assimilation of the alien possible?, Charsky wonders. The *improvisatore* replies by reminding Charsky of his own belief, the very one that has led to his suggestion, that inspiration can be neither commanded nor explained but arises mysteriously. If so, the Italian asks, how can Charsky, of all people, demand an explanation of the *improvisatore*'s inspiration?

> Every talent is inexplicable…. Why is it that a thought emerging from a poet's head is already equipped with four rhymes and measured in concordant, uniform feet? Similarly, no one except the improvisatore can comprehend this alacrity of impressions, this close tie between one's own inspiration and another's will. (Pushkin, 255)

If I could explain how I did it, the *improvisatore* contends, it would not be inspiration at all, just a craft. Rather than deny the ideas that apparently make his art impossible, he embraces them while turning them to his own advantage. The apparent inescapability of Charsky's trap makes the *improvisatore*'s escape all the more impressive. Instantaneously, he commands the uncommandable without its ceasing to be uncommandable. Of course, that is what spectator improvisation by its nature does.

But even spectator improvisation has limits. It cannot assimilate *any* contingency. Unpoetic or self-contradictory topics qualify as moves in the game, but a physical assault would not. The rules allow for only certain kinds of surprises. Otherwise, one is not playing the game at all. To play the game, one must play by the rules.

Or is it somehow possible to assimilate rule-breaking itself?

### Meta-Games

In fact, it is possible. Odd as it may sound, some games involve moves from *outside* the game. In fact, that is their point.

As spectator improvisations involve unanticipated suggestions, games of this sort involve unanticipated challenges to their rules. They meet those challenges by changing their rules. The point of the game is to evolve into a different game. Paradoxically enough, one is making a move inside such a game only if one makes a move outside it.

Spectator improvisations require challenges *in* the game but here contingency is modeled with challenges *to* the game. Not the player but the game itself—or its designer—must assimilate the alien. The suggestion may come from the designer (or would-be new designer) who makes the change or, as in a game of improvisation, from a challenger testing whether the designer can accommodate the possible innovation.

Such games are really meta-games. They make a game out of the process of making a new game. To be sure, rules govern that very process, but not the same rules that operate within the starting or concluding game. These *interim rules* are rules about changing rules. As a game has its rules, the meta-game has its meta-rules.

It works like this: begin with a game. Suggest, or allow someone else to suggest, a complication not envisaged by the rules. The challenge is to come up with a new game incorporating that complication.

One might start with a game modeling a famous battle, say Austerlitz or Waterloo. Each player commands a certain number of infantry and cavalry units, represented by pieces on a game board. The game consists in refighting the battle. Can the Austrians and Russians win at Austerlitz, or Napoleon at Waterloo?

Having learned this game, one might suggest variations. Perhaps add artillery? Or introduce hills, mud, and villages to the terrain? Or sudden storms? Each suggestion might lead to new rules. Perhaps in the original game cavalry can move five "hexes" per turn and infantry three. Artillery might be restricted to one, and all may be slowed by climbing a hill. In this way, one might capture the advantage high ground confers.

But how does one judge whether a rule change constitutes a success? Typically, meta-rules to answer that question specify (a) that the new game be at least as playable and interesting as the old, and preferably more so, and (b) that the new game must be a recognizable variation on the old one, with the change in rules as small as possible. To add artillery, one does not add dice as well. If one models sudden storms by rolling dice, one does not also add a raingear fashion contest. Doing so would alter the game more radically than is necessary. One must sense that the old game has assimilated the alien, not that one is playing a wholly new game. A sort of Ockham's razor principle applies. Similarly, the one offering the challenge must make a suggestion that derives from the game as it exists. One cannot demand that a designer add dress-up to tic-tac-toe.

For obvious reasons, such meta-games appeal to game-lovers. Having exhausted a favorite game, players get to make it interesting in a new way: the game is "defamiliarized."[9] In fact, many games anticipate this process by allowing for play at higher levels of complexity as they are learned. Moreover, by turning the game into the starting point of a meta-game, players get to be designers as well. The new game will therefore intrigue in two distinct ways, as a game to be played and as the successful solution to an earlier (meta-)game. If meta-gaming holds primary interest, the new game may be played only minimally, merely to show that it is playable.

An interesting variation may therefore accomplish numerous purposes. It keeps an old game interesting, allows for meta-gaming, and above all makes the new game *one's own*. It may have started out as the invention of Parker Brothers or Avalon Hill, but now it is partly my own creation. Literary translators often enjoy the same pleasure.

Meta-tennis, anyone? Who can come up with the best variation on Scrabble? Perhaps one could use two contiguous boards, allowing words to branch off from the center of either, and gain extra points for joining the two branches? Or how about arranging four square boards as a larger square? One needs to solve all sorts of problems: Does joining two boards create two contiguous triple word scores, or should one just assume that the last row of one board coincides with the first row of the other, so that only one can contain letters? Does play with four boards require four hundred tiles, and if two players compete on four boards, does each control two racks?

Can one play Monopoly with choice of route? To do so, why not add two more streets, running diagonally and crossing at the center, so that more than one path leads to any point and any point can be bypassed? If one's opponent can avoid one's best properties this way, perhaps it will pay to allocate resources differently?

So common are meta-games that one can buy computerized versions allowing players to design their own variations. Sometimes the gaming company itself comes up with new versions every few months, so that to play effectively one has to learn not only the game

---

9    For an interesting piece on possible changes to tic-tac-toe and other games, see Bernard DeKoven, "Changing the Game" in GDR, 518-37.

as originally designed but also the game of adjusting to changes in the game. *Dungeons and Dragons, Magic: The Gathering,* and other games sold by Wizards of the Coast work in just this way.[10] For the player, the game is always new, and tournaments test skill not only at the game but also at the meta-game. Players dream up their own variations, post them online, or send them as suggestions they hope Wizards will adopt. For the gamemaker, meta-gaming ensures continuing sales.

### The Mikado in Wonderland

Gilbert and Sullivan's Mikado, who aspires "to make the punishment fit the crime," would condemn billiard sharps to play "on a cloth untrue, with a twisted cue, and elliptical billiard balls."[11] That would indeed be hard, but not unplayable. It would be a variation of billiards, the sort that might result from meta-gaming. Start with billiards, but give the table hillocks and valleys. Perhaps allow the player to use not a single cue, but, as in golf, a set of cues that enable one to escape the equivalent of a sand trap. And so on. The billiards we know would then be just one of a family of games—the one where the table just happens to be flat—much as Euclidian space is one of several possible spaces and Newtonian physics a mere special case allowed for by Einstein's.

Without mentioning Gilbert and Sullivan, Gregory Bateson imagines such a version of croquet. He concludes correctly that it could be made into a game. But I think Bateson errs in his analysis of the croquet match Alice plays with flamingoes as mallets, hedgehogs as balls, and soldiers forming hoops. You will recall that over and over again "just as she had got it [the flamingo's] neck nicely straightened out, and was going to give the hedgehog a blow with its head, it *would* twist itself round and look up in her face … and, when she had got its head down, and was going to begin again, the hedgehog had unrolled

---

10    The inventor of *Magic*, Richard Gardner, stresses that meta-gaming was built into the game from the start in numerous ways: deck design before playing a deck, new card sets with modified rules in each expansion, and different formats in which different expansions were legal. See Gardner, "The Design Evolution of *Magic: The Gathering*," in GDR, 538-555.

11    *The Complete Plays of Gilbert and Sullivan* (New York: Modern Library, n.d.), 384.

itself, and was in the act of crawling away...."[12] Such a game would be unplayable, Bateson argues, because flamingoes, hedgehogs, and soldiers are alive:

> [S]uppose the croquet lawn was bumpy ... or the heads of the mallets were just wobbly instead of being alive, then the people could still learn and the game would only be more difficult—it wouldn't be impossible. But once you bring live things into it, it becomes impossible. (SEM, 30-31)

But lots of games involve live things. What else is fox hunting all about? Humans, as well as flamingoes, are alive, so what about war games and improvisations? Besides, one obviously *could* make a game out of the situation Alice faces, perhaps the game of testing how creatively or calmly people can face apparently impossible tasks. Let us call it "Rhodes Scholarship Interview."

Nevertheless, I think Bateson is right that Alice's game is impossible, but for a different reason. The reason is not the presence of living beings but the fact that in *Alice*, Carroll has implicitly created the meta-game of making variations on croquet and then offered a particularly difficult suggestion for the meta-gamer to handle.[13]

Carroll was himself an accomplished meta-gamer, who invented variations on checkers, billiards, and croquet. "Castle Croquet," for instance, is played with "eight balls, eight arches, and four flags; 4 of the balls are called 'soldiers,' the others 'sentinels'.... Each player has to bring his soldier out of the castle, and with it 'invade' the other castles ... re-enter his own, and touch the flag, and then to touch it with his sentinel ... and whoever does all this first wins."[14] The rules run to three pages.

In *Alice*, Carroll tacitly challenges the reader to assimilate a set of difficult variations on croquet. Unless the reader can imagine rules

---

[12]   *The Annotated Alice*, ed. Martin Gardner (New York: Bramhall House, 1960), 111-12.

[13]   As *Through the Looking Glass* plays with whimsical variations on chess.

[14]   Lewis Carroll, *The Lewis Carroll Picture Book: A Selection from the Unpublished Writings and Drawings of Lewis Carroll, Together with Reprints from Scarce and Unacknowledged Work*, ed. Stuart Dogson Collingwood (n.p.: Ebiron, 2005; facsimile reprint of London: T. Fisher Unwin, 1899), 272. See also the note in *The Annotated Alice*, 111.

for "flamingo croquet," Carroll has won the meta-game. So far as I am concerned, he has. That is because Rhodes Scholarship Interview does not satisfy the second meta-game rule: it is not close enough to the original game; indeed, it really isn't a variation on croquet at all.

### A Table of Games

Let us sum up what we have seen so far about games and unpredictability:

| Game | Includes statistically chance events | Includes statistically unpredictable events or kinds of events | Involves presentness | Makes spectators into actors | Includes challenges to the game from outside the game |
|------|------|------|------|------|------|
| Chess | No | No | Yes & No | No | No |
| Roulette | Yes | No | Mini-mally | No | No |
| Baseball | No | Yes | Yes | No | No |
| Improvisation | No | Yes | Yes | Yes | No |
| Meta-games | No | Yes | No | No | Yes |

Chess strives to be a game of pure skill. One never rolls dice. In tournament chess, a clock limits the time per move. But does the clock exist in order to create presentness, or is that a mere byproduct of precluding the use of infinite delay to force a draw?[15]

---

[15]   Stephen Sniderman points out that games always contain unwritten rules, often concerning time. No rule of tic-tac-toe prevents someone from losing by endless stalling, but such a tactic violates an implicit rule, as every player understands. See Sniderman, "Unwritten Rules," in GDR, 476-502.

We usually think of roulette as a game of pure chance, which ensures suspense and therefore presentness. But nothing depends on presence of mind in placing a bet. Of course, many players have (mistakenly) considered roulette a game of skill that does depend on presence of mind. The addicted gambler Dostoevsky attributed his losses to the sheer intense presentness of play, which prevented him from keeping to his "system."

Baseball is a game of skill and presentness, but allows for unpredictable chances. Spectator improvisations are games of skill that essentially involve the unforeseen, derive suspense from presentness, and make the spectators into players. The whole interest of meta-games lies in assimilating challenges to the game itself.

### Dostoevsky's Literary Game

Let us briefly consider a sort of literary game that Dostoevsky invented. He devised what he called a new literary genre that would not just appear in a periodical but would *be* a periodical. Including its periodical form in its title, he called it *The Diary of a Writer: A Monthly Publication*. As he explained at the outset, every issue had to a) include a variety of literary genres, b) make a thematic whole out of diverse contents, c) occupy a specified length and appear at a specified time, and d) use events in the real world that have taken place since the previous issue—events that in principle *could not* have been foreseen—as material, theme, and starting point. Each issue shows a creative mind struggling with recalcitrant material. Before our eyes, the author applies his bag of tricks to make literature out of contingency.

Dostoevsky makes the challenge hard enough so that some issues fail in whole or in part. Successes therefore convey a sense of real triumph. Suspense is genuine.

*The Diary of a Writer* also allowed spectators to be actors. Dostoevsky invited readers to suggest themes, and several issues work as responses to their letters. He refers to his readers as his "co-authors." Moreover, as the work developed, its initial set of rules also evolved, so the work became a sort of meta-game.[16]

---

[16]    On this odd work of Dostoevsky, see BoG; and Morson, *Dostoevsky's Great Experiment*, the "introductory study" to AWD1, 1-117.

## Witticisms as Play

Let us approach witticisms as a form of play. Like games, they assert control over a contingent world. As a genre, witticisms vindicate the superiority of mind, even—in fact, especially—in extremities of difficulty where mental presence must overcome a disadvantage. They resemble the sort of improvisatory game in which one must handle an unexpected challenge and, on the spot, come up with an appropriate response. The harder the challenge, the faster and less predictable the reply, the greater the wit's mastery of social circumstances, and the cleverer his facility with verbal resources, the better the witticism—and the more surely the game has been won.

Like the game of improvisation, the witticism dramatizes the mind's encounter with contingency. Both depend on presentness. *The successful witticism expresses the triumph of mind and its adequacy to any social situation.* In an instant, the wit masters all the complexities of a set of social circumstances and formulates a perfectly a propos remark that illuminates them.

Speed is therefore important, and stories about great witticisms often include words or phrases like "immediately," "without a pause," or "promptly." Such terms reflect the importance of presentness. It would not do to describe how someone insulted Dorothy Parker and, after scratching her head and pausing a while, Dorothy tried out a few replies until at last she found a good one.

For the same reason that improvisations demand a difficult challenge, witticisms thrive in socially challenging moments. A surprising social situation seems to permit no good response and therefore offers the wit an opportunity to display the power of mind. The opportunity is fleeting, and so the more quickly the wit responds, the more the adequacy of mind to circumstance is displayed. Conversely, the common lament "I shoulda said" testifies that afterthought cannot substitute for presentness. Diderot called the answer thought of too late as "staircase wit" (*l'esprit d'escalier*). "I can always make excellent impromptu replies, if only I have a moment to think," wrote Rousseau, sounding like Groucho Marx.[17]

---

[17]    In chapter 3 of *The Confessions of Jean-Jacques Rousseau,* trans. J. M. Cohen (Harmondsworth, UK: Penguin, 1953), 113. My thanks to Herbert (Chip) Tucker for this reference.

Witticisms typically involve *stories*. The wit faces a test, and the story tells how he passed it. That is why the same witticisms often appear in anthologies both of anecdotes and quotations. In the former, the witticism concludes the story, while in the latter the witticism often appears first, followed by the editors' explanation of the circumstances that led up to it.

### The Provocateur

Not just anyone can tell the story of a witticism. For example, the wit usually cannot tell it about himself, because then it would demonstrate not presence of mind but an all-too-common pretense to it. That is why wits often attribute their own mots to another: "Someone once said…" (and rather humorless "misquotation" debunkers conclude that the wit took the line from elsewhere).

Johnson required Boswell. A true master of witty stories, Boswell also understood how a biography favored their telling. Often, wits demonstrate presence of mind by noticing facts about a situation that others have missed. If the storyteller begins by mentioning those facts, they cannot come as a surprise to the reader. But Boswell can mention them pages before, so that readers, like people present at the occasion, will have seen them but not grasped their significance.

A long biography allows each anecdote to be short. The more we know about Johnson, the less we need to be told what provokes him. To be sure, if anecdotes too closely resembled earlier ones, they would lack the crucial element of surprise that testifies to intelligence. But if they are sufficiently varied, the reader can appreciate not only the cleverness of each witticism but also the added surprise that yet another surprise can happen. How amazing that Johnson can generate so many profound remarks all reflecting his personality yet differing from each other! Moreover, as witticisms accumulate, they can reflect how a personality gradually alters. As the biography comes to the aid of each witticism, so the witticisms taken together help form the biography.

Sometimes Boswell narrates how Johnson made a clever insult, such as when he disparaged Lord Chesterfield: "This man I thought had been a lord among wits; but, I find, he is only a wit among lords."[18]

---

[18]    Frank R. Shapiro, ed., *The Yale Book of Quotations* (henceforth YBQ) (New

But Boswell can also play a more complex role. As a spectator of an improvisation may also play a part in it, so Boswell not only relates the story but also becomes the disparaged character in it. He is both narrator and insultee. It is as if Lord Chesterfield had told the story of Johnson's witty insult:

> Boswell: I do indeed come from Scotland, but I cannot help it.
> Johnson: That, Sir, I find, is what a very great many of your countrymen cannot help. (ODQ, 428)

Still more effectively, Boswell often plays a third role—which is a second role within the story—the provocateur. He not only narrates to perfection his own diminishment, but has also had the wit to foresee exactly what would inspire Johnson to diminish him so quotably. Johnson demonstrates one kind of wit, and Boswell another. He plays George Burns to Johnson's Gracie Allen. Only a fool fails to give the straight man credit. And only someone who does not appreciate wit undervalues the skill demonstrated in preserving the sense of presence that has made the witticism so surprising. After all, the very fact that a story is being told conveys advance warning that something narratable happened, the sort of warning that people present could not have had. To make his story funny, Boswell has to overcome that disadvantage. And overcoming disadvantages is what wit is all about.

### Two Corollaries

(1) Precisely because witticisms demonstrate power to handle the unforeseen, one can diminish a wit's reputation by exposing advance preparation. That was the point of Whistler's famous retort to Oscar Wilde when they heard a clever comment:

> Wilde: I wish I had said that.
> Whistler: You will, Oscar, you will. (MDQ, 482)

(2) Certain locales, especially salons, serve as conventional settings for witticisms. The salon becomes a sort of playground or "magic circle," a marked-off space and time for an occasion governed by rules for verbal and nonverbal behavior. So much are salons the favored locale for wit that witticisms themselves may retrospectively transform

---

Haven: Yale University Press, 2006), 402 (from the Life).

a locale or social situation into a sort of salon. The less like a salon a situation may be, the wittier it is to make it into one.

### Verbal Duels and Instantaneous Games

Like spectator improvisers, wits often invite challenges to discourse wittily on a suggested theme. So Dorothy Parker, challenged to speak on the dull topic of "horticulture," replied: "You can lead a horticulture but you cannot make her think" (YBQ, 580). Wilde (or in some tellings Disraeli) once offered to speak on any subject. Someone suggested "the Queen," and he promptly responded: "The Queen is not a subject."[19]

Perhaps the most successful witticisms involve a response to an earlier insult or witticism, which serves as the challenge. This challenge is all the more difficult because, unlike the case of Pushkin's *improvisatore*, it has not been invited and comes unexpectedly. By a sort of mental judo, one must turn the energy of a surprise attack to one's advantage, and do so on the spot. Consider these famous examples:

> 1) Clare Booth Luce, meeting Dorothy Parker in a doorway, motioned her in and smirked, saying, "Age before beauty." Parker walked right in, saying "Pearls before swine." (MDQ, 480)
>
> 2) Lady Astor told Churchill that if she were his wife, she'd put poison in his coffee. "If you were my wife," he answered, "I'd drink it." (MDQ, 478)
>
> 3) A descendant of the Athenian hero Harmodius reproached the general Iphicrates, the son of a cobbler, with his low birth. "The difference between us," Iphicrates replied, "is that my family begins with me, whereas yours ends with you." (MDQ, 479)
>
> 4) George Gershwin said to Oscar Levant, "If you had it all over again, would you fall in love with yourself?" Levant replied, "Play us a medley of your hit." (MDQ, 480)

Example (4) works relatively simply. One insult answers another. Because the initiator of the exchange chooses the time, he has placed

---

[19]    See Mardy Grothe, *Viva la Repartee: Clever Comebacks and Witty Retorts from History's Greatest Wits and Wordsmiths* (New York: HarperCollins, 2005), 39-40; and MDQ, 162.

the other at a disadvantage. Therefore the responder wins the contest simply by doing as well as the challenger.

Iphicrates's response represents a particular subgenre of witty reply, the clever man's response when his low birth is insulted. Erasmus tells one such story:

> A young man, said to look strikingly like Augustus, was asked by the emperor if his mother had ever been to Rome. The young man replied: "My mother never, my father constantly."[20]

Iphicrates does not contest the premise that birth matters by asserting that brains are more important. Rather, by turning the insult into a challenge, he demonstrates *why* brains matter. Iphicrates reminds Harmodius that noble families begin with an accomplished, but by definition less than nobly born, founder. A fool can be noble *only* by birth. The accomplished man of low birth therefore resembles the noble's ancestor, who is the very reason for his high birth, more closely than the noble himself does.

The young man in Erasmus's story follows the logic of Augustus's suggestion but shows that it leads just as easily to the conclusion that it is Augustus's mother who is the whore. Such responses prove the superiority of mind over birth while demonstrating the mind's triumph over circumstance.

Churchill's riposte not only demonstrates rapid agility and the readiness to use Lady Astor's premises, he also turns her very words against her. When she supposes that if she were Churchill's wife, she would poison him, she means that if she had the opportunity to kill him, she would. But Churchill discovers in this supposition not just opportunity but also the thought of marriage to such a woman. His insult uses her phrase and so produces all the satisfaction of poetic justice.

Dorothy Parker does an amazing number of clever things at once. She responds to one insult with a greater one (as swinishness is worse than age or lack of beauty); overcomes a disadvantage with her prompt reply; accepts the premise that the order of passing through the doorway determines the duel's winner; answers one famous quotation

---

[20]    *The Adages of Erasmus*, selected by William Barker (Toronto: University of Toronto Press, 2001), 9, 26.

with another; imitates the verbal form of the original quotation; and plays on the key terms while doing so. Though superficially similar as "noun before noun," the two phrases display different deep structures. "Age before beauty" condenses "Age should go before beauty," whereas "pearls before swine" abbreviates "Do not cast thy pearls before swine." In the first sentence, the initial noun is a subject, in the second a direct object; in the first, it is what is less desirable and in the second more. That is why the same (or apparently the same) wording can be imitated with opposite significance. Moreover, because Parker strides in while delivering her riposte, she ensures that Luce, even if she could think of an answer, will not have a chance to make it. She thereby turns not only Luce's choice of words but her sarcastic gesture to her advantage. Caught unawares, Parker manages all this without missing a beat: such presence of mind explains why her reply has come to define triumph in verbal dueling.

We refer to the sport of wit, and Parker's reply suggests why. Sports time takes place here and now and tests one's ability to respond without planning, and so does wit. Both contests entail intense presentness, but situations like Parker's add one more element because, unlike Luis Aparicio fielding a difficult bounce, she had to respond as soon as she realized that a game was being played. It is as if Aparicio was taken unawares when a game began with a ball hit to him while he was still in the locker room.

In such cases, the game is over almost as soon it has begun, and before we have registered that it has begun. *Instantaneous games*, as we might call them, demonstrate all the more skill on the part of the fielder or wit.

### The Deathbed

Because the best witticisms overcome the most formidable obstacles, the most favorable locale is often the apparently least favorable one. Deathbed cleverness impresses because no place less resembles a salon, and so the ability to treat it as one demonstrates remarkable presence. This, too, is a sort of instantaneous game over as soon as the fact that it is a game is established.

Not all famous last words are witticisms— some are heroic statements, others pull on the heartstrings, and still others evoke an aphoristic sense of mystery—but many witticisms are famous last words:

1) "This is no time for making new enemies." (Voltaire, asked to renounce the devil on his deathbed; YBQ, 169)

2) "You might make that a double." (Murderer Neville Heath when offered a drink before his execution; MDQ, 316)

3) "No, it is better not. She will only ask me to take a message to Albert." (Disraeli, offered a visit by Queen Victoria to his deathbed; MDQ, 315)

4) "Either that wallpaper goes, or I do." (Oscar Wilde; MDQ, 317; given as "One of us must go" in ODQ, 473)

5) "Die, my dear doctor, that's the very last thing I shall do!" (Lord Palmerston; MDQ, 316)

Each dying man maintains his identity. Even to the last Voltaire and Wilde remain wits, the murderer shows no restraint, and the two politicians demonstrate why wit goes with political acumen, since both require presence of mind. Disraeli imagines being sent to deliver yet another diplomatic message to a foreign power. Wilde treats his own death as a matter of interior decorating, by paying attention to the wallpaper, and as an occasion for cleverness, by devising the superb if ghastly pun on "goes." As Voltaire takes advantage of the conventional presence of a deathbed priest, Palmerston does the same with a physician. For both, death is just another social occasion.

Palmerston not only puns on an idiom, as Wilde does, but also exploits a curious linguistic fact. Although "die" is an active verb used in the active voice, dying is not something one does but something one undergoes. Perhaps language should have us say, "he was deaded," or at least, "it died to him."

## Gallows Wit

If any place less resembles a salon than the deathbed, it is the scaffold, and so the place of execution has also become a conventional, because unconventional, locale for wit. What can be less amusing than hanging, guillotining, or roasting over a slow fire? Even without torture, execution involves shame as well as death, and the condemned person faces not family and friends but an executioner and, often, hostile spectators.

Most stories about the last words of a man condemned describe and evoke terror. Very few people are witty. Now consider that the evening before his execution during the Terror of 1793, the French astronomer John Sylvain Bally supposedly said: "It's time for me to enjoy another pinch of snuff. Tomorrow my hands will be bound, so as to make it impossible" (MDQ, 196). Treating execution as no more than an inconvenience preventing the use of snuff belongs to the province of the wit, who can be intimidated by no circumstance and so can always play. What would evoke terror in another provides the wit yet another opportunity for mental agility. It is a challenge, but, like all gamesters, the wit appreciates challenges.

And here is another way such wit impresses: it demonstrates supreme courage. Both wit and courage demand mental presence when most difficult. Not everyone can make sport of his or her own imminent dismemberment. Overwhelmed soldiers are, as we say, cut to pieces, but one Spartan hero at Thermopylae, told that the Persians were so numerous that their arrows blocked out the sun, replied: all the better, for then we shall fight in the shade.

We usually do not think of martyrdom as an occasion for play, but for the truly witty and courageous, it can become one.

> 1) Saint Lawrence, being burned alive on a gridiron, said at one moment that he might be turned over, since he was done enough on that side.[21]
>
> 2) Thomas More, mounting the scaffold: "I pray you, master Lieutenant, see me safe up, and my coming down, let me shift for myself" (ODQ, 548).
>
> 3) More, drawing his beard aside before placing his head on the block: "This has not offended the king" (YBQ, 537).

Which of us, suffering the most extreme agony, would have the presence of mind to think of one's own roasting alive as a scene of daily food preparation? More's pun on "shift" makes the place of execution into another salon. So courageous is he, and so convinced of his salvation, that he can afford to jest at the last moment. And as if that were not enough, he hazards a second joke by distinguishing his head, which has offended the king and so must be cut off, from his beard, which is entirely innocent.

---

[21] Herbert Lockyer, *All the Last Words of Saints and Sinners* (Grand Rapids: Kregel, 1969), 152.

More's jests invoke an ultimate mystery, the housing of an immaterial mind and an immortal soul in a perishing, dismemberable body. "To shift for oneself" in the idiomatic sense involves exercising will, but a corpse "shifts" on its own. The body shifts literally and the mind metaphorically, and between the two lies the whole imponderability of consciousness. To treat the head as something no different from the beard, or the beard as if it, like the head, could choose to give offense, plays on the same mystery.

Danton allegedly made three famous remarks before his execution:

> 1) "If I left my balls to Robespierre and my legs to Couthon, that would help the Committee of Public Safety for a while."[22]

> 2) "At least they can't stop our heads from kissing in the basket." (Danton to his fellow victim Hérault de Séchelles, after a guard had stopped them from giving each other a last embrace on the scaffold; HIQ, 525)

> 3) "Don't forget to show my head to the people. It's a pretty sight." (Danton to the executioner; HIQ, 525)

The first comment turns execution into a duel of insults. They begin by condemning me to dismemberment; in response, I follow their logic by mentioning their defective parts. The second shows the presence of mind to make the scaffold into a drawing room by convicting the executioner of a lapse in etiquette. About the third comment, the editors of *History in Quotations* observe: "Danton was an outstandingly ugly man, and such self-mockery, just seconds before his death, is breathtaking" (HIQ, 525). To be sure, but something else is involved. Like More, Danton alludes to the head as containing the mind. What makes a head valuable is *what is no longer there* after execution and, though worth seeing, can never be seen.

The triumph of mind over brute force belongs to the wit. Games keep the alien at bay, and the game of wit on the scaffold assimilates what is most alien to human life—death itself—into the mind-made game world.

If only death itself could be overcome so easily!

---

[22]    HIQ, 525. Robespierre was allegedly impotent, and Couthon a cripple.

# Index

In this index an "f" after a page number indicates a separate reference on the next page; an "ff" indicates separate references on the next two pages. A continuous discussion is indicated by two page numbers separated by a hyphen. *Passim* indicates a cluster of references in close but not continuous sequence.

This index used the following abbreviations: AK = *Anna Karenina*, B = Bakhtin, BK = *The Brothers Karamazov*, C&P = *Crime and Punishment*, D = Dostoevsky, T = Tolstoy, W&P = *War and Peace*.

CPSIA information can be obtained
at www.ICGtesting.com
Printed in the USA
BVHW041058050720
583012BV00004B/155